Treatment of the Borderline Adolescent: A Development Approach
by James F. Masterson

Psychopathology: Contributions from the Biological, Behavioral,
and Social Sciences
edited by Muriel Hammer, Kurt Salzinger, and Samuel Sutton

Abnormal Children and Youth: Therapy and Research
by Anthony Davids

Principles of Psychotherapy with Children
by John M. Reisman

Aversive Maternal Control: A Theory of Schizophrenic Development
by Alfred B. Hilbrun, Jr.

Individual Differences in Children
edited by Jack C. Westman

Ego Functions in Schizophrenics, Neurotics, and Normals: A Systematic Study
of Conceptual, Diagnostic, and Therapeutic Aspects
by Leopold Bellak, Marvin Hurvich, and Helen A. Gediman

Innovative Treatment Methods in Psychopathology
edited by Karen S. Calhoun, Henry E. Adams, and Kevin M. Mitchell

The Changing School Scene: Challenge to Psychology
by Leah Gold Fein

Troubled Children: Their Families, Schools, and Treatments
by Leonore R. Love and Jaques W. Kaswan

Research Strategies in Psychotherapy
by Edward S. Bordin

The Volunteer Subject
by Robert Rosenthal and Ralph L. Rosnow

Innovations in Client-Centered Therapy
by David A. Wexler and Laura North Rice

The Rorschach: A Comprehensive System
by John E. Exner

Theory and Practice in Behavior Therapy
by Aubrey J. Yates

THEORY AND PRACTICE
IN BEHAVIOR THERAPY

THEORY AND PRACTICE IN BEHAVIOR THERAPY

AUBREY J. YATES

A WILEY-INTERSCIENCE PUBLICATION

JOHN WILEY & SONS   New York • London • Sydney • Toronto

Library of Congress Cataloging in Publication Data:

Yates, Aubrey J
Theory and practice in behavior therapy.

(Wiley series on personality processes.)
  "A Wiley-Interscience publication."
  Includes indexes.
  1. Behavior therapy.   I.   Title.
RC489.B4Y33   616.8'914   74-30018
ISBN 0-471-97230-4

Printed in the United States of America
10 9 8 7 6 5 4 3 2

To Duncan and Ella Howie

Series Preface

This series of books is addressed to behavioral scientists interested in the nature of human personality. Its scope should prove pertinent to personality theorists and researchers as well as to clinicians concerned with applying an understanding of personality processes to the amelioration of emotional difficulties in living. To this end, the series provides a scholarly integration of theoretical formulations, empirical data, and practical recommendations.

Six major aspects of studying and learning about human personality can be designated: personality theory, personality structure and dynamics, personality development, personality assessment, personality change, and personality adjustment. In exploring these aspects of personality, the books in the series discuss a number of distinct but related subject areas: the nature and implications of various theories of personality; personality characteristics that account for consistencies and variations in human behavior; the emergence of personality processes in children and adolescents; the use of interviewing and testing procedures to evaluate individual differences in personality; efforts to modify personality styles through psychotherapy, counseling, behavior therapy, and other methods of influence; and patterns of abnormal personality functioning that impair individual competence.

IRVING B. WEINER

Case Western Reserve University
Cleveland, Ohio

Preface

At the time of the publication of *Behavior Therapy* (Wiley, 1970), some 15 months after the manuscript was completed, it was already clear that the substantive elements of the book would be rapidly outdated and that, ideally, a revised and updated edition would be needed within 5 years. After a short rest period I began, therefore, to collect post-1968 published material systematically with that aim in view, hoping to be in a position to revise the text when I was next on study leave in 1973–1974.

The generous award of a Commonwealth Research Fellowship by the Association of Universities and Colleges of Canada appeared at first sight to make this goal possible. The fellowship was tenable in the Department of Psychology at Queen's University, Kingston, Ontario, and it entailed no formal commitments other than, presumably, to justify the distinction of receiving the award.

Behavior Therapy could not unreasonably be said to have been a handbook of work carried out under this rubric, because its coverage of the literature through 1968 was virtually complete. It very soon became apparent, however, that a revision of the book along the lines of a handbook was well-nigh impossible, perhaps even undesirable. Aside from the sheer magnitude of the task, the inevitable delay in publication of the huge book that would have resulted would have meant that, on publication, it would be significantly out of date, if judged as a handbook. It could be argued, indeed, that the production of such a handbook is now beyond the capacity of one person, unless he worked at it on a fulltime basis over several years.

In such a situation there are three possible avenues of approach. One is a multiauthored handbook. A second approach is the production of annual or biennial review publications that attempt to review and evaluate recent work. Several such annuals are now available, consisting either of reprints of important papers or of original contributions—the latter, especially, are undoubtedly of great value. The third approach (which I have adopted in this book) is to write a more personal critique of important issues in behavior therapy. In this book I have endeavored to put forward some views about behavior therapy that, whether accepted or not by individual therapists, could probably be said to be controversial. The significance of this is outlined in the first chapter and lies mainly in the fact that behavior therapy has now passed beyond the stage of being a rather esoteric approach and become a way of life for large numbers of therapists. Indeed, behavior therapy is now almost as popular, and as much in the public eye, as psychoanalysis once was, and its recent history bears a rather striking resemblance to the history of psychoanalysis (which is not, of course, surprising, since both have taken on the semblance of "movements," with father-figures, heretics, internal disputes, and so on). It seems to me important, therefore, that the nature of behavior therapy should be examined from time to time. It will be obvious to the reader that my own views differ significantly from those of some distinguished behavior therapists. My primary intention in writing this book is not to produce converts or followers (I find such notions abhorrent) to my point of view, but rather to try to jolt people into at least examining just what it is they are doing and why they are doing it (rather than doing something else). At the same time I have tried to include a good deal of substantive material in the book, so that it could be regarded as a partial updating of *Behavior Therapy.*

The book represents the substance of a series of seminars given at Queen's University at the beginning of 1974 to graduate students in clinical psychology and to interested staff. I would like to express my gratitude to those who attended the course and criticized the viewpoint I presented. To Professor James Inglis of Queen's University I owe a special debt of gratitude—for twisting my arm to give the seminars, for reintroducing me to

Claude Bernard's classic book, and for many other favors too numerous to mention. I am deeply indebted to the Association of Universities and Colleges of Canada—without the freedom granted by their fellowship, it would not have been possible to complete this book in the time available. I am indebted to my wife who acted over several years as a part-time research assistant. The Department of Psychology at Queen's University (Head: Professor P. C. Dodwell) generously provided me with a place to hang my hat and many other facilities.

AUBREY J. YATES

University of Western Australia
September 1974

Acknowledgments

Permission to reprint the following material is gratefully acknowledged:

Quotations, pp. 7–8: From London, P., The end of ideology in behavior modification. *American Psychologist*, 1972, **27**, 913–920. Copyright 1972 by the American Psychological Association. Reprinted by permission.

Quotation, p. 10: from Lazarus, A. A., *Behavior Therapy and Beyond*. New York: McGraw-Hill, 1971, p. xii.

Quotation, p. 10: from Lazarus, A. A., Multimodal behavior therapy: treating the "basic id." *Journal of Nervous and Mental Disease*, 1973, **156**, 404–411. © (1973) The Williams & Wilkins Co., Baltimore.

Quotations, pp. 15–17: From Kuhn, T. S., *The Structure of Scientific Revolutions*. Chicago: University of Chicago Press, 1962 (2nd ed., 1970), pp. 10, 11, 13, 15, 23, 28, 39, 47–48, 56.© 1962, 1970 by the University of Chicago.

Quotations, pp. 20–23: from Bernard, C. *An Introduction to the Study of Experimental Medicine* (1865). New York: Dover, 1957, pp. 22, 23, 24, 25, 32, 55, 134–135, 137.

Quotation, pp. 37–38: from Goldfried, M. R., and Pomeranz, D. M., Role of assessment in behavior modification. *Psychological Reports*, 1968, **23**, 75–78. Reprinted with permission of author and publisher.

Quotation, pp. 39–41: from Wolpe, J., Supervision transcripts: III. Some problems in a claustrophobic case. *Journal of Behavior Therapy and Experimental Psychiatry*, 1972, **3**, 301–305. Copyright 1972, Pergamon Press, Oxford.

Quotations, p. 71: from Azrin, N. H., and Foxx, R. M., A rapid method of toilet training the institutionalized retarded. *Journal of Applied Behavior Analysis*, 1971, **4**, 89–99.

Quotation, p. 96: from Ingham, R. J., and Andrews, G., Stuttering: the quality of fluency after treatment. *Journal of Communication Disorders*, 1971, **4**, 279–288. Reprinted with permission of author and publisher (North-Holland Publishing Company, Amsterdam).

Quotation, p. 101: from Bloodstein, O., The anticipatory struggle hypothesis: implications of research on the variability of stuttering. *Journal of Speech and Hearing Research*, 1972, **15**, 487–499. Reprinted with permission of author and publisher (American Speech and Hearing Association, Washington, D.C.).

Quotation, pp. 107–108: from Sklar, B., A feedback model of the stuttering problem: an engineer's view. *Journal of Speech and Hearing Disorders*, 1969, **34**, 226–230. Reprinted with permission of the author and publisher (American Speech and Hearing Association, Washington, D.C.).

Quotations, p. 109: from Stromsta, C. Interaural phase disparity of stutterers and nonstutterers. *Journal of Speech and Hearing Research*, 1972, **15**, 771–780. Reprinted with permission of the author and publisher (American Speech and Hearing Association, Washington, D.C.).

Quotation, p. 128: from Premack, D., Mechanisms of self-control. In W. A. Hunt (Ed.), *Learning Mechanisms in Smoking*. Chicago: Aldine, 1970, pp. 107–123.

Quotation, pp. 152–153: from Watson, J. B. Behaviorism. *The Encyclopaedia Britannica*, Supplementary Volume I, 1926 (p. 346). Reprinted by permission, © *Encyclopaedia Britannica*, 13th edition (1926).

Quotation, p. 160: from Cotler, S. B., Sex differences and generalization of anxiety reduction with automated desensitization and minimal therapist interaction. *Behavior Research and Therapy*, 1970, **8**, 273–275. Reprinted with permission of the author and publisher (Pergamon Press, Oxford).

Table 1 (Chapter 1): data from Lazarus, A. A., Multimodal behavior therapy: treating the "basic id." *Journal of Nervous and Mental Disease,* 1973, 156, 404–411, tabulated data on p. 409.©(1973) The Williams & Wilkins Company, Baltimore.

Figure 1 (Chapter 2): data from Marlatt, G. A., Demming, B., and Reid, J. B., Loss of control drinking in alcoholics: an experimental analogue. *Journal of Abnormal Psychology,* 1973, **81**, 233–241, Figure 1. Copyright 1973 by the American Psychological Association. Reprinted by permission.

Figure 1 (Chapter 3): data from Collins, R. W., Importance of the bladder-cue buzzer contingency in the conditioning treatment for enuresis. *Journal of Abnormal Psychology,* 1973, **82**, 299–308, Figure 1. Copyright 1973 by the American Psychological Association. Reprinted by permission.

Figure 2 (Chapter 3): data from Finley, W. W., Besserman, R. L., Bennett, F. L., Clapp, R. K., and Finley, P. K., The effect of continuous, intermittent, and "placebo" reinforcement on the effectiveness of the conditioning treatment for enuresis nocturna. *Behavior Research and Therapy,* 1973, **11**, 289–297, Figure 1. Reprinted by permission of the authors and publisher (Pergamon Press, Oxford).

Figure 3 (Chapter 3): data from Starfield, B., Functional bladder capacity in enuretic and non-enuretic children. *Journal of Pediatrics,* 1967, **70**, 777–781, Figure 1.

Figures 1 and 2 (Chapter 4): data from Martin, R. R., Kuhl, P., and Haroldson, S., An experimental treatment with two preschool stuttering children. *Journal of Speech and Hearing Research,* 1972, **15**, 743–752, Figures 1 and 2. Reprinted with permission of the authors and publisher (American Speech and Hearing Association, Washington, D.C.).

Figure 1 (Chapter 5): data from Hunt, W. A., and Matarazzo, J. D., Three years later: recent developments in the experimental modification of smoking behavior. *Journal of Abnormal Psychology,* 1973, **81**, 107–114, Figure 1. Copyright 1973 by the American Psychological Association. Reprinted by permission.

Figure 2 (Chapter 5): data from Lichtenstein, E., Harris, D. E., Birchler, G. R., Wahl, J. M., and Schmahl, D. P., Comparison of rapid smoking, warm smoky air, and attention placebo in the modification of smoking behavior. *Journal of Consulting and*

Clinical Psychology, 1973, **40**, 92–98, Figure 1. Copyright 1973 by the American Psychological Association. Reprinted by permission.

Figure 1 (Chapter 6): data from Wollersheim, J. P., Effectiveness of group therapy based upon learning principles in the treatment of overweight women. *Journal of Abnormal Psychology*, 1970, **76**, 462–474, Figure 2. Copyright 1970 by the American Psychological Association. Reprinted by permission.

Figure 2 (Chapter 6): data from Stuart, R. B., A three-dimensional program for the treatment of obesity. *Behavior Research and Therapy*, 1971, **9**, 177–186, Figure 1. Reprinted by permission of author and publisher (Pergamon Press, Oxford).

Figure 1 (Chapter 7): from Van Egeren, L. F., Psychophysiological aspects of systematic desensitization: some outstanding issues. *Behavior Research and Therapy*, 1971, **9**, 65–77, Figure 1. Reprinted by permission of author and publisher (Pergamon Press, Oxford).

Table 1 (Chapter 7): from Van Egeren, L. F., Feather, D. W., and Hein, P. L., Desensitization of phobias: some psychophysiological propositions. *Psychophysiology*, 1971, **8**, 213–228, Table 2.

Figure 1 (Chapter 8): data from Roberts, A. H., Kewman, D. G., and MacDonald, M., Voluntary control of skin temperature: unilateral changes using hypnosis and feedback. *Journal of Abnormal Psychology*, 1973, **82**, 163–168, Figure 1. Copyright 1973 by American Psychological Association. Reprinted by permission.

Figures 2 and 3 (Chapter 8): data from Budzynski, T. H., Stoyva, J. M., Adler, C. S., and Mullaney, D. M. *EMG* biofeedback and tension headache: a controlled outcome study. *Psychosomatic Medicine*, 1973, **35**, 484–496, Figures 3 and 4.

Figure 4 (Chapter 8): data from Bleecker, E. R., and Engel, B. T., Learned control of ventricular rate in patients with atrial fibrillation. *Psychosomatic Medicine*, 1973, **35**, 161–175, Figure 1.

Figure 5 (Chapter 8): data from Elder, S. T., Ruiz, Z. R., Deabler, H. L., and Dillenkoffer, R. L. Instrumental conditioning of diastolic blood pressure in essential hypertensive patients. *Journal of Applied Behavior Analysis*, 1973, **6**, 377–382, Figure 2.

Figure 6 (Chapter 8): data from Jacobs, A., and Felton, G. S. Visual feedback of myoelectric output to facilitate muscle relaxation in normal persons and patients with neck injuries. *Archives of Physical Medicine and Rehabilitation*, 1969, **50**, 34–39, figure on p. 37.

Figure 7 (Chapter 8): data from Platt, L. J., and Basili, A. Jaw tremor during stuttering block: an electromyographic study. *Journal of Communication Disorders*, 1973, **6**, 102–109, Figure 2.

Contents

CHAPTER 1

The Role of Theory in the Practice of Behavior Therapy

BEHAVIOR THERAPY AND ITS CRITICS

The historical development of behavior therapy has been described in detail in an earlier book (Yates, 1970a, pp. 3–23), and Freedberg (1973) has provided a historical perspective for even earlier antecedents. These developments could be said to have reached their culmination in the almost simultaneous publication of four substantial summaries and interpretations of the status of behavior therapy in 1969–1970 (Bandura, 1969; Franks, 1969; Kanfer and Phillips, 1970; Yates, 1970a). In the subsequent 5 years, the pace has accelerated at a frantic rate, even beyond the trends indicated in a review by Ernst (1971). Four major journals wholly devoted to behavior therapy are now in existence, with new journals forecast[1]; and it would not be any exaggeration to assert that at least 500 papers are published each year directly dealing with some area of behavior therapy. At least 20–30 books (if all shapes and sizes are counted) on behavior therapy are published each year, together with numerous monographs, books of readings, and "how-to-do-it" manuals. Training courses oriented solely toward behavior therapy have increased rapidly

---

[1]The four journals (initial year of publication indicated in parentheses) are *Behavior Research and Therapy* (1963), *Journal of Applied Behavior Analysis* (1968), *Behavior Therapy* (1970), and the *Journal of Behavior Therapy and Experimental Psychiatry* (1970).

(Benassi and Lanson, 1972). More than 1800 persons (all of them either behavior therapists in clinical practice or people deeply interested in the possibility of using behavior therapy approaches in their work situation) attended a 1973 conference on behavior therapy held in Los Angeles (the conference has been an annual event for several years and is likely to continue to be held on this basis); only 1 month later there was a large attendance on the other side of the American continent for the annual conference in Miami of the Association for Advancement of Behavior Therapy (in addition, several other annual conferences are held on the American continent, including Canada; in South America; in Europe; and even, less frequently, in Australia). Behavior therapy flourishes in the United States, Canada, South America, Australia, England, and Europe, with national and local societies springing up at an ever-increasing rate. Truly, behavior therapy appears to have displaced psychoanalysis (if not, indeed, psychodynamic psychology as a whole) as the "in thing" (it would not be at all surprising if, in California, every film star now has to have his or her own behavior therapist, just as once he or she needed his or her own psychoanalyst).

Nonetheless, it is possible to discern a rising tide of criticism and dissent in relation to the ever-widening applications of behavior therapy. In the United States this criticism has reached as far as the halls of Congress and the state legislatures, resulting in the withdrawal of research funds, the forced abandonment of therapy programs, and the outright banning by law of some of the techniques used by behavior therapists on the grounds that they are violating the rights of patients or other persons (such as prisoners). It is unfortunate that much of this criticism rests on misconceptions about behavior therapy, which has been found guilty by false association with techniques such as sterilization programs applied to black retarded persons and psychiatric shock treatment programs such as the application of insulin shock therapy to psychotic patients without their informed consent. These kinds of criticisms (important as their practical consequences for behavior therapy may be) are not dealt with here. Several examples are given, however, of recent criticisms made of behavior therapy on practical and philosophical grounds, to indicate that all is clearly not idyllic in the new Garden of Eden.

Klein, Dittman, Parloff, and Gill (1969) have severely criticized the *practices* of both Wolpe and Lazarus after directly observing their clinical and teaching procedures. A reading of the numerous case transcriptions published by Wolpe[2] tends to verify the criticism of Klein et al. that most of the uncontrolled variables to which behavior therapists attributed the "successes" claimed by psychodynamic psychologists are present in abundant degree in the procedures used by Wolpe and Lazarus, as described in his case conferences (suggestion effects, patient/therapist uncontrolled interaction effects, and so on).

Locke (1971) has severely criticized Wolpe on both practical and theoretical grounds. Locke first identifies the basic premises of behaviorism (determinism, epiphenominalism, and rejection of introspection), and then provides evidence that he claims demonstrates that Wolpe has systematically violated at least the last two premises repeatedly in his clinical practice.

Portes (1971) has criticized behavior therapy for deriving its treatment procedures from theoretical considerations (contrasting this situation with that pertaining to psychoanalysis, which he claims developed in the reverse fashion, deriving its theory from empirical observations made while treating patients). Furthermore, he criticizes behavior therapists for ignoring what he regards as two of the most crucial aspects of human behavior, namely, *meanings* and *self-reflectiveness*. His other criticisms are similar to those made by Locke.

It is not necessary here to do more than point out these criticisms and the fact that spirited rejoinders have been made (for example, by Eysenck, 1970, 1971, 1972; Waters and

---

[2]These transcripts can be found scattered through the volumes of the *Journal of Behavior Therapy and Experimental Psychiatry*. An excerpt from one of them is given at the beginning of Chapter 2 of this book.

McCallum, 1973) to which the interested reader is referred. More importantly, perhaps, the very *definition* of behavior therapy seems to be at issue among behavior therapists themselves. Thus Eysenck (1964) defined behavior therapy as: "the attempt to alter human behavior and emotion in a beneficial manner according to the laws of modern learning theory" (p. 1). Although a perusal of subsequent accounts of behavior therapy shows that Eysenck's definition has been very widely accepted, the present writer provided a very different definition of behavior therapy:

. . . The attempt to utilize systematically that body of empirical and theoretical knowledge which has resulted from the application of the experimental method in psychology and its closely related disciplines (physiology and neurophysiology) in order to explain the genesis and maintenance of abnormal patterns of behavior; and to apply that knowledge to the treatment or prevention of those abnormalities by means of controlled experimental studies of the single case, both descriptive and remedial (Yates, 1970a, p. 18).

It will be noted that this definition, although it refers to theory, makes no reference whatever to *learning* theory as a *sine qua non* of behavior therapy. This definition regards behavior therapy as, in essence, a *methodological prescription;* that is, behavior therapy represents (or should represent) a unique and particular way of approaching the patient with respect to describing and dealing with his particular problem. The definition does *not* deny an important role to learning theory in many disorders of behavior, with respect both to explanation and to therapy; what it does deny is that the use of learning theory is the essence of behavior therapy, as claimed in Eysenck's definition.[3]

THE CLINICAL PRACTICE OF BEHAVIOR THERAPY

These criticisms of behavior therapy do not, however, relate only to the relationship between theory and practice in behavior

---

[3]For a fuller discussion of this and other misconceptions about behavior therapy see Yates (1970b).

therapy; nor to the definition of behavior therapy. The very rapid growth in the number of practicing behavior therapists gives rise to the question: What do behavior therapists in clinical practice actually do that justifies them in calling themselves "behavior therapists," rather than "psychotherapists"? When a patient presents himself with a statement that he needs help, what exactly does the practicing behavior therapist do that distinguishes him from other therapists? The answer to this question is unknown and cannot be deduced from published case reports in the literature, which represent only a very small, and no doubt biased, sample of what actually goes on in the consulting rooms of behavior therapists. The question is, however, of vital importance in view of the claims made by behavior therapists that what they do is different from, superior to, and produces better results than what is done by more "conventional" therapists.

The nature of the problem may perhaps, be clarified by placing it within the framework of the historical development of behavior therapy. One of the most critical factors leading to that development was the rejection of psychiatric diagnosis and its replacement by what might be called the behavioral model. The stages from appearance to (as it were) disappearance of the patient in these two models may be contrasted as follows:

Stage	Medical Model	Behavioral Model
I	Clinical investigation	Behavior analysis
II	Diagnosis + implications (i) etiology (ii) treatment (iii) prognosis	Target behavior selection
III	Treatment (i) notional (ii) empirical (iii) rational	Behavior modification
IV	Outcome evaluation (validation)	Outcome evaluation (validation)

With respect to the *behavioral model*, some critical questions arise that need answers urgently, but that are all too often ignored by behavior therapists:

1. What is meant by behavior analysis and how should (or does) the behavior therapist go about it?
2. What is the basis, following behavior analysis, for the selection of target behaviors? After selection, should the target behaviors be tackled successively, simultaneously, or as a gestalt?
3. Having selected one or more target behaviors, how does the clinician decide what he is now going to *do* with the patient? Apply a standard technique? Use a new technique he has not used before? Do something other than apply a technique? Most importantly, *what is his rationale for selecting and using a technique*? Or, more generally, for whatever he decides to do?
4. How does the clinician decide when to terminate whatever therapeutic procedures he is applying? What criteria does he apply to decide that the patient is sufficiently "improved" that therapy can end?

Underlying all these questions is the fundamental issue concerning the significance of theory in the clinical practice of behavior therapy. This problem arises at all of the stages outlined above—behavior analysis, selection of target behaviors, and the selection of the technique to use, or whatever other approach may be decided on. In most of this book little is, in fact, said about clinical practice as such. Rather, the role of theory in behavior therapy is considered in a much broader sense.

BEHAVIOR THERAPY AS A TECHNOLOGY

The importance of theory in the practice of behavior therapy has been strongly disputed by London (1972), by Arthur (1971), and by Lazarus (1971), all of whom favor, in one form or another, what might be called the development of a *technology* of behavior therapy and view theory with indifference or even open hositility. The views of each is considered in turn.

In a paper with the provocative title, "The end of ideology in behavior therapy," London (1972) made the following points:

1. The argument that the *practice* of behavior therapy should be derived from theory and/or laboratory experimentation was a *prestige* argument. Psychoanalysis had achieved fame largely through its complex and daring theorizing—hence to have a hope of displacing it, behavior therapy needed theoretical underpinnings also (London ignores the argument of Portes, 1971, that psychoanalytic theory developed out of its practice).

2. Learning theory was the obvious candidate at the time behavior therapy was developing.

3. However, "explanatory concepts are only necessary to explain what is going on—and until you know that, you do not need a theory, at least much of one" (p. 914).

4. Furthermore, argued London, "the only important question about systematic treatment is that of the simultaneous relevance of the treatment technique to the person's manifest trouble and to the rest of his life" (p. 915).

5. Nevertheless, the nettle of theory is firmly grasped by London: "But what about theory? If behavior modification lacks theory, then is it not reduced to a technology rather than a science? Yes, it is, and I believe that is what it should be, just as medicine is technology rather than science" (p. 916).

6. Theory is perfectly acceptable (perhaps even essential) in its proper place and at the proper time, according to London. But, he maintains, behavior therapists have never, in fact, had a theory to apply. What they have had, and what they have "applied," is only an *ideology* or rallying point. The much trumpeted "theory " in behavior therapy amounted only to a stress on the *functional analysis* of problems that has produced a proliferation of techniques for which no theory is necessary until they can be shown to work—and perhaps not even then. In any case, he argues, "theory will largely grow from practice and

practice from instrumentation, in its broadest sense" (p. 916–917).

7. Furthermore, it is largely untrue that technique develops out of theory; indeed, the reverse may sometimes be the case.

London (1972) goes on to distinguish between *metaphors* and *paradigms*, drawing on the work of Kuhn (1962) in particular. Both metaphors and paradigms are less sophisticated than *laws* and *theories*. Systematic desensitization and flooding represent, for London, examples of metaphors, whereas modeling and shaping techniques are examples of paradigms, the difference arising from the fact that in the case of a paradigm the workings are well understood, whereas in the case of metaphors they are not. Neither metaphors nor paradigms are important to clinical practice at the present time:

What *is* important, at this juncture, is the development of systematic practice and of a technology to sustain it . . . new equipment, new drugs, new gimmickry and gadgetry, should now be the basis for systematically developing new methods of behavior modification and for streamlining the established techniques with controlled experimental testing. Instead of looking for new principles, or justifying worn-out ones, we should look for new applications. What could we do to treat such-and-such if we had such-and-such machinery? What would be required to build it? To test it? And then, finally, to determine what it means? (p. 918).

To hammer home his point, London asserts that "The critical point is that *good technology* always undermines bad theory" (p. 918), and "theory has worn itself out in behavior modification and . . . technology, essentially of treatment, should now be a primary focus" (p. 919, and, finally, "The first issue, scientifically, as well as clinically, is the factual one—Do they work? On whom? When? The how and why come later" (p. 919).

Like London, Arthur (1971) has argued strongly in favor of an engineering approach to behavior modification and has pointed out that it is a mistake to believe that applications of science derive from theories and are contingent on theoretical advances.

He distinguishes three kinds of scientific activity—theoretical
science, empirical science, and engineering science: "academic
training in basic experimental research is not a substitute or even
precondition for more effective engineering and technology of
behavior that many academics seem to think it is" (p. 33). He
points to the reluctance of clinical psychologists to be regarded
as, or become, "engineers" of behavior in a real sense, that is, by
using machines, computers, and so on, because they think this
may dehumanize them. In another paper, Arthur (1972) seems to
make a very sharp distinction between theory-oriented and
action-oriented research, almost as if the two were incompatible.
Thus he argues that there are essential aspects of theoretical
scientific research that make it specifically inappropriate for
clinical decision making:

1. A theoretical study fails to assess the practical possibilities
of results obtained.
2. A laboratory study fails to take account of the moderating
effect of real-life variables.
3. The theoretical concepts used (e.g., anxiety) may bear little
relationship to the "real" anxiety patients endure.
4. The results of a theoretical study do not provide a basis for
taking action.
5. A theoretical study does not demonstrate the superiority of
its findings over alternative approaches.

Action-oriented research (which appears to be equivalent to
engineering), on the other hand:

1. Will often indicate a precise solution to a given problem.
2. Will enable the efficiency of a course of action to be
established.
3. May produce improved quality of outcome.
4. May indicate clearly the relative value of different
procedures.

Like London, therefore, Arthur concludes that what is needed at the present time in the clinical field is more action and less theory.

Lazarus' "technical eclecticism" or, as he now calls it, "multimodal behavior therapy" represents perhaps the most extreme version of the technological approach, especially coming, as it does, from one of the leading practitioners of behavior therapy. His approach is clearly illustrated in his book, *Behavior Therapy and Beyond* (1971), in which he says:

The emphasis of the volume is upon techniques rather than upon theories. . . . Technical eclecticism does not imply a random melange of techniques taken haphazardly out of the air. It is an approach which urges therapists to experiment with empirically useful methods instead of using their theories as a priori predictors of what will and will not succeed in therapy. (p. xii).

In a recent paper, Lazarus (1973) has given a particularly clear example of his current multimodal procedures. These are based on the assumption that:

most clinicians would probably agree with the pragmatic assumption that the more a patient learns in therapy, the less he is likely to relapse afterwards. Thus, an alcoholic treated only by aversion therapy would be more likely to relapse than his counterpart who had also received relaxation therapy. The benefits that accrue from aversion therapy plus relaxation training would be further potentiated by the addition of assertive training, family therapy and vocational guidance (p. 405).

Lazarus identified seven modalities that should always be investigated and that, by putting together their first letters, form an acronym with the (no doubt intended) ironical title of BASIC ID. That is, every patient-therapist interaction involves:

B—Behavior
A—Affect
S—Sensation
I—Imagery
C—Cognition
I—Interpersonal Relations
D—Drugs

(The last one—drugs—was apparently added as an afterthought to enable the acronym to be completed; it is difficult to imagine that the therapist-patient relationship will *always* involve drugs.) "Durable results are in direct proportion to the number of specific modalities deliberately invoked by any therapeutic system" (p. 407).

Lazarus provides a case illustration that shows clearly what may be involved in multimodal behavior therapy. In this case the *modality profile* (as Lazarus calls it) involved behavioral analysis in six of the seven modalities (excluding only drugs), with 31 subcategories. The eclectic nature of the treatment for this one patient is indicated by the specification and use of 27 distinct techniques, from abdominal breathing exercises to Gendlin's focusing methods. The range of behaviors treated and techniques used is shown in Table 1. According to Lazarus, these procedures were able to be blended together smoothly and logically into meaningful interventions. Furthermore, the modality profile is subject to constant revision during the course of therapy. The treatment of this patient lasted 13 months, and the outcome was described as "favorable."

The viewpoints considered above clarify another aspect of behavior therapy that has come increasingly to the fore in the last few years. It was pointed out (Yates, 1970a, pp. 388–394) that four distinct positions could be discerned concerning the relationship between behavior therapy and psychotherapy:

1. That there are fundamental differences between the two approaches that are irreconcilable.

2. That there are both similarities and differences that make the two approaches complementary.

3. That behavior therapy, when it is successful, is so because of elements in it that are of the essence of psychotherapy.

4. That psychotherapy, when it is successful, is so because of elements in it that are of the essence of behavior therapy.

It is the second viewpoint that has gained ground in recent years, though the exact relationship alleged to exist takes several different forms. Sometimes behavior therapy is given a subsidi-

Table 1. Problem Areas and Treatment Techniques in Multimodal Therapy (Single Patient)

Modality	Problem	Proposed Treatment
Behavior	Inappropropriate withdrawal responses	Assertive training
	Frequent crying	Nonreinforcement
	Unkempt appearance	Grooming instructions
	Excessive eating	Low calorie regimen
	Negative self-statements	Positive self-talk assignments
	Poor eye contact	Rehearsal techniques
	Mumbling of words with poor voice projection	Verbal projection exercises
	Avoidance of heterosexual situations	Re-education and desensitization
Affect	Unable to express overt anger	Role playing
	Frequent anxiety	Relaxation training and reassurance
	Absence of enthusiasm and spontaneous joy	Positive imagery procedures
	Panic attacks (usually precipitated by criticism from authority figures)	Desensitization and assertive training
	Suicidal feelings	Time projection techniques
	Emptiness and aloneness	General relationship building
Sensation	Stomach spasms	Abdominal breathing and relaxing
	Out of touch with most sensual pleasures	Sensate focus method
	Tension in jaw and neck	Differential relaxation
	Frequent lower back pains	Orthopedic exercises
	Inner tremors	Gendlin's focusing methods (8, p. 232)
Imagery	Distressing scenes of sister's funeral	Desensitization
	Mother's angry face shouting "You fool!"	Empty chair technique

12

Table 1. Problem Areas and Treatment Techniques in Multimodal Therapy (Single Patient) (continued)

Modality	Problem	Proposed Treatment
	Performing fellatio on God	Blow up technique (implosion)
	Recurring dreams about airplane bombings	Eidetic imagery invoking feelings of being safe
Cognition	Irrational self-talk: "I am evil." "I must suffer." "Sex is dirty." "I am inferior."	Deliberate rational disputation and corrective self-talk
	Syllogistic reasoning, overgeneralization	Parsing of irrational sentences
	Sexual misinformation	Sexual education
Interpersonal relationships	Characterized by childlike dependence	Specific self-sufficiency assignments
	Easily exploited/submissive	Assertive training
	Overly suspicious	Exaggerated role taking
	Secondary gains from parental concern	Explain reinforcement principles to parents and try to enlist their help
	Manipulative tendencies	Training in direct and confrontative behaviors

Source: Lazarus, 1973.

ary role, preparing the ground at a superficial level, as it were, for the more serious digging that can then proceed along psychodynamic lines. Or behavior therapy may be regarded as a genuine equal partner, with each kind of therapy being suited to particular kinds of disorders (though behavior therapy is often allotted the less complex disorders, such as "simple" phobias). Not infrequently, the same practitioner will utilize both behavior therapy and psychotherapy simultaneously with the same patient. Perhaps the most extreme example of this is to be found in a recent study by Astor (1973) who carried out behavior therapy on a patient as a prelude to pyschoanalysis. Weitzenhoffer (1972) and Barber and his colleagues (Spanos, De Moor, and Barber, 1973) have made detailed comparisons between the procedures used in therapy by behavior therapists and hypnotists. These comparisons would, presumably, be congenial at least to London and Arthur (though certainly not to Lazarus), since they stress the technology of therapy rather than its theoretical aspects.

London argued that the disappearance of theory from behavior therapy would be beneficial; he, Arthur, and Lazarus argued for a technology of behavior therapy, finding out (it is not stated how) what works best in particular types of problems and then developing these technical (and technologically based) procedures to the highest possible level of efficiency. All three agreed that the predominance of theory has hampered the development of behavior therapy as a clinical or applied endeavor, and argued that development of a technology is not dependent on the development of theoretical sophistication. These arguments cannot be sustained, as a careful examination of the work of Kuhn (1962) reveals.

London made a distinction between *metaphors* (citing systematic desensitization as an example) and *paradigms* (citing the Skinnerian approach as an example). He defines a paradigm as "an attempt to construct a direct model or example of how something works" (p. 917), and he clearly thinks that he has derived this definition from Kuhn's work on the use of paradigms in science. But London has completely misunderstood Kuhn's account of the nature and role of paradigms in science. Because the notion of paradigm, as used by Kuhn, has been widely misused by psychologists (especially writers of textbooks) in recent years, a detailed account of Kuhn's use of the term is appropriate.

The main points of Kuhn's position follow.

Paradigms are "accepted examples of actual scientific practice—examples which include law, theory, application and instrumentation together—[which] provide models from which spring particular coherent traditions of scientific research" (p. 10). Examples of paradigms cited by Kuhn include Copernican astronomy, Newtonian dynamics, and corpuscular optics. Paradigms can be very broad or relatively narrow (e.g., Maxwell's theorems).

The common characteristic of paradigms is that the paradigm is *accepted* as a common framework within which scientists doing "normal science" work: "Men whose research is based on shared paradigms are committed to the same rules and standards for scientific practice" (p. 11).

The foregoing definition clearly rules out the interpretation of paradigms made by London, for a prevailing paradigm will be accepted as valid for the time being by *all* scientists within the overall discipline, whether working within the particular paradigm or not. By no stretch of the imagination could it be said that all psychologists accept the validity of the Skinnerian approach, and thus it cannot possibly qualify as a paradigm in Kuhn's sense.

It is, in fact, quite clear that all psychology is still in the *preparadigm* stage. As Kuhn points out: "the preparadigm period, in particular, is regularly marked by frequent and deep debates over legitimate methods, problems, and standards of solution, though these serve rather to define schools than to produce agreement" (p. 47–48). In making this statement, Kuhn was *not* referring to psychology, but clearly it does almost precisely describe the present position in psychology.

Kuhn provides a particularly illuminating example of paradigm growth from the history of physical optics. As he points out, three main paradigms have been accepted by scientists as working models: present day—light as photons (Einstein, Planck); nineteenth century—light as tranverse wave motion (Young); eighteenth century—light as corpuscular (Newton) Of especial interest, however, is the preparadigm position in physical optics. Before Newton there was no paradigm, only competing views. The appearance of Newton's paradigm, however, forced scientists from then on to work within a restricted framework—competing views were simply phased out by being ignored:

Anyone examining a survey of physical optics before Newton may well conclude that, though the field's practitioners were scientists, the net result of their activity was something less than science. Being able to take no common body of belief for granted each writer on physical optics felt forced to build his field anew from its foundations. In doing so, his choice of supporting observation and experiment was relatively free, for there was no standard set of methods or of phenomena that every optical writer felt forced to employ and explain. Under these circumstances, the dialogue of the resulting books was often directed as much to the members of other schools as it was to nature (p. 13).

After Newton, of course, this situation no longer obtained. If "psychology" (or even "behavior therapy") is substituted for "physical optics" in the above quotation, the present position in psychology is perfectly described.

If it is accepted that psychology is still in the preparadigm stage, does it then follow that theorizing is premature and that behavior therapists should therefore concentrate on developing a technology of behavior therapy? Again, an example from Kuhn will help to refute this proposition. The example is taken from the problem of explaining electrical phenomena. In the preparadigm phase, there were many empirical observations made concerning electrical phenomena, but serious disagreement (just as in psychology at present) as to which phenomena were fundamental or basic, and, indeed, even the *nature* of the phenomena were misread. Thus one school held that *attraction* and *friction* were the fundamental phenomena to be investigated—*repulsion* was considered to be mechanical, not electrical in nature, and *conduction* effects were simply ignored. For a second school, attraction and repulsion were fundamental phenomena, and conduction was ignored. For yet a third school, conduction was regarded as the fundamental phenomenon, but attraction and repulsion were ignored or explained away.

Thus in the absence of a paradigm, scientists could not agree on what the important data were. As Kuhn puts it: "in the absence of a paradigm . . . all of the facts that could possibly pertain to the development of a given science are likely to seem equally relevant" (p. 15). All these differences about which phenomena were regarded as basic disappeared only when Franklin's work led to a theory that incorporated all the phenomena and provided a common paradigm which then dictated what scientists should look for and what kind of experiments they should carry out. "Paradigms gain their status because they are more successful than their competitors in solving a few problems that the group of practitioners has come to recognize as acute" (p. 23).

Kuhn, in fact, is especially critical of the view that empiricism must precede theory. As an example, he refers to the fact that: "the electron-scattering maxima that were later diagnosed as indices of electron wave-length had no apparent significance when first observed and recorded. Before they became measures of anything, they had to be related to a theory that predicted the wave-like behavior of matter in motion" (p. 39). Kuhn also denies that laws such as Boyle's law, Coulomb's law, or Joule's formula can be discovered without the existence of a paradigm:

> We often hear that they [the laws] are found by examining measurements undertaken for their own sake and without theoretical commitment. But history offers no support for so excessively Baconian a method. Boyle's experiments were not conceivable (and, if conceived, would have received another interpretation or none at all) until air was recognized as an elastic fluid to which all the elaborate concepts of hydrostatics could be applied (p. 28).

In relation to the discovery of oxygen, Kuhn maintains that: "what Lavoisier announced in his papers from 1777 on was not so much the discovery of oxygen as the oxygen theory of combustion. That theory was the keystone for a reformulation of chemistry so vast that it is usually called the chemical revolution" (p.56).

Kuhn's analysis of the history of advances in science by way of paradigms has not, of course, gone unchallenged (Lakatos and Musgrave, 1970). It has even been suggested quite seriously that young scientists should be protected from evidence of the often irrational and intuitive behavior of the great scientists, lest their belief in the rational and objective nature of science itself be undermined (Brush, 1974). Although the present writer finds Kuhn's analysis of compelling relevance to the current scene in psychology, others may not.

Enough has been said to show that psychology is still in the preparadigm stage and that it is highly likely that it will not advance significantly until a paradigm is found which will be accepted by all psychologists as valid, and that this paradigm will not appear if psychologists abandon theorizing and merely concentrate on being empiricists. It should also be pointed out, however, that a paradigm, when accepted, is not a complete theory, nor is a paradigm necessarily able to be readily validated. For example, Newton's paradigm proved to be quite extraordinarily difficult to explicate, and only one agreed prediction from Einstein's paradigm has yet been checked. Nevertheless, the paradigm changes the activities of scientists decisively once it is accepted, and it is accepted primarily because it unifies critical observations that previous paradigms can no longer accommodate, or, in the case of an initial paradigm, because it brings order out of chaos. Most importantly, perhaps, once the paradigm is accepted, there is no "going back"—certain activities that were quite legitimate scientific activities before the acceptance of a paradigm would lead to professional ruin as a scientist if indulged in after acceptance of the paradigm (in psychology by contrast, the enormous influence exercised by the Skinnerian approach, or, more generally, by behaviorism, has not prevented the reemergence of imagery as a major area of study).

The acceptance of the preparadigm status of psychology still leaves open the question of how to proceed in trying to solve the problems of individuals in society. Kuhn's analysis of what goes on in the preparadigm state indicates clearly that it would not only be unncecessary to abandon the therapeutic endeavor until a paradigm is found, but that such a decision would contradict what is known about the development of science. He has shown that, in the preparadigm state, both theory *and* practice proliferate rather than stagnate, the difference between pre- and post-paradigm states lying in the *discipline* with which scientists work. Furthermore, the initial paradigm will arise only out of this undisciplined activity.

It does not, therefore, follow from the foregoing analysis that, in the absence of a generally accepted theoretical base, behavior therapists must rely solely for the present on blind technology, thrashing about multimodally in the dark until a technique is discovered by chance that appears to "work" (Kuhn is particularly contemptuous of such blind empiricism). There are several immediate suggestions that may be made to enable behavior therapists to proceed in clinical work in a rational and systematic manner. First, a great deal can be learned by behavior therapists by careful consideration of the approach of experimental *physiologists* in relation to medicine, as exemplified in the work of Claude Bernard. Second, and developing out of this, the application of the experimental study of the single case, as developed by Shapiro and others, provides a rational basis for handling the presenting problems of individual patients. Third, the use of "theory" in a rather special and restricted sense may increase the power of the approach advocated by Shapiro and Bernard—although, in fact, "theory," as it is used here, is only a special instance of Bernard's approach.

BERNARD AND THE EXPERIMENTAL METHOD

Claude Bernard was one of the truly great men of the nineteenth century, and his ideas on how to do research in biology revolutionized physiology, neurophysiology, and experimental pathology, not to mention criminal pathology, exemplified in the twentieth century detective work of Spillsbury. Essentially, the experimental method for Bernard consisted of four stages:

1. Making an observation of some aspect of nature's functioning (the observation may arise by chance or through deliberate arrangement of a set of conditions).
2. Asking an appropriate question about how the observed fact may be interpreted—this activity invariably involving hypothesis-making.
3. Setting up experimental conditions in such a way that as clear an answer as possible might be obtained in terms of deductions made from the hypothesis.
4. From this experiment, noting the new phenomena that result.

Bernard stressed the distinction between hypothesis making and the observation of data. In the former, the investigator must be active and creative; in the latter, objective and uninvolved:

An experimenter...........is a man inspired by a more or less probable but anticipated interpretation of observed phenomena to devise experiments which, in the logical order of his anticipations, shall bring results serving as controls for his hypothesis or preconceived idea...........Of necessity, we experiment with a preconceived idea. . . . But when the conditions of an experiment are once established . . . the experimenter is confronted with a real observation which he has induced and must note, like any other observation, without any preconceived idea. The experimenter must now disappear or rather change himself instantly into an observer; and it is only after he has noted the results of the experiment exactly, like those of an ordinary observation, that his mind will come back, to reason, compare and decide whether his experimental hypothesis is verified or disproved by these very results (p. 22).

Bernard particularly stressed the importance of "ideas" or hypotheses: "I consider it, therefore, an absolute principle that experiments must always be devised in view of a preconceived idea, no matter if the idea be not very clear nor very well defined" (p. 23), and again: "People who condemn the use of hypotheses and of preconceived ideas in the experimental method make the mistake of confusing invention of an experiment with noting its results" (p. 24). He was as scornful as Kuhn of pure empiricism: "Men who gather observations are useful only because their observations are afterward introduced into experimental reasoning; in other words endless accummulation of observations leads nowhere" (p. 25). He gives an amusing example of this: a group of scientists wished to observe everything excreted by a cat during a specified period of time. It happened that, unknown to the experimenters, the cat was pregnant, and, when it gave birth to kittens during the period of observation, the experimenters dutifully noted the kittens down as excretions.

Thus, says Bernard: "an anticipative idea or an hypothesis is, then, the necessary starting point for all experimental reasoning. Without it, we could not make any investigation at all nor learn anything; we could only pile up sterile observations" (p. 32). Bernard was well aware, of course, that hypothesis making could lead to biased observation; it is the combination of creative hypothesis making and objective experimental observation that produces advance in knowledge.

A careful examination of both Bernard's precepts and of the many examples he gives of his approach to actual experimental problems will show that his model of research is one that could very profitably be followed by behavior therapists at the present time. The method can, in fact, be regarded as a general statement of the experimental investigation of the single case. Bernard is particularly sceptical of averaging procedures and group mean comparisons, and he gives an amusing example to illustrate his point, which has a startlingly modern ring to it:

If we collect a man's urine during twenty-four hours and mix all this urine to analyze the average, we get an analysis of a urine which simply does not exist; for urine, when fasting, is different from urine during digestion. A startling instance of this kind was invented by a physiologist who took urine from a railroad station urinal where people of all nations passed, and who believed he could thus present an analysis of *average* European urine!" (pp. 134–135).

For Bernard, there is no such thing as error—every observation has its explanation:

In my opinion, statistics can never yield scientific truth, and therefore cannot establish any final scientific method. A simple example will illustrate my meaning. Certain experimenters...........published experiments by which they found that the anterior spinal roots are insensitive; other experimenters published experiments by which they found that the same roots are sensitive. These cases seemed as comparable as possible; here was the same operation done by the same method in the same spinal roots. Should we therefore have counted the positive and negative cases and said: the law is that the anterior roots are sensitive, for instance, 25 times out of a 100? Or should we have admitted, according to the theory called the law of large numbers, that in an immense number of experiments we should find the roots equally often sensitive and insensitive? Such statistics would be ridiculous, for there is a reason for the roots being insensitive, and another reason for their being sensitive; this reason had to be defined; I looked for it, and I found it; so that we can now say: the spinal roots are always sensitive in given conditions and always insensitive in other equally definite conditions" (p. 137).

Bernard's approach bears a remarkable resemblance to the two principal single-case approaches to the description and remediation of abnormal forms of behavior, namely, the work of Shapiro, on the one hand, and the work of the operantly-inclined behavior therapists, on the other. Consider, for example, the experiment reported by Bernard, following a casual observation that puzzled him. He observed that a group of rabbits brought into his laboratory displayed clear and acid urine. The puzzle arose from the fact that rabbits, which are herbivora, usually have cloudy, alkaline urine, whereas carnivora have clear and acid urine. Bernard's straightforward hypothesis was that the rabbits must be in an unusual nutritional condition (that of carnivora) not normally found in rabbits. He further hypothesized that this condition arose from the rabbits having been transformed, by fasting, into carnivorous animals, living on their own blood. He tested his hypothesis by systematically alternating conditions in which they fasted or ate grass and found that, when they fasted, their urine was clear and acid; whereas when they ate grass, their urine was cloudy and alkaline. The devotee of the operant literature on behavior modification will recognize this procedure as an example of the A–B–A reversal design beloved of these workers,100 years before they invented it.

This example also illustrates another innovation of Bernard's which was "rediscovered" more than 100 years later— what he calls the counterproof. Bernard actually defines counterproof in A–B–A terms. Thus he writes:

proof that a given condition always precedes or accompanies a phenomenon does not warrant concluding with certainty that a given condition is the immediate cause of that phenomenon. It must still be established that, when this condition is removed, the phenomenon will no longer appear. If we limited ourselves to the proof of presence alone, we might fall into error at any moment and believe in relations of cause and effect where there was nothing but simple coincidence. As we shall later see, coincidences form one of the most dangerous stumbling blocks encountered by experimental scientists in complex sciences like biology. It is the *post hoc, ergo propter hoc* of the doctors, into which we may very easily let ourselves be led, especially if the result of an experiment or an observation supports a preconceived idea (p. 55).

However, in instituting a counterproof as the crucial test of his hypothesis concerning the reason for the rabbits' urine being clear and acid, Bernard used a procedure quite different from the A–B–A design. What he did, in fact, was to feed his rabbits meat and predict that their urine would be clear as it was when they were fasting, but not when they were eating grass. Thus he fed his rabbits on cold boiled beef (which, he says, they eat very nicely when given nothing else) and indeed their urine did become clear and acid in this condition. Actually, Bernard went even further than this, for when he sacrificed the animals and performed an autopsy to see if the meat was ingested in the same way as in carnivora (a *further* test of his hypothesis) he made some unexpected observations which set him off again.

THE EXPERIMENTAL INVESTIGATION OF THE SINGLE CASE

It is not necessary to follow Bernard further, but it should be noted that the method of the experimental investigation of the single case pioneered by Shapiro in the early 1950s resembles the approach of Bernard to an extraordinary degree, although it appears that Shapiro was not aware of Bernard's work at the time he developed his approach. Because Shapiro's work has been described in some detail elsewhere (Yates, 1970a, pp. 15–17), and because a much fuller account is available in Inglis (1966), not to mention the many articles published by Shapiro himself, which have not received the attention they merit, his approach is not fully considered here. Nor, for the same reasons, is time spent describing the single-case approach as practised by the operant psychologists, of which countless examples are now available in the behavior modification literature (especially in the *Journal of Applied Behavior Analysis*). The case for $n = 1$ research has also been made at some length by Yates (1970a). Attention may be drawn, however, to some crucial points that have come to the fore in recent years.

Single-case methodology has developed greatly over the past 5 years. Very recently, detailed accounts have been published about various designs for $n = 1$ research, notably by Leitenberg (1973), Barlow and Hersen (1973), Liberman, Davis, Moon, and Moore (1973), and McNamara and MacDonough (1972). The strategies described by Leitenberg, and by Barlow and Hersen, and used in behavior modification practice, fall into three main groups:

1. *reversal and withdrawal designs* (the familiar A–B–A design and its more complex variants).
2. *multiple baseline designs*, in which several behaviors are treated sequentially in an overlapping manner.
3. *multiple schedule designs*, in which one specific form of behavior is shown to be under the differential control of various schedules of reinforcement.

The statistical and inferential problems associated with single-case studies have come under increasing attention, culminating in the important recent paper by Gentile, Roden, and Klein (1972), that shows how analysis of variance procedures may (if desired) be applied appropriately to testing hypotheses in successive reversal designs for single-subject experiments.

Several important single-case studies have been published in recent years that show clearly the payoff that may result from the intensive single-case study in which essentially Bernard's method of putting questions systematically to nature, rather than simply trying schedules of reinforcement on an *ad hoc* basis, has been utilized. Some of these studies emanate, interestingly enough, from rather unexpected sources. Among those that bear close scrutiny are the study by Alexander, Chai, Creer, Miklich, Renne, and Cardoso (1973) on the elimination of chronic cough by response suppression shaping; the study by Ayllon, Smith, and Rogers (1970) on the behavioral management of school phobia; the study by Cohen, Liebson, and Faillace (1971) on the role of reinforcement contingencies in chronic alcoholism; the dramatic study by Ludwig, Marx, Hill, and Browning (1969) on the control of violent behavior by faradic shock; and the study by Sachs, Martin, and Fitch on the use of visual feedback to control digital performance in a functionally deaf, cerebral palsied child.

Several studies have highlighted the need for individual analysis and experimental treatment and illustrate clearly the dangers of simply considering the patient as a member of a homogeneous group of patients to whom a standard form of treatment can be applied. Among these may be included the study by Barrett (1969) on four mentally defective brothers who, on standardized tests, performed very similarly, but whose behavioral individuality (the term is Barrett's) showed up very clearly on the Barrett/Lindsley operant discrimination apparatus (Barrett concluded that these individual variations had specific implications for treatment programming); Browning's (1971) study, also with defective children, that demonstrated the need for individually designed remedial programs; and the similar demonstration by Hingten and Churchill (1969) in relation to mute autistic children.

THE USE OF THEORY IN CLINICAL BEHAVIOR THERAPY

The approach of Bernard in physiology and of Shapiro in psychology involved essentially the art of asking the right questions, on the one hand, and of devising objective, experimentally based ways of obtaining answers to these questions, on the other. Because psychology is still in the preparadigm stage, however, it is difficult to argue that formal theories are available at present that will be helpful in answering the questions asked (even though theories proliferate in psychology). Thus it is not surprising that clinical behavior therapists have not made much use of formal psychological theories in devising therapy approaches to individual patients. Nevertheless, where use *can* be made of existing theories, the payoff is likely to be substantial in suggesting specific ways of changing the behavior of the patient. As an illustration, the writer may, perhaps, be excused for using one of his own clinical/experimental studies that demonstrates the important role theory may play when it relevant to the problem in hand (Yates, 1958). The patient in question was a young lady with four severe tics—nasal, eyeblink, throat-clearing, and stomach-contraction, that appeared to have originated simultaneously as a group when she underwent anesthetization for dentistry at the age of 11. She felt that she was being suffocated when the gas-inhalation unit was placed over her nose and mouth, and clearly the four tics could be regarded as originally an unconditioned fear response to this traumatic event. This explanation of the genesis of the tics as conditioned avoidance responses that somehow reduced the fear was, in fact, unnecessary (though interesting) in terms of the derivation of a treatment technique. The patient was, of course, a real clinical patient presenting for treatment, and little time was available for deciding what to do—a not atypical situation in clinical practice. What was done, in fact , was to derive a method of treatment from the then predominant learning theory of Clark Hull. Hull's basic equation is still well known:

$$S\bar{E}_R = (_SH_R \times D) - (I_R + _SI_R)$$

In general terms, $_S\bar{E}_R$ refers to effective excitatory potential, $_SH_R$ to habit strength, D to drive, I_R to reactive inhibition, and $_SI_R$ to conditioned inhibition. In relation to the presenting problem (the tics) of the patient, $_S\bar{E}_R$ would refer to the patient's momentary ability to produce the tics at a given moment in time, and this would be a function of the relative balance of the excitatory forces (habit strength and drive) and inhibitory forces (reactive and conditioned inhibition) of the equation.

The theoretical argument from which the treatment program was derived follows.

At the time the patient presented, it was assumed that I_R and $_SI_R$ were effectively zero and that the patient's performance was a function of D and $_SH_R$ only—as D (drive or anxiety) increased, so $_S E_R$ (reaction potential) increased. Thus in the face of anxiety-arousing situations, the patient's performance rate would increase as a function of the level of D.

Now, a whole body of literature, based on the results of studies with both rats and humans, had led Hull to include in his formula the two theoretical constructs of I_R and $_SI_R$. Reactive inhibition I_R increases as a function of repetitions of a response and declines during intervals between responding. If the interval between responses is too short to allow the dissipation of all I_R then it accumulates over trials and, eventually, if it achieves sufficient magnitude, will force the animal (or person) to stop responding. In itself this is, of course, a trivial finding—it is equivalent merely to saying that if a sprinter runs the 100 meters 10 times in rapid succession, he will run more slowly on each occasion. With sufficient rest he will recover his original times. However, Hull argued further that the accumulation of I_R is an aversive state and that, therefore, the dissipation of I_R during a period of not responding will be reinforcing and, furthermore, that it will be the response of not responding that will be strengthened. Conditioned inhibition $_SI_R$ is therefore itself a habit, but one with the important property of being incompatible with the response which has produced the involuntary rest pause (*IRP*), as it was called.

To produce an *IRP*, it was found that massed practice of the response was required; that is, the interval between successive evocations of the response should be as small as possible, thus preventing the dissipation of I_R.

The deduction made from Hull's theory was, therefore, quite straightforward: if the patient was required to repeat the tics under conditions of massed practice, she would accumulate I_R to the point at which *IRP*s would occur, during which I_R would dissipate, generating increments of $_SI_R$. If $_SI_R$ could be increased in this manner to the point at which "not being able to perform the tic" ($_SI_R$) was equal in strength to "ability to perform the tic" ($_SH_R$), then the tic should be reduced effectively to zero in its overt manifestation.

Now, the particular point to be noted about this experiment (for it was presented to the patient as such) is that the use of massed practice was specifically derived from theoretical considerations and would almost certainly not have been used if Hull's theoretical model (and the associated empirical evidence) had not been available. After all, "practice makes perfect" (and, indeed, had done so in this patient), and the natural expectation would have been either further increases in the patient's ability to perform the tic or a completely trivial finding of decrement during practice, followed by complete recovery after a short rest. Indeed, throughout the study, every time the patient returned after a rest period (which, late in the study, might extend over days or even weeks), it was anticipated that the tic would have recovered to its original strength (in fact, however, a kind of reverse reminiscence effect in which significant decrements took place during rest was found). The crucial element in the whole therapeutic rationale was Hull's construct of $_SI_R$ (conditioned inhibition)—without this construct to mediate the procedure, there would really have been no justification for subjecting the patient to the ordeal of prolonged periods of practicing the very responses of which she wished to be relieved.

This example illustrates a further important point relating to the clinical practice of behavior therapy. There was no problem of behavioral analysis here, of course, although it is true that the analysis of the patient's tics (where, when, and with what frequency the four responses were manifested, their degree of interrelatedness, and so on) was inadequate by modern standards. the decision concerning what to do about the presenting problem was based on a consideration of the implications of Hull's model. However, there remains the problem of evaluating the outcome of the therapy or techniques used. Briefly, currently, behavior therapists appear to approach the question of the validation of therapy procedures in respect of *clinical* patients in one of two ways.

The first of these is derived from procedures that were criticized strongly by the present writer (Yates, 1970a) and is related to the use of standard behavior therapy techniques applied to defined, supposedly homogenous groups of patients for the purpose of comparing the results obtained with alternative standard nonbehavior therapy techniques applied to matched groups of patients. Thus the behavior therapist, having satisfied himself that these studies provide evidence that, for example, systematic desensitization is an appropriate therapy for phobias, and is significantly superior to other techniques, will, faced with a patient with a phobia, decide to use systematic desensitization and will then evaluate the outcome (including assessments made during treatment) in terms of one, several, or many dependent variables such as change in status of main and subsidiary phobias, general adequacy of adjustment, sexual and family relationships, and work record. This approach is unsatisfactory because it is essentially a version of the medical model—that is, a patient is categorized as having a defined disorder, a standard form of treatment is then applied, and a result is obtained that indicates that the patient is improved, unchanged, or worse, on a number of indices of behavior (physiological, verbal, or performance). If the patient is worse, some other technique or techniques are tried, or the patient is discharged. Although this may seem to be an unfair representation of what behavior therapists in clinical practice actually do, it is contended that a careful examination (or even experimental study) of the actual practices of clinical behavior therapists (as opposed to accepting their verbal protestations of what they do) would show that this pattern is, in fact, very common.

The therapy approach just described is typically found in the practice of those behavior therapists who make extensive use of such techniques as systematic desensitization or covert sensitization, that is, procedures deriving essentially from the approach of Wolpe. The fact that details of the procedures may be varied as they are applied to an individual patient does not negate the point made, any more than it would in the case of the analogous use of drugs, in which the body weight of the patient is considered in determining the individual dosage to be given. A quite different approach, one certainly much closer to what is being recommended here, is found in the work of those behavior therapists utilizing the operant approach. Here, of course, the emphasis is much more on bringing a particular response class under experimental control and demonstrating this by the use of reversal, multiple baseline, and multiple schedule designs. There is, however, a serious methodological difficulty involved in this approach, which has never been squarely faced by its proponents. The reversal design is said to be an appropriate design because it shows that the behavior in question is under experimental (which is equivalent to reinforcement) control; that is, the undesirable behavior is first shown to be manifested under certain conditions; the introduction of a specified contingency is shown to eliminate or reduce the undesired behavior; and the withdrawal of the contingency is shown to lead to the reinstatement of the undesired behavior (the reference here is, of course, only to the simplest design situation). This line of approach involves the assumption that irreversible behavior change can never really be achieved, whereas it is commonly hoped by most behavior therapists that undesirable behaviors can be permanently eliminated in the sense that they cannot be recovered in their original form—the problems of enuresis and stuttering will serve as obvious examples in which this would be the hoped-for outcome. Thus those using the operant approach paradoxically usually express disappointment if not bewilderment when, so they believe, having caused an undesirable behavior to disappear by the introduction of an appropriate contingency, they are unable to reinstate it when the contingency is withdrawn—a finding that is more common in the literature (and even more so in studies rejected for publication—often precisely on these grounds) than is generally admitted or recognized.

It is suggested here that there is a third approach to the problem of validating behavior therapy interventions. The question may be asked: given the presenting problem, and given the procedures used, is the patient improved, unchanged, or worse (by whatever criteria are specified)? or, given the presenting problem, and having changed specified behavior by introducing or withdrawing specified contingencies, can validity be demonstrated by reinstating the behavior? However, the question may be approached instead by way of deducing predictions from hypothesis as to what should happen under specified conditions and looking to see if what is predicted does in fact happen. The criterion of validity then becomes not whether the patient improved, stayed the same, or got worse; nor can the abnormal behavior be reinstated; but rather was the deduction verified or not? Thus the criterion of validity becomes what may be called an *internal* criterion; that is, whether changes in the patient's behavior do or do not agree with what was predicted would occur in terms of the hypothesis and deductions made from it. The treatment of the patient then becomes a true single-case experimental investigation, but one that has no simple outcome in terms of whether the patient "gets better" or not. The approach suggested, although being much closer to the procedures of the operantly inclined behavior therapists than to the procedures used by the followers of Wolpe and Lazarus, does differ in important respects from the approach of the operant behavior therapists, most notably, of course, in its explicit use of hypothesis formulation in terms of some general model or theory. As already pointed out, however, it is probable that the number of occasions on which explicit theory can be meaningfully used, as in the case of the tic study, may be relatively small at present. In relation to routine clinical use, therefore, this recommended approach probably reduces to a combination of the Shapiro strategy with the Bernard philosophy, that is, that the clinical practice of behavior therapy essentially should involve asking the right questions and devising appropriate means of answering those questions, if possible by way of the explicit use of theory and hypothesis construction leading to precise experimental investigation. Although many clinical behavior therapists may say (indignantly perhaps) that this is, in fact, what they do, the writer begs leave to doubt it. In line with Lazarus' extreme position, there is little doubt that the clinical behavior therapist is looking mainly for standard techniques that he can apply in standard fashion to standard patients. This does not appear to be the best way to advance the practice of behavior therapy.

REFERENCES

Alexander, A. B., Chai, H., Creer, T. L., Miklich, D. R., Renne, C. M., and Cardoso, R. de A. The elimination of chronic cough by response suppression shaping. *Journal of Behavior Therapy and Experimental Psychiatry*, 1973, **4**, 75–80.

Arthur, A. Z. Psychology as engineering and technology of behavior. *Canadian Psychologist*, 1971, **12**, 30–36.

Arthur, A. Z. Theory- and action-oriented research. *Journal of Consulting and Clinical Psychology*, 1972, **38**, 129–133.

Astor, M. H. Hypnosis and behavior modification combined with psychoanalytic psychotherapy. *International Journal of Clinical and Experimental Hypnosis*, 1973, **21**, 18–24.

Ayllon, T., Smith, D., and Rogers, M. Behavioral management of school phobia. *Journal of Behavior Therapy and Experimental Psychiatry*, 1970, **1**, 125–138.

Bandura, A. *Principles of behavior modification*. New York: Holt, Rinehart and Winston, 1969.

Barlow, D. H., and Hersen, M. Single-case experimental designs. *Archives of General Psychiatry*, 1973, **29**, 319–325.

Barrett, B. H. Behavioral individuality in four cultural-familially retarded brothers. *Behavior Research and Therapy*, 1969, **7**, 79–91.

Benassi, V., and Lanson, R. A survey of the teaching of behavior modification in colleges and universities. *American Psychologist*, 1972, **27**, 1063–1069.

Bernard, C. *An introduction to the study of experimental medicine (1865).* New York: Dover, 1957.

Browning, R. M. Treatment effects of a total behavior modification program with five autistic children. *Behavior Research and Therapy*, 1971, **9**, 319–327.

Brush, S. G. Should the history of science be rated X? *Science*, 1974, **183**, 1164–1172.

Cohen, M., Liebson, I. A., and Faillace, L. A. The role of reinforcement contingencies in chronic alcoholism: An experimental analysis of one case. *Behavior Research and Therapy*, 1971, **9**, 375–379.

Ernst, F. A. Behavior therapy and training in clinical psychology: A student's perspective. *Journal of Behavior Therapy and Experimental Psychiatry*, 1971, **2**, 75–79.

Eysenck, H. J. The nature of behavior therapy. In H. J. Eysenck (Ed.), *Experiments in behavior therapy*, London: Pergamon, 1964. Pp. 1–15.

Eysenck, H. J. Behavior therapy and its critics. *Journal of Behavior Therapy and Experimental Psychiatry*, 1970, **1**, 5–15.

Eysenck, H. J. Behavior therapy as a scientific discipline. *Journal of Consulting and Clinical Psychology*, 1971, **36**, 314–319.

Eysenck, H. J. Behavior therapy is behavioristic. *Behavior Therapy*, 1972, **3**, 609–613.

Franks, C. M. *Behavior therapy: Appraisal and status.* New York: McGraw-Hill, 1969.

Freedberg, E. J. Behavior therapy: A comparison between early (1880–1920) and contemporary techniques. *Canadian Psychologist*, 1973, **14**, 225–240.

Gentile, J. R., Roden, A. H., and Klein, R. D. An analysis-of-variance model for the intrasubject replication design. *Journal of Applied Behavior Analysis*, 1972, **5**, 193–198.

Hingten, J. N., and Churchill, D. W. Identification of perceptual limitations in mute autistic children: identification by use of behavior modification. *Archives of General Psychiatry*, 1969, **21**, 68–71.

Inglis, J. *The scientific study of abnormal behavior.* Chicago: Aldine, 1966.

Kanfer, F. H., and Phillips, J. S. *Learning foundations of behavior therapy.* New York: Wiley, 1970.

Klein, M. H., Dittman, A. T., Parloff, M. B., and Gill, M. M. Behavior therapy: observations and reflections. *Journal of Consulting and Clinical Psychology*, 1969, **33**, 259–266.

Kuhn, T. S. *The structure of scientific revolutions.* Chicago: University of Chicago Press, 1962. (2nd ed., 1970)

Latakos, I., and Musgrave, A. (Eds.) *Criticism and the growth of knowledge.* London: Cambridge University Press, 1970.

Lazarus, A. A. *Behavior therapy and beyond.* New York: McGraw-Hill, 1971.

Lazarus, A. A. Multimodal behavior therapy: Treating the "basic id." *Journal of Nervous and Mental Disease,* 1973, **156,** 404–411.

Leitenberg, H. The use of single-case methodology in psychological research. *Journal of Abnormal Psychology,* 1973, **82,** 87–101.

Liberman, R. P., Davis, J., Moon, W., and Moore, J. Research design for analyzing drug-environment-behavior interaction. *Journal of Nervous and Mental Disease,* 1973, **156,** 432–439.

Locke, E. A. Is "behavior therapy" behavioristic? (an analysis of Wolpe's psychotherapeutic methods). *Psychological Bulletin,* 1971, **76,** 318–327.

London, P. The end of ideology in behavior modification. *American Psychologist,* 1972, **27,** 913–920.

Ludwig, A. M., Marx, A. J., Hill, P. A., and Browning, R. M. The control of violent behavior through faradic shock. *Journal of Nervous and Mental Disease,* 1969, **148,** 624–637.

McNamara, J. R., and MacDonough, T. S. Some methodological considerations in the design and implementation of behavior therapy research. *Behavior Therapy,* 1972, **3,** 361–378.

Portes, A. On the emergence of behavior therapy in modern society. *Journal of Consulting and Clinical Psychology,* 1971, **36,** 303–313.

Sachs, D. A., Martin, J. E., and Fitch, J. L. The effect of visual feedback on a digital exercise in a functionally deaf, cerebral palsied child. *Journal of Behavior Therapy and Experimental Psychiatry,* 1972, **3,** 217–222.

Spanos, N. P., De Moor, W., and Barber, T. X. Hypnosis and behavior therapy: Common denominators. *American Journal of Clinical Hypnosis,* 1973, **16,** 45–64.

Waters, W. F., and McCallum, R. N. The basis of behavior therapy, mentalistic or behavioristic? A reply to E. A. Locke. *Behavior Research and Therapy,* 1973, **11,** 157–163.

Weitzenhoffer, A. M. Behavior therapeutic techniques and hypnotherapeutic methods. *American Journal of Clinical Hypnosis,* 1972, **15,** 71–82.

Yates, A. J. The application of learning theory to the treatment of tics. *Journal of Abnormal and Social Psychology,* 1958, **56,** 175–182.

Yates, A. J. *Behavior therapy.* New York: Wiley, 1970. (a)

Yates, A. J. Misconceptions about behavior therapy: A point of view. *Behavior Therapy,* 1970, **1,** 92–107. (b)

CHAPTER 2

Behavior Analysis

REJECTION OF THE PSYCHIATRIC APPROACH

In *Behavior Therapy* a detailed account was provided of the background to the rejection of psychiatric diagnosis by behavioristic clinical psychologists, a development that is understandable only when placed in its proper historical context, a context that involved fundamental dissatisfaction with the role the clinical psychologist was usually compelled to play within the mental health system (Yates, 1970, pp. 4–13). A brief recapitulation of the main points of that review will set the scene for the development of behavior analysis as a viable alternative to psychiatric diagnosis.

Psychiatric diagnosis fell into disfavor because it came to be regarded as an alien and illegitimate transplant from the field of physical medicine, where it had been brilliantly successful, to the field of mental medicine, where it was regarded by many psychologists as irrelevant to what are more properly termed disorders of behavior. In physical medicine diagnosis was relevant and important because it often enabled the physician to determine etiology, rational treatment, and prognosis. In the area of behavior disorders, however, a diagnostic label usually did not enable causation to be stated, had no implications for rational treatment, and might merely indicate a very unfavorable prognosis, which was comforting neither to patient nor physician. More generally, of course, disorders of behavior did not seem to be, in fact, mental diseases, comparable to physical diseases except that they involved the mind rather than the body, and hence the diagnostic exercise seemed futile.

As already pointed out, however, this disenchantment with diagnosis as a primary aim of examination of the presenting patient was related to a much more general dissatisfaction with the role of the clinical psychologist as a kind of pseudopsychiatrist, aping the activities of the psychiatrist by learning his language and utilizing his frame of reference. Thus when the psychiatrist used an unstructured interview situation to discover facts about the patient, the clinical psychologist used a structured situation (questionnaires) but with essentially the same aim. When the psychiatrist used depth interviews to probe the dynamics of the patient's motivation, the clinical psychologist attempted to achieve the same end by using projective tests. When the psychiatrist used neurological examination techniques to probe for brain damage or deterioration, the clinical psychologist used formal tests of brain damage or deterioration. In each case, however, the aim of the psychologist was primarily to answer questions put to him by the psychiatrist (is this patient depressed or an early case of schizophrenia, brain-damaged or not, deteriorated from an earlier higher level of functioning?). The clinical psychologist tended to make little use of his own special knowledge of psychology as the science of behavior, in part because if he did he would not be able to communicate successfully with the psychiatrist, whose formal training in human behavior and its determinants was usually sketchy, to say the least. As a person considerably lower in the pecking order in mental health, the psychologist to survive in the system had to conform to the rules of the game as laid down by the psychiatrist, rather than being able to contribute as a specialist in his own right.

These factors (and others detailed in Yates, 1970, pp. 4–13) led eventually both to the rejection of this subordinate role of the clinical psychologist in general and the routine use of diagnosis in particular. At the time *Behavior Therapy* was written, however, viable alternatives to psychiatric diagnosis were only beginning to be developed in detail, as is evident from the fact that only one small paragraph was devoted to behavior analysis in that book (Yates, 1970, p. 418) and that was placed appropriately in the final chapter on Future Trends. Now, only 5 years later, there would be no difficulty whatever in writing a whole book on the subject of behavior analysis. In this chapter it is possible only to give some examples of what has already been achieved and to show the relevance of theory and/or hypothesis testing to behavior analysis. The role of Shapiro has already been mentioned (Chapter 1) and described in detail elsewhere (Yates, 1970, pp. 15–17). This chapter concentrates on other approaches to behavior analysis.

APPROACHES TO BEHAVIOR ANALYSIS

Before considering the various models for behavior analysis that have been advanced in recent years, the basic nature of the problem may be illustrated by an actual example, provided by Goldfried and Pomeranz (1968):

Consider the hypothetical case of a 50-year-old man who comes to therapy because he has difficulty in leaving his house. The situation has reached the point where merely contemplating getting out of bed results in such anxiety that most of his time is spent in a prone position and he therefore must be constantly looked after by his wife. Further questioning reveals that his most salient fear is having a heart attack which he states is the reason for remaining at home and in bed. Upon carrying the assessment further—this time evaluating the nature of his current life situation—it is found that this man has recently been promoted in his job to a position where he now has the responsibility for supervising a large staff. Prior to this promotion, he led a fairly normal life and his fears of having a heart attack were non-existent.

Other assessment procedures reveal that the client has always had the tendency to become anxious in unfamiliar situations, and he is the type of person who would prefer to have other people look after him and care for him. Additionally, questioning his wife reveals that she does not find the current situation entirely noxious; rather, she feels important and needed now that she has to care for her husband, and she lavishes much attention and affection on him in his incapacitated state (pp. 83–84).

Examined carefully, this case will be found to contain all the factors relating to behavior analysis that have subsequently been stressed as relevant to the endeavor: dealing with overt behavior patterns versus verbal reports, the examination of reinforcers maintaining behavior, the assessment of general personality traits, real-life situational analysis, and so on. The basic question that arises, of course, in all behavior analysis is: what is the nature of the disorder and how are decisions arrived at concerning which target behavior (or behaviors) to select for treatment? In this instance, for example, should the patient, his wife, or both be treated? The answers are now fairly clear, but they were certainly not so clear when behavior analysis first emerged as an alternative to psychiatric diagnosis.

The Range of Behavior Analysis

The extraordinary range of activities that may be subsumed under the rubric of behavior analysis may be illustrated by two examples, taken, as it were, from opposite ends of the spectrum. The first example relates to an attempt to analyze the behavior of mental defectives in a nonsocial, highly controlled situation. Barrett and Lindsley (1962) used a task involving two lights (C_1) and C_2), each of which was activated (M_1 and M_2) by a manipulandum (a lever). The association C_1M_1 was reinforced on a FR-10 schedule, whereas the associations C_1M_2, C_2M_1, and C_2M_2 were not reinforced. Using this simple device, Barrett and Lindsley were able to investigate the acquisition of response differentiation, stimulus discrimination, and motivational level. Thus *response differentiation* was said to be acquired if, after training, the association C_1M_1 exceeded C_1M_2; *stimulus discrimination* if C_1M_1 exceeded C_2M_1; and both *response differentiation* and *stimulus discrimination* if C_1M_1 exceeded C_2M_2. *General motivational level* was defined as the total number of responses per session. The system could not only be used to measure "assets," however; it could also determine deficits in behavior. Thus a high rate of C_2M_2, accompanied by a reduction in rate of C_1M_2 and C_2M_1 would indicate *overgeneralization*. It is interesting to note that highly individualized response patterns were found in the mental defectives studied.

This example of behavior analysis may be compared with an example of what goes on in the clinic of one of the founding fathers of behavior therapy, Joseph Wolpe. In recent years Wolpe has published several transcripts of training sessions from his clinic, and these are very revealing with respect to his approach to behavior analysis. The following partial transcript of an actual session is taken from Wolpe (1972) and deals with the analysis of problems arising during the course of treatment of a patient who was claustrophobic.

In this excerpt from a supervisory session several points should be noted. In the first place, although the student had already treated the patient's fear of driving with notable success, she nonetheless, because of her earlier psychoanalytic orientation, leapt at speculative hypotheses when the patient suffered a setback during her efforts at treating his claustrophobia. These hypotheses were put forward as if "on principle", not because the circumstances of the setback pointed to them. In fact, the setback closely followed locking the patient in the trunk of a car as a therapeutic measure. It was this, evoking considerable anxiety, that was the starting point for a reconditioning of both claustrophobic anxiety and pervasive anxiety.

Another point is that the enclosure in the car trunk was brief. Brief strong anxiety stimuli often increase anxiety-conditioning; while prolonged exposure (flooding) can be beneficial, paradoxical as it may seem. However, this is not a matter on which it is at present possible to generalize. Flooding is not always effective. There is much to be learned about the necessary conditions for it to succeed. Clinical experience, both in the Behavior Therapy Unit and elsewhere, indicates that it is probably wise to present the flooding stimulus in the first place at an intermediate intensity. Research at Oxford . . . suggests that pro- longed weak anxiety arousal may be optimal.

The immediate effect of the patient's enclosement in the trunk was a high level of anxiety. This subsided and then build up again in the course of a few days, probably on the basis of cognitive reminiscence of the experience. Anxiety conditioning, due to anxiety evoked by imagined stimuli is a common phenomenon that is hardly ever mentioned.

FIRST STUDENT: I want to talk about my claustrophobic and agoraphobic patient. Driving is not the main problem any more. As a result of flooding with imaginary scenes he can now go where he ordinarily needs to go without anxiety. Perviously he was anxious a couple of miles from base. He still can't go 30 miles, but his mind is not occupied with this. Now he keeps on bringing up other problems. One is about relationships at work. Also, he again has a 30–40 anxiety level most of the time.[1]

WOLPE: What was he down to before?

FIRST STUDENT: Around 10 or 5. When he first came for treatment, he said he was at 30–40 anxiety units all the time. Then after several treatments with flooding he was improving at the driving. Even before his driving distance improved his anxiety was better. He went down the week after the first session to the 5–15 SUDS range—not very relaxed, of course, but not bothered much either. But in the last 2 weeks his anxiety has risen again. Several things are contributing. First of all, he wants to get married. He doesn't know to whom, but the idea frightens him to death.

WOLPE: What frightens him to death?

FIRST STUDENT: The idea of a long term commitment frightens him. He said, 'How could I commit myself to a very serious relationship?' I said, "You have committed yourself to this therapy." And he agreed that this was not stressful to him.

WOLPE: So this does not explain why his anxiety level has gone up?

FIRST STUDENT: No. Then I got to probing into what might have happened lately. He spoke about stress at work. He feels that he is not very capable. He's teaching a course now, and if while he is lecturing some student challenges him about an idea, he becomes so defensive that he'll start an argument with the student.

[1]The reference is to subjective units of disturbance (SUDS)

WOLPE: Are you putting this forward as the reason for his having a 40 level of continuous anxiety?

FIRST STUDENT: No. The reason is that he feels that he is on the defensive all the time, that he is really not as clever as they think he is.

WOLPE: Three weeks ago, did he have a different view?

FIRST STUDENT: No, when he came here, he had the same view as now.

WOLPE: Then what's your explanation? He originally came here with a 40 level of anxiety and after treatment it went down to 5, and then it went back again to 40. Now, why?

FIRST STUDENT: It all started when I put him in the trunk of his car, when I was closing him in the trunk with a mind to do an *in vivo* flooding for his claustrophobia.

WOLPE: Since then he has been worse. Apparently, you reconditioned the continuous anxiety by locking him in the trunk?

FIRST STUDENT: Yes. Three weeks ago.

WOLPE: With such a clear association, why first consider such peripheral possibilities as fear of marriage?

SECOND STUDENT: Wasn't it two weeks ago that you asked him, "What do you think worked?" and one of the things he said was, "I've finally found someone I trust—it's the first time I've ever trusted anybody." Perhaps putting him in the trunk killed that trust.

WOLPE: That could be an important factor. But let's first look at the flooding *per se*.

FIRST STUDENT: I didn't flood him.

WOLPE: You put him in the trunk."[2] (Wolpe, 1972, pp. 301–303)

The extreme difference between the two approaches is quite apparent. In the one case a very strictly controlled experimental situation is set up; only overt nonverbal behavior is examined; and there is no verbal interaction whatever between subject and (the word is used deliberately) experimenter. In the second case both verbal and nonverbal behaviors are being examined; there is almost total reliance on the patient's verbalizations as valid indicators of an emotional state called anxiety; and it is doubtful whether the behavioral analysis could in any sense be called experimental. In both cases the ultimate aim is to produce information that could be utilized in changing the patient's real-life behavior. It is true, of course, that the patients in question presented with very different problems; nevertheless, it is doubtful whether Lindsley, faced with Wolpe's patient, would have analyzed his behavior in the way that Wolpe and his students did, and vice versa.

It is quite clear from the foregoing examples that behavior analysis means many different things, and it seems certain that no one set of rules will suffice to cover all possible approaches. Nevertheless, there have been several attempts to provide a general framework for behavior analysis. Three of these are examined briefly: the behavior-analytic model of Goldfried and his colleagues, the behavioral diagnosis model of Kanfer and Saslow, and the modality profile of Lazarus.

The Behavior-Analytic Model of Goldfried

The work of Goldfried and his colleagues (Goldfried and D'Zurilla, 1969; Goldfried and Kent, 1972; Goldfried and Pomeranz, 1968) on what they have labeled "a behavioral-analytic model for assessing competence" actually represents the development of an alternative form of personality assessment to that currently in vogue in the personality field (the use of formal tests), although they have explicitly related the model to behavior analysis as a prolegomena to behavior modification. Goldfried and Kent (1972), for example, compare the assumptions of traditional and behavioral personality assessment in relation to conceptions of personality, selection of test items, and interpretation of test responses. They also compare the two approaches in terms of comparative levels of inference and comparative predictive efficiency. Thus in relation to the *conception of*

[2]It should be made clear that the transcript does not end at this point.

personality, the traditional model focuses on characteristics such as traits that an individual "has" and that are assumed to remain invariant across situations; whereas the behavioral model concentrates on what an individual "does" in a specified situation and examines changes in his behavior as a function of change in that situation. With respect to *selection of items*, the traditional model assumes that the items making up a personality test may not be very important as to content, for the personality trait will impose itself on whatever items are present; whereas the behavioral model lays great stress on the careful selection of relevant items so that the behavior manifested can be appropriately tied to stimulus antecedents. With respect to the *interpretation of test responses*, the traditional model assumes that the responses may be interpreted as reflecting the operation of stable personality traits; whereas the behavioral model assumes that the responses constitute a sample of possible responses to a specific situation.

As a result of these differential assumptions, Goldfried and Kent argue that the two approaches differ significantly in their method of analyzing behavior difficulties. If, for example, the problem is one of anxiety in relations with the opposite sex, the traditional approach would be to measure anxiety as a personality trait and then infer social anxiety of greater or lesser degree in social situations involving the opposite sex, according to the score obtained on the anxiety test. The behavior analyst would start from the other end by sampling the patient's responses to situations involving the opposite sex (although Goldfried and Kent assume that a test rather than real-life sampling may still be used) and from these responses infer a general (or perhaps, more specific) level of competence in such situation, but no general trait of anxiety in such relationships would necessarily be inferred. The different assumptions lead to different kinds of predictive activity on the part of the clinician. In the traditional method of personality assessment, the predictions would be made from samples of the supposed underlying trait of anxiety; whereas in the behavioral approach, the predictions would be made from the patient's performance in simulated (or real) situations involving social interaction with the opposite sex.

Goldfried and D'Zurilla (1969) have exemplified this approach in a study involving the assessment of *behavioral competence.* This involves the analysis of specified situations such as interpersonal relationships in five stages: *situational analysis* (the collection of a pool of problem situations in the area under study), *response enumeration* (the collection of the range of responses possible in each of these situations), *response evaluation* (specifying the degree of adequacy of each of the possible responses); the development of *measuring instrumentation,* and the demonstration of the *validity and reliability* of the instrument. A given subject could then be assessed as to his social competence by comparison with a relevant sample of his peers by comparing his reaction to these social situations with the established norms.

Goldfried's approach represents a genuine alternative to personality assessment but, although clearly relevant to behavioral analysis prior to modification, retains many of the features of traditional personality assessment, for example, in the way reliance still tends to be placed on responses to questionnaires as compared with how the subject performs in the problem situation itself.

Behavioral Diagnosis Model of Kanfer

A rather different approach is represented in the work of Kanfer and Saslow (1969) who, in effect, define behavior analysis as: "an attempt to identify classes of dependent variables in human behavior which would allow inferences about the particular contemporary controlling factors, the social stimuli, the physiological stimuli, and the reinforcing stimuli, of which they are a function" (p. 419). For them, there are three aspects to behavior analysis: the specification of the behavior patterns that require changing, the specification of the conditions under which the behavior was acquired and of the factors which are now maintaining it, and the specification of practical procedures for changing the behavior patterns in question.

They break down these general requirements into seven more detailed stages of analysis:

The problem situation is subjected to an initial analysis. At this stage, the presenting problem may be classified as behavioral excess (for example, compulsive hand washing) or behavioral deficit (for example, male sexual impotence). Kanfer and Saslow also stress the importance of determining what behavioral assets the patient possesses. This is followed by *clarification of the problem situation.* the meaning of which is self-evident in general terms, but hardly as to specifics. Following these two basic stages, however, Kanfer and Saslow then go on to describe the other stages of behavior analysis which are merely listed to show what they believe must be involved: *motivational analysis* (which includes the patient's ranking of incentives and stimuli which are aversive); *developmental analysis* (including biological changes such as visual defects, sociological changes, and behavioral changes); *analysis of self-control*; *analysis of social relationships*; and *analysis of the social-cultural-physical environment.*

The purpose of all this activity is stated by Kanfer and Saslow to be the discovery of specific target behaviors for treatment and the discovery of specific treatment operations. They lay particular stress on the need to recognize that the patient operates in a complex of situations; the need to recognize the effects of any change in the patient's behavior on his environment that may be produced by the therapy; the effect on treatment possibilities of limitations in the patient's repertoire (e.g., low intelligence); the need for individualized analysis; and in many cases, the need to change the environment of the patient, or his peers, as much as to work with the patient himself.

Multimodal Behavior Analysis of Lazarus

Until comparatively recently, Lazarus has stressed the eclecticism of his *therapeutic* approach, but his most recent work lays particular stress on the use of a very wide range of behavioral assessment techniques (Lazarus, 1973). As pointed out in Chapter 1, these can be subsumed under his BASIC ID acronym. For Lazarus, behavior analysis involves systematic attention, both before and during the course of treatment to all these factors, his justification being that: "the major advantage of a multimodal orientation is that it provides a systematic framework for conceptualizing presenting complaints within a meaningful context" (Lazarus, 1973, p. 407). It is perhaps not without irony that he compares his behavior analysis approach to the recently developed problem-oriented record approach in medicine.

Consideration of these three approaches to behavior analysis (Goldfried, Kanfer, Lazarus) reveals two outstanding points: how very different they are from the approach originally advocated by Shapiro, that is, the *experimental* investigation of the single case; and how closely they resemble, in the multitude of procedures and assessments that are recommended as routinely applicable to all patients, the battery approach to psychological testing that was all the rage in the 1940s and 1950s, and disenchantment with which was one of the main factors in the development, both of Shapiro's approach, and indeed of behavior modification itself.

Behavior Analysis as Experimental Control

Much closer to the Shapiro approach, and indeed one which is much more heavily represented in a systematic way in the published literature, is the behavior analysis model of those who utilize operant approaches to therapy. Baer, Wolf and Risley (1968) stated quite unequivocally that: "an experimenter has achieved an analysis of behavior when he can exercise control over it" (p. 94), by which they mean, in applied terms at least, an attempt to show that the experimenter can turn the behavior on and off at will. They readily admit, however, that: "application, to be analytic, demonstrates control when it can and thereby presents its audience with a problem of judgment" (p. 94). The control to which they are referring involved at the time at which they wrote, the use of the A - B - A reversal design, on the one hand, or the multiple-baseline technique, on the other. As has already been pointed out, these techniques have since been developed to a considerable degree of sophistication, and new designs introduced. It is worth noting here that in this approach behavior analysis and behavior modification are not clearly separated, the one merging into the other. It would be no exaggeration to say that probably the best way to teach behavior analysis at present would be to have students of behavior modification examine carefully all the papers published in the *Journal of Applied Behavior Analysis* since its inception in 1968.

The more technical and methodological aspects of behavior analysis are very complex matters that are not considered here. A general review of methodological problems in the design and implementation of behavior therapy research has been provided recently by McNamara and MacDonough (1972), though it is not particularly helpful from the practical viewpoint; important experimental papers on observer reliability and validity have begun to appear (e.g., Wahler and Leske, 1973; Thomas, 1973; Romanczyk, Kent, Diament, and O'Leary, 1973), attesting to the increasing attention being paid to this particular problem. Much can be learned about behavior analysis, however, from a careful examination of recent work in selected areas of behavior modification, where the problem of behavior analysis has loomed large. Two major areas of special interest are those of alcoholism and depression.

BEHAVIOR ANALYSIS IN OPERATION

Alcoholism

As Miller (1973) has pointed out, there is still an extraordinary lack of hard data concerning the drinking habits of alcoholics.

Most of the information that is available is based on indirect evidence, gleaned from unreliable sources. For example, information is often obtained from verbal reports of alcoholics themselves who are attempting to report on how they behaved at just the time when they are in no condition to observe their own behavior reliably and validly. Other evidence comes from relatives and friends, from arresting officers, and from hospital personnel whose reports are very likely biased. Clinical judgments by psychiatrists and psychologists are made when the patient is in a state of sobriety rather than when he is affected by alcohol (or, alternatively, when the patient is so inebriated that his physiological state is of primary concern). One of the major achievements of behavior analysis has been the examination of the drinking and social behavior of the alcoholic when alcohol is freely available. The significance of this work lies partly in its dispelling of some common beliefs about the behavior of the alcoholic in the presence of alcohol and partly in its relevance to theories about alcoholism.

Considerable light has been thrown on the classical loss-of-control belief or hypothesis (otherwise known as the one-drink hypothesis) by careful behavioral analysis. This hypothesis makes three basic assertions about alcoholics.

1. The alcoholic is unable to resist drinking in the presence of others who are drinking.

2. The alcoholic will always drink if alcohol is available.

3. If the alcoholic takes a single drink, physiological changes will occur that will compel him to take another drink to effect changes in the physiological state produced by the first drink (an alternative form of this proposition states that the second and subsequent drinks are taken to maintain or enhance the physiological state produced by the first drink).

Behaviorally, the loss-of-control hypothesis states that if the alcoholic takes one drink, he will be unable to stop drinking. The hypothesis, if true, has two important implications: the aim of treatment must be total abstinence, for even one drink will produce complete relapse; and it is impossible to train an alcoholic to be a social drinker, that is, a person who can drink in moderation without losing control. It is necessary to emphasize that this hypothesis is very widely accepted, and any suggestion that it may be false produces a state bordering on apoplexy among medical experts on alcoholism. That this is so may easily be seen by reference to the extraordinary reaction to the famous (or infamous) paper by Davies (1972) who presented cases of both treated and untreated alcoholics who had become, and had remained, social drinkers for long periods without any evidence of relapse. A furious debate ensued in which the journal found itself impelled to publish dozens of letters whose authors denied that Davies' patients could have been alcoholics (since, *ex hypothesi*, they would have relapsed if they had been). This position was maintained in a further stream of letters when Davies showed that his patients did meet the criteria of alcoholism laid down as defining the disorder by his critics. This conservative, pessimistic position was apparently overwhelmingly reaffirmed as recently as late 1973 at a world congress on alcoholism held in London.

Nevertheless, behavior analysis has provided very strong evidence that all three major propositions of the loss-of-control hypothesis are false. Gottheil, Alterman, Skoloda, and Murphy (1973), following earlier pilot investigations, studied 66 alcoholics aged 25–55 who were not psychotic, had no serious medical or neurological disease, and who were volunteers. They were placed in small groups on a closed ward and observed over a period of 6 weeks. In the first week, no alcohol was available. A 4-week program requiring fixed-interval drinking decisions (FIDD) was then introduced in which the subject was given the opportunity of drinking 0, 1, or 2 ounces of ethyl alcohol at one-half hour intervals 13 times per day (thus a maximum of 26 ounces could be drunk each day). The alcohol could be drunk straight or with water and had to be consumed on the spot, if accepted. Drinking behavior, situational discomfort, sleep disturbance, and degree of socialization were measured repeatedly. The results showed that 29 (44%) of the alcoholics did not drink at all in the presence of free alcohol during the 4-week period; 22 (33%) drank throughout; and 15 (23%) began drinking but stopped before the program ended. There seemed to be no doubt at all that those alcoholics who began drinking and then stopped met all of the criteria for alcoholism (12 had experienced blackouts; 11 the "shakes"; 4 delirium tremens; 3 convulsions). Those alcoholics who drank continuously showed wide individual differences in their patterns of drinking. Those who stopped drinking during the program did *not* show significant withdrawal symptoms and did not appear to be uncomfortable while watching others drink.

Marlatt, Demming, and Reid (1973) argued that if the drinking rate in alcoholics could be shown to be a function of *expectancy* (i.e., whether what was being drunk was thought to contain alcohol, regardless of whether it did, in fact, contain alcohol), then serious doubt would be cast on the loss-of-control hypothesis that the first drink triggered physiological changes that produce uncontrolled drinking. In their study alcoholics and nonalcoholics were given drinks that were a mixture of tonic and vodka or tonic alone and were told either that the drink contained alcohol or that it consisted of tonic only (they had determined previously that a mixture of one part vodka and five parts tonic cannot reliably be judged as to whether it contains alcohol). The experimental situation was disguised as a comparative taste test of three brands of tonic, on the one hand, and three brands of a mixture of vodka and tonic, on the other. Having been given their instructions, the subjects were left alone to taste the samples as often as they wished in order to make their comparative judgments. Objective measurements were available for the amount consumed, sip rate, and amount consumed per sip. In addition, the subjects were asked to estimate the alcoholic content of the drinks, and assessments were made of each subject's post-experimental blood alcohol level.

The results were extremely clear-cut and revealing with respect to the loss-of-control hypothesis. It was found that the amount consumed was a function of the instructional set induced. Thus subjects who were told they were drinking tonic and who were, in fact, drinking tonic, consumed an average of 10.94 oz; those told they were drinking tonic but whose drinks contained vodka consumed an average of 10.24 oz. However, subjects who were told the drinks contained alcohol but were, in fact, consuming only tonic drank an average of 23.87 oz; whereas those who were told the drinks contained alcohol and whose drinks did, in fact, contain vodka consumed an average of 22.13 oz. Thus the amount drunk was clearly a function of the *belief* that the drink was alcoholic and not whether it was, in fact, alcoholic. Under all four conditions, the alcoholics drank most of what they consumed during the first 3 minutes of the 15-minute period, with a steady decline in amount drunk being evident during the remaining 12 minutes, as is evident from Figure 1. It is important to note in connection with this result that subjects were not aware

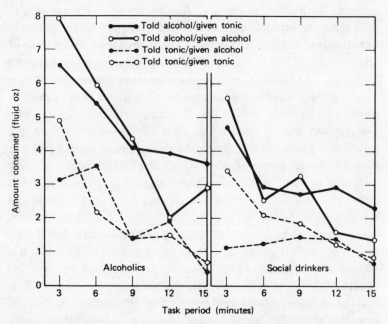

Figure 1. Amount of total beverage consumed by alcoholics and social drinkers during task period (based on amount consumed per sip by each subject in 3-minute blocks).

that the session would terminate after 15 minutes. Marlatt found that instructional set also determined how much alcohol a subject estimated was in his drink. Finally, it was found that for those subjects actually ingesting alcohol, the blood alcohol level was significantly higher for alcoholics as compared with nonalcoholics at the end of the session, regardless of the instructional set. The results of this study argue very strongly against all aspects of the loss-of-control hypothesis insofar as the alcoholics did not drink equally heavily during the whole of the test period, even where alcohol was still available, but rather tapered off rapidly and drank as a function of induced belief about the presence of alcohol, which argues against the physiological-priming aspect of the loss-of-control hypothesis.

Finally, with respect to this hypothesis, Sobell, Sobell, and Christelman (1972) have demonstrated that alcoholics themselves do not subscribe to the one-drink hypothesis and that they will not necessarily "compulsively" leave a hospital environment to gain access to liquor, even though free to do so while engaging in experimental studies that involve the ingestion of an amount of alcohol that might be expected, according to the loss-of-control hypothesis, to prime them towards excessive drinking.

The serious doubts cast on the validity of the loss-of-control hypothesis by these studies and the clinical evidence provided by Davies and others opens the way for consideration of the possibility that at least some alcoholics can be taught to bring their drinking habits under self-control, and there is now encouraging evidence that such control may be achieved, although it is undeniable that it is not easy to do so (Lovibond and Caddy, 1970; Mills, Sobell, and Schaefer, 1971; Orford, 1973; Sobell and Sobell, 1973a, 1973b.) A cautionary note has, however, rightly been sounded by Keehn (1970) who has suggested that uncontrolled drinking patterns may be situation specific. This note represents, of course, a substantial modification of the loss-of-control model, but it suggests caution in interpreting the foregoing results. However, Keehn, Bloomfield, and Hug (1970), using a version of Cautela's reinforcement

survey schedule, showed that alcoholics have alcohol prefer-
ences and suggested that alcohol may sometimes, even in
alcoholics, be indulged in not because it is reinforcing in itself,
but because it leads to other reinforcers. Drinking, for example,
may be the only way in which the alcoholic can obtain social
reinforcers (Premack principle), but this behavior would also
represent a significant modification of the loss-of-control
hypothesis.

Other behavior analysis studies in the area of alcoholism have
been concerned with trying to define the behavioral characteristics of alcoholics without these results in and of themselves
necessarily having specific treatment implications. Nevertheless,
the studies are based on the premise that a great deal more hard
evidence is needed relating to the behavior of alcoholics before
rational remedial action can be taken.

The first type of study is concerned with the operant analysis of
the drinking patterns of alcoholics in situations that are
laboratory analogs but are closer to being laboratory studies
than real-life analogs. Two groups of workers have made major
contributions here: Mendelson and Mello and Nathan and his
colleagues.

Mendelson and Mello had earlier studied the behavioral effects
of the administration of alcohol to nonalcoholic volunteers, but
they particularly wished to study the drinking behavior of
alcoholics *in situ*. Specifically, if an alcoholic is given free access
to alcohol via a dispensing machine and if he is simultaneously
given free access to money from a dispensing machine, what
pattern of behavior will he demonstrate if to obtain the alcohol
and/or money he is required to work for either reinforcer under
the control of various schedules? (It will be noted that the
experimental situation is a close analog of the real-life problem of
the alcoholic who is often reported to work steadily to
accummulate funds and then leave his job and go on a binge.)

A study by Mendelson and Mello (1966), which illustrates their
approach, involved two chronic alcoholics who had been
deprived of alcohol for some time. They were given access to an

apparatus that dispensed alcoholic drinks (10cc increments of 86 proof bourbon) or displayed reinforcement points exchangeable for money, according to which reinforcer was chosen via a selector switch. Responses were made by pressing a button that changed color according to which reinforcement schedule was currently in operation. Four types of reinforcement schedule were randomly programmed: fixed ratio, reinforcement was given after 360, 240, 120, or 60 presses; fixed interval, reinforcement was given for the first response after a 1-, 2-, or 3-, minute interval; extinction, no responses were reinforced for a 1-minute period; and differential reinforcement of no response (DRO)—the subject must not respond during the 30-second period the DRO is in operation; if the subject does respond during this period, the clock resets and the DRO continues. If no response is made during the period, a new schedule starts. This experiment lasted for 11 days; during this period, the subject could work the machine at any time of day or night.

The main findings were that:

1. Both subjects rapidly ingested enough alcohol to raise blood alcohol levels to 150–300 mg per 100 cc.

2. Both subjects showed only mild intoxication, although blood alcohol levels were well above that which would produce disorientation in nonalcoholics.

3. Both subjects tended to maintain their blood alcohol level at a constant level, although operant rates fluctuated markedly.

4. Both subjects showed significant *increases* in anxiety and depression while drinking (supporting previous evidence that intoxication is *not* anxiety reducing).

5. Both subjects reported *decreased* drive to drink as time went on.

6. Neither subject stopped drinking by tapering off.

7. Both subjects tended to hoard alcohol rather than drink it immediately.

Studies by Nathan and his colleagues (Nathan, Titler, Lowenstein, Solomon, and Rossi, 1970; Nathan and O'Brien,

1971) were concerned with the interaction between drinking behavior patterns and socialization/isolation patterns. In the first study (Nathan et al. 1970), 12 severe alcoholics were studied in groups of four on a ward that consisted of individual rooms and a group area. To obtain alcohol the subject had to work by pressing a lever on a FR-150 schedule for 1 point and had to accumulate 20 points (3000 presses) to gain access to 20cc of beverage alcohol. Following a 6-day no-alcohol period (during which, however, he could earn points by working), a variable drinking access period was introduced; half the time the subject was kept in isolation, and during the other half he could socialize if he wished. The experimental period was followed by a 6-day no-access-to-alcohol period. Operant lever pressing rates, responses to a behavior inventory, a ward sociogram, mood adjective checklist, ataxia, physical status, vital signs, and blood alcohol level were all assessed repeatedly.

The results showed that the subjects worked for reinforcement during the predrinking period; stopped working and spent their money on alcohol at the beginning of the access-to-alcohol period; and then balanced work and drinking. They showed *increased* anxiety and depression, and they tended to remain socially isolated even though they said they did not like isolation.

The second study (Nathan and O'Brien, 1971) was rather similar to the previous one, the main change being that during the isolation period the subject could use the points gained either for alcohol or to obtain social interaction. The study also compared skid row alcoholics with steady drinkers from the same environment but not showing extreme symptoms of skid row alcoholics. The results were very similar to those found in the earlier study for the skid row alcoholics, but not for the steady drinkers who drank less, had lower blood alcohol levels, and used their points to purchase social interaction as well as alcohol. The differences were able to be correlated with real-life work patterns—skid row alcoholics worked to earn money and then stopped working and went on a spree; the others tended to remain in steady employment.

These studies are valuable in providing hard data about alcoholics' behavior and once more in refuting some commonly held beliefs (e.g., that alcohol reduces anxiety and depression).

The work of Schaefer and Sobell and their colleagues (e.g., Sobell, Schaefer, and Mills, 1972; Schaefer, Sobell and Mills, 1971) utilized an even closer approximation to the real-life drinking situation than the studies so far considered. They set up a simulated bar atmosphere with 4-hour sessions in which the subject could drink anything up to the equivalent in one session of 16 oz of 86-proof liquor. The behaviors recorded included mean number of drinks ordered, type of drink (straight, mixed, beer), magnitude of sips, time per drink and time between sips. They found that alcoholics ordered more drinks than nonalcoholics; showed a definite preference for straight drinks over mixed drinks (the reverse was the case for nonalcoholics); took larger sips of all kinds of drinks; and consumed their drinks 3 times as quickly as nonalcoholics. These results are not surprising; however, it was also found, contrary to common belief, that the alcoholics had longer time intervals between drinks than did nonalcoholics (at least within straight drinks and beer). A clear implication of this unexpected finding is that it is unnecessary to train alcoholics to drink more slowly (they already do); rather, the emphasis should be on training them to take smaller sips each time they do drink.

It is clear that careful behavior analytic studies have already paid a handsome dividend in the study of the behavior patterns of alcoholics. They have demonstrated that alcoholics do not necessarily lose control of their drinking as soon as they imbibe one drink, that they do not succeed in reducing anxiety and depression by drinking, that they do not necessarily drink to enable them to socialize more successfully, and that their drinking patterns are not quite what they are commonly believed to be. Some myths have been dispelled or should have been (beliefs about alcoholics, which are often heavily influenced by moral judgements about the evils of alcohol, die hard), and even these preliminary results (for they should be treated as no more than first steps toward a comprehensive behavior analysis) have some obvious implications for treatment that are already being put into effect (Mills et al., 1971; Sobell and Sobell, 1973a, 1973b).

Depression

The behavior analysis of depression is of relatively recent origin. The principal change that has occurred to produce this heightened interest has been the attention paid to the *functional analysis* of depression. As is the case with alcoholism, however, the analysis is not carried out *in vacuo* but is clearly related to theorizing about the nature of depression (i.e., defining the factors that produce and maintain depressed behaviors) and the implications that the functional analysis may have for therapy.

Two general papers have been published dealing with the functional analysis of depression. Moss and Boren (1972), drawing on earlier observations by Ferster (1966), have described in detail the possible ways in which depressed behavior may be initiated and maintained. These fall into two general classes; the first involves the theory that depression of behavior may be produced by *insufficient positive reinforcement;* the second, that depressed behavior may be under *aversive control.* The two classes are not, of course, mutually exclusive. Taking the insufficient positive reinforcement hypothesis first, Moss and Boren argue that this controlling variable may manifest itself under any or all of three sets of conditions:

1. A high behavior/reinforcement ratio manifested by insufficient frequency, insufficient magnitude, or insufficient duration of reinforcement; or by a high response cost, which may be summarized by saying that depression of behavior may occur when the individual has to work too often, too much, or too long to obtain reinforcement.

2. Withdrawal of a positive reinforcer, the withdrawal being permanent (e.g., death of a loved one); prolonged (e.g.

separation); or brief (e.g., time out from reinforcement).

3. Interruption of a chain of behavior leading to reinforcement, for example, loss of a job during a period when the person is working hard toward a long-term goal (such as promotion). Depression may arise under these conditions even if a better-paying job is obtained.

The second class (aversive control) is much less clearly spelled out by Moss and Boren, but essentially it involves the notion that depression of behavior may result when emitted behavior continually leads to aversive consequences. Depressed behavior may represent extinction of responding in the face of repeated punishment, or it may represent escape behavior from, and subsequently avoidance of, an aversive situation. [3]

Within the general schema proposed by Moss and Boren there is room for considerable dispute. Lazarus (1968), one of the first behavior therapists to write systematically on depression, espoused the viewpoint, subsequently elaborated by Moss and Boren, that depression resulted from the loss of reinforcers. Costello (1972), however, put forward the alternative hypothesis that it was not loss of reinforcers *per se* that produced depressed behavior, but rather the *loss of reinforcer effectiveness*, a view essentially equivalent to Moss and Boren's third subcategory (interruption of a chain of behaviors leading to reinforcement), although Costello considers that loss of reinforcer effectiveness may also result from endogenous, biochemical or neurological changes: "The reinforcer effectiveness of all the components of the chain of behavior is contingent upon the completion of the chain at either an overt or covert level" (Costello, 1972, p. 241). Lazarus (1972) has maintained his position, but the point to note is that behavioral analysis of depressed behavior may help to resolve the question and that behavioral therapy may very well take different directions, depending on which hypothesis is accepted.

[3]Ferster (1973), in a long and complicated paper, has described these possibilities in considerable detail, but on an entirely theoretical basis.

A rather different viewpoint of depressed behavior is that put forward recently by Libet and Lewinsohn (1973) who argue that depressed behavior results from inadequate social skills that manifest themselves in two ways: the depressed person has proved less successful in acquiring and exercising social skills that lead to social reinforcement and, similarly, has proved less skillful in refraining from emitting social behaviors that lead to aversive social consequences. This model is, of course, not inconsistent with the Moss and Boren model, for Ferster would undoubtedly argue that the defective social skills are themselves the product of the individual's reinforcement history. But it would clearly have different remedial implications, for in the one case the depressed behavior results from a novel change in the person's environment, whereas, in the other case the depressed behavior results from a long history of differential reinforcement. In the former case the depressed behavior might be changed by changing the person's environment, whereas in the latter case it might be more appropriate to teach the person new forms of social behavior.

Turning briefly to the possibility that depressed behavior is associated with a history of aversive consequences for behavior rather than a lack of reinforcers, note should be taken of the learned-helplessness model proposed by Seligman. This model is based on animal research which has shown that animals subjected to shocks they cannot avoid exhibit deficits in initiating responses that will produce escape from shock and have difficulty in associating responding with reinforcement. They tend to behave as if reinforcement (shock termination) is response independent; that is, they are unable to produce reinforcement by their own behavior—hence the term, learned helplessness. Miller and Seligman (1973) applied this model to depression and argued that it involves the depressive viewing reinforcement as response independent and hence a specific cognitive distortion of the perception of the ability of one's own responses to change the environment in such a way as to produce reinforcement. Miller and Seligman (1973) have tested this model in a study in which changes in expectancies of success were studied following reinforcement in chance and skill tasks. In skilled tasks, nondepressed subjects showed greater changes in success expectancy than did depressed subjects whereas no difference was found on the chance tasks.

Several studies have attempted to determine by functional analysis of behavior the variables responsible for generating and maintaining depressed behavior (Lewinsohn, Lobitz, and Wilson, 1973; Nutter, Cruise, Spreng, Weckowicz and Yonge, 1973; Williams, Agras, and Barlow, 1972). Attempts are being made to utilize the functional analyses described above in the treatment of depressed patients (Jackson, 1972; Reisinger, 1972; Robinson and Lewinsohn, 1973a, 1973b; Shipley and Fazio, 1973; Todd, 1972). It would be premature to attempt to draw firm conclusions from the results of these preliminary therapeutic studies, but it may be noted that, as with alcoholism, there is an unmistakeable influence of theory or hypothesis testing involved in the functional analyses. Behavior cannot be analyzed blindly or in a purely empirical manner; given this, it seems essential that the theorizing or hypothesizing underlying even behavioral analysis be made as clear and unambiguous as possible.

CONCLUSION

The account given above of recent work on behavior analysis in two major areas of abnormal behavior (alcoholism and depression) is very instructive. In both instances an examination of the literature reveals very clearly that it is impossible to carry out more than the most superficial behavior analysis without becoming involved in theorizing or hypothesis making. Indeed, in the case of alcoholism the work on behavioral analysis started out, partly at least, in efforts to verify or disprove certain assumptions which, up to that point, had dominated the approach to therapy—the results of behavior analysis were such as to lead to significant modifications of those assumptions and hence to modified approaches to therapy. In the case of depression, a good deal of theory construction went on before any of the behavioral analyses were carried out, and that theory construction largely dictated the kind of behavioral analysis that was carried out. Thus far the work in these two areas supports the contention that theory construction is inextricably bound up with empirical work and that the two cannot be divorced. The examples of studies quoted in Chapter 1, however, in which the experimental study of single cases was involved (such as Ayllon's work on school phobia) show clearly that theory or hypothesis testing is involved there too. Thus the essential link between Kuhn, Bernard, and Shapiro becomes evident. Kuhn's work on the role of theory is relevant when *group* studies are involved and a *general* model is being formulated to account for a disorder (such as alcoholism and depression); Bernard's stress on formulating and testing a specific hypothesis is relevant when the experimental investigation of the single case along lines advocated by Shapiro is involved.

There is no incompatibility between these two levels of behavioral analysis, but the nature of the theorizing/hypothesis making will differ according to the aims of the experimenter, that is, whether he is seeking general determining factors applicable to explanation in general of a particular disorder, or whether he is seeking to account for the behavior of an individually presenting patient.

REFERENCES

Baer, D. M., Wolf, M. M., and Risley, T. R. Some current dimensions of applied behavior analysis. *Journal of Applied Behavior Analysis*, 1968, **1**, 91–97.

Barrett, B. H., and Lindsley, O. R. Deficits in acquisition of operant discrimination and differentiation shown by institutionalized retarded children. *American Journal of Mental Deficiency*, 1962, **67**, 424–436.

Costello, G. C. Depression: Loss of reinforcers or loss of reinforcer effectiveness? *Behavior Therapy*, 1972, **3**, 240–247.

Davies, D. L. Normal drinking in recovered alcohol addicts. *Quarterly Journal of Studies on Alcohol*, 1962, **23**, 94–104.

Ferster, C. B. Animal behavior and mental illness. *Psychological Record*, 1966, **16**, 345–356.

Ferster, C. B. A functional analysis of depression. *American Psychologist,*1973, **28**, 857–870.

Goldfried, M. R. and D'Zurilla, T. J. A behavioral-analytic model for assessing competence. In C. D. Spielberger (Ed.), *Current topics in clinical and community psychology*. New York: Academic Press, 1969. Pp. 151–196.

Goldfried, M. R., and Kent, R. N. Traditional versus behavioral personality assessment: A comparison of methodological and theoretical assumptions. *Psychological Bulletin*, 1972, **77**, 409–420.

Goldfried, M. R., and Pomeranz, D. M. Role of assessment in behavior modification. *Psychological Reports*, 1968, **23**, 75–87.

Gottheil, E., Alterman, A. I. , Skoloda, T. E., and Murphy, B. F. Alcoholics' patterns of controlled drinking. *American Journal of Psychiatry*, 1973, **130**, 418–422.

Jackson, B. Treatment of depression by self-reinforcement. *Behavior Therapy*, 1972, **3**, 298–307.

Kanfer, F. H., and Saslow, G. Behavioral diagnosis. In C. M. Franks (Ed.), *Behavior Therapy: Appraisal and Status*. New York: McGraw-Hill, 1969, pp. 417–444.

Keehn, J. D. Reinforcement of alcoholism: Schedule control of solitary drinking. *Quarterly Journal of Studies on Alcohol*, 1970, **31**, 28–39.

Keehn, J. D., Bloomfield, F. F., and Hug, M. A., Use of the reinforcement survey schedule with alcoholics. *Quarterly Journal of Studies on Alcohol*, 1970, **31**, 602–615.

Lazarus, A. A. Learning theory and the treatment of depression. *Behavior Research and Therapy*, 1968, **6** , 83–89.

Lazarus, A. A. Some reactions to Costello's paper on depression. *Behavior Therapy*, 1972, **3**, 248–250.

Lazarus, A. A. Multimodal behavior therapy: Treating the "basic id." *Journal of Nervous and Mental Disease*, 1973 **156**, 404–411.

Lewinsohn, P.M., Lobitz, W. C., and Wilson, S. "Sensitivity" of depressed individuals to aversive stimuli. *Journal of Abnormal Psychology*, 1973, **81**, 259–263.

Libet J. M. and Lewinsohn, P. M. Concept of social skill with special reference to the behavior of depressed persons. *Journal of Consulting and Clinical Psychology*, 1973, **40**, 304–312.

Lovibond, S. H., and Caddy, G. Discriminated aversive control in the moderation of alcoholics' drinking behavior. *Behavior Therapy*, 1970, **1**, 437–444.

McNamara, J. R., and MacDonough, T. S. Some methodological considerations in the design and implementation of behavior therapy research. *Behavior Therapy*, 1972, **3**, 361–378.

Marlatt, G. A., Demming, B., and Reid, J. B. Loss of control drinking in alcoholics: An experimental analogue. *Journal of Abnormal Psychology,* 1973, **81**, 233–241.

Mendelson, J. H., and Mello, N. K. Experimental analysis of drinking behavior of chronic alcoholics. *Annals of the New York Academy of Science,* 1966, **133**, 828–845.

Miller, P. M. Behavioral assessment in alcoholism research and treatment: Current techniques. *International Journal of the Addictions,* 1973, **8**, 831–838.

Miller, W R., and Seligman, M. E. P. Depression and the perception of reinforcement. *Journal of Abnormal Psychology,* 1973, **82**, 62–73.

Mills, K. C., Sobell, M. B., and Schaefer, H. H. Training social drinking as an alternative to abstinence for alcoholics. *Behavior Therapy,* 1971, **2**, 18–27.

Moss, G. R., and Boren, J. H. Depression as a model for behavioral analysis. *Comprehensive Psychiatry,* 1972, **13**, 581–590.

Nathan, P. E., and O'Brien, J. S. An experimental analysis of the behavior of alcoholics and nonalcoholics during prolonged experimental drinking: A necessary precursor of behavior therapy? *Behavior Therapy,* 1971, **2**, 455–476.

Nathan, P. E., Titler, N. A., Lowenstein, L. M., Solomon, P., and Rossi, A. M. Behavioral analysis of chronic alcoholism. *Archives of General Psychiatry,* 1970, **22**, 419–430.

Nutter, R. W., Cruise, D. G., Spreng, L. F., Weckowicz, T. E., and Yonge, K. A. Effect of monetary incentive on concept attainment in depressed subjects. *Canadian Psychiatric Association Journal,* 1973, **18**, 13–20.

Orford, J. A comparison of alcoholics whose drinking is totally uncontrolled and those whose drinking is mainly controlled. *Behavior Research and Therapy,* 1973, **11**, 565–576.

Reisinger, J. J. The treatment of "anxiety-depression" via positive reinforcement and response cost. *Journal of Applied Behavior Analysis,* 1972, **5**, 125–130.

Robinson, J. C., and Lewinsohn, P. M. Experimental analysis of a technique based on the Premack principle changing verbal behavior of depressed individuals. *Psychological Reports,* 1973, **32**, 199–210. (a)

Robinson J. C., and Lewinsohn, P. M. Behavior modification of speech characteristics in a chronically depressed man. *Behavior Therapy,* 1973, **4**, 150–152. (b)

Romanczyk, R. G., Kent, R. N., Diament, C., and O'Leary, K. D. Measuring the reliability of observational data: A reactive process. *Journal of Applied Behavior Analysis,* 1973, **6**, 175–184.

Schaefer, H. H., Sobell, M. B., and Mills, K. C., Baseline drinking behavior in alcoholics and social drinkers: Kinds of drinks and sip magnitude. *Behavior Research and Therapy,* 1971, **9**, 23–27.

Shipley, C. R., and Fazio, A. F. Pilot study of a treatment for psychological depression. *Journal of Abnormal Psychology,* 1973, **82**, 372–376.

Sobell, M. B., and Sobell, L. C. Individualized behavior therapy for alcoholics. *Behavior Therapy*, 1973, **4**, 49–72. (a)

Sobell, M. B., and Sobell, L. C. Alcoholics treated by individualized behavior therapy: One year treatment outcome. *Behavior Research and Therapy*, 1973, **11**, 599–618. (b)

Sobell, M. B., Schaefer, H. H., and Mills, K. C. Differences in baseline drinking behavior between alcoholics and normal drinkers. *Behavior Research and Therapy*, 1972, **10**, 257–267.

Sobell, L. C., Sobell, M. B., and Christelman, W. C. The myth of "one drink." *Behavior Research and Therapy*, 1972, **10**, 119–123.

Thomas, E. J. Bias and therapist influence in behavioral assessment. *Journal of Behavior Therapy and Experimental Psychiatry*, 1973, **4**, 107–111.

Todd, F. J. Coverant control of self-evaluative responses in the treatment of depression: A new use of an old principle. *Behavior Therapy*, 1972, **3**, 91–94.

Wahler, R. G., and Leske, G. Accurate and inaccurate observer summary reports. *Journal of Nervous and Mental Disease*, 1973, **156**, 386–394.

Williams, J. G., Barlow, D. H., and Agras, W. S. Behavioral measurement of severe depression. *Archives of General Psychiatry*, 1972, **27**, 330–336.

Wolpe, J. Supervision transcripts: III. Some problems in a claustrophobic case. *Journal of Behavior Therapy and Experimental Psychiatry*, 1972, **3**, 301–305.

Yates, A. J. *Behavior therapy*. New York: Wiley, 1970.

CHAPTER 3

Have We Solved the Problem of Enuresis?

Until comparatively recently, the therapeutic approach to the problem of nocturnal enuresis was dominated by the belief that it represented a failure to develop cortical control of an extremely powerful natural voiding reflex. The operation of this powerful reflex involves detrusor muscle activity that triggers automatically once a specified amount of urine accumulates in the bladder. The process could be regarded as an evolutionary protective device since failure to void automatically in the infant would, of course, be fatal. In the normal developmental sequence, it was believed that maturational factors involving corticla development were essential to the achievement of cortical control, since even the most intensive program of training will not successful before about the age of 12 months. It was also postulated that conditioning processes were involved in both night- and daytime control, but little or no emphasis was placed on the role of social, reinforcement factors or, in other words, wetting as a operant form of behavior. Development of the control of urination was considered akin to the development of the skill of locomoting or even breathing.

CORTICAL CONTROL MODEL OF ENURESIS

The line of reasoning that produced this model and its implications for the treatment of nocturnal enuresis follows:

Given that the child is born with a powerful natural voiding reflex, the achievement of both daytime and nocturnal control involves several stages of increasing mastery over the natural reflex, each of which is presumed to involve complex high-level patterns of conditioned responses at the cortical level, dependent in part on maturation, in part on learning: Increased bladder capacity is required to accommodate the increasing amounts of urine produced as growth of other bodily processes occurs: Within the bladder, the activity of the detrusor muscle changes its function. Under normal advanced control of urination, the detrusor muscle does not show a linear increase in activity as the bladder fills, but rather adapts continuously so that pressure remains relatively constant as volume increases. Should volume exceed a certain level, however, the detrusor muscle will begin to contract rhythmically, and failure of adaptation will begin to occur. Eventually, the detrusor muscle will "run wild," and reflex urination will occur, which means simply that the protective mechanism remains available in case of emergency (e.g., if the person is unconscious). It is assumed that the adaptation of detrusor muscle function is controlled at higher cortical levels than those involved in reflex urination. This represents, of course, a specific example of the more general proposition of Hughlings Jackson that the function of the cortex is to exercise control over the primitive parts of the brain. This control is normally established first in the waking state, and the child then has to solve the problem of transferring this control to the nighttime situation so that adaption of the detrusor muscle occurs when he is asleep. It should be pointed out that successful transfer involves continued adaptation over much longer periods of time than is usually found during the day, this being clearly reflected in the differential incidence of urination during the day and at night.

During the daytime also the child has to acquire other skills relating to urination:

1. He must learn to initiate urination voluntarily and when only small or moderate amounts of urine are present in the

bladder—the child does not usually wait until the detrusor muscle ceases to adapt before going to the toilet.

2. He must acquire the skill of inhibiting the flow of urine voluntarily after it has been initiated.

3. He must, if necessary, be able to hold a full bladder briefly, that is, inhibit reflex urination, until he can get to a toilet.

During sleep, however, a different skill is required should urine volume increase beyond the capacity of the detrusor muscle to adapt. In order to avoid reflex urination, the child must acquire the skill of awakening to increased detrusor muscle activity, but before the muscle "runs wild" and produces bed wetting.

The achievement of both daytime and nocturnal control is, not unnaturally, thought to be extremely complex, if only because it is well established that reflex urination is itself a very complicated process. Muellner (1958, 1960) has argued that the voluntary initiation of urination in the waking state involves the following sequence of events: voluntary steadying of the diaphragm, contraction of the lower abdominal muscles, and relaxation of the pubococcygeus of the levator ani, all of which results in a rapid lowering of the neck of the bladder. This in turn leads to an increase in intra-abdominal pressure, followed by detrusor contraction and internal followed by external sphincter relaxation. Little is known with respect to the inhibitory control exercized during sleep, as is shown by the rather vague suggestion that "sentinel points" are established in the cortex that are alerted when detrusor muscle activity exceeds adaptation values (Jones, 1960).

Within this model it was admitted that, once the above pattern of cortical control had been established, extraorganismic factors would also come, via learning, to play a role in patterns of urination in the waking state (e.g., the sight of toilet facilities might "remind" the person to urinate when objective bladder volumes and pressures are low) but these factors were assigned a relatively low priority in relation to the acquisition of the skill itself.

To summarize thus far, control of bladder functioning was regarded as a high-level acquired skill, involving physiological maturation, cortical conditioning, and the integration of internal feedback cues with the discrimination of external (social and environmental) cues. In effect, the child learns to *anticipate* reflex urination primarily by responding to internal cues with social and environmental control being regarded as of secondary importance.

The *failure* to acquire bladder control was, by extension of this model, attributed primarily to deficiencies in the development of the internal control system involved in successful control and described mainly in terms of a maturational or developmental failure involving higher cortical control systems or even failure at lower levels. Cystometric studies tended to implicate deficiencies in detrusor muscle adaptation leading to the attribution of a neurogenic bladder to the enuretic child. It was argued that enuretics were characterized by an abnormal depth of sleep such that the child did not awaken to uninhibited detrusor muscle activity before the reflex voiding occurred; EEG studies as well as depth-of-sleep studies were carried out in attempts to confirm that cortical functioning was abnormal in enuretic children. All these studies appeared to offer some confirmation that enuretics had low bladder capacity and abnormal detrusor muscle function, although the evidence was not conclusive and was even less clear with respect to depth of sleep and EEG abnormality.

The evidence appeared sufficiently persuasive, however, that remedial techniques all concentrated on developing the supposed higher cortical control that was said to be lacking in enuretics. Thus Mowrer and Mowrer (1938) developed the pad-and-bell technique as a logical outcome of Mowrer's theoretical analysis of the nature of the defect. Before treatment, when the child is wetting at night (usually without awakening), increasing detrusor muscle tension (TDT) acts as an unconditioned stimulus (US) to produce the unconditioned urination response (UR). In the Mowrer conditioning technique TDT (as US_1) produces urination (UR_1) that in turn, via a contact across the wires of the pad, rings the bell (US_2). The ringing of the bell has two immediate effects: it wakes the child (UR_2) and inhibits urination by producing reflex sphincter contraction (UR_3). However, as this process is repeated, TDT (now acting as a conditioned stimulus, CS) itself eventually comes to wake the child (CR_1) and inhibit urination (CR_2). Because TDT involves a gradient of intensity, it was argued that, with training, the process would move backward in time and the child would wake without having urinated, *before* the bell was activated, that is, while it was still dry. If this CS could be stably established by the Mowrer technique, the child would be effectively dry—though how the child subsequently achieved (if, indeed, he did) the *normal* criterion of sleeping through the night *and* not wetting, as the normal child does, was never satisfactorily accounted for by Mowrer's model. The criticisms of Mowrer's model and treatment made by Lovibond (1964), the development of his alternative model (an aversive instrumental conditioning model), and the modification of Mowrer's treatment technique (by the development of the twin-signal method) do not affect the essential point, namely, that the problem was considered to be one of the establishment of high-level cortical control over a powerful natural reflex.

SOCIAL REINFORCEMENT MODEL OF ENURESIS

Now, the models proposed by Mowrer and by Lovibond were constructed in efforts to explain the failure of some children to become dry at night. Nothing was said about daytime wetting because enuretic children who are otherwise normal almost always achieve daytime continence. However, there is another class of children in whom daytime incontinence (usually, but not invariably, also wetting during sleep) represents a serious problem, namely, moderate or severe mental defectives. In these children it was argued by Ellis (1963) originally and subsequently by Azrin and his colleagues (Azrin, Bugle and O'Brien, 1972; Azrin and Foxx, 1971; Foxx and Azrin, 1973) that: "Normal toileting is not simply a matter of learning to respond to bladder and bowel pressures by relaxing the sphincter but rather is a complex operant and social learning process that has been hindered by a reduced learning capacity and by institutionaliza-tion" (Azrin and Foxx, 1971, p. 89). The implication drawn from this argument was that a program should be developed in relation to daytime incontinence in which positive reinforcement would be given for eliminating appropriately, and aversive consequences (described by Azrin and Foxx as "inhibitory training") would follow incontinent behavior. Azrin and his colleagues were not, of course, the first to institute such remedial programs with mental defectives (for a review of the earlier studies, see Yates, 1970, pp. 332–333) but they have provided what might truly be called a technology for such programs. The importance of their work for present purposes lies not so much in this development as in their further conclusion that the same model can be applied to incontinence during sleep in both mental defectives and normals. If this claim can be sustained, then it raises important questions about the theoretical explanations given by Mowrer and by Lovibond with respect to the failure to achieve control and why *their* techniques succeed. The work that treats wetting as an operant falls into two main categories: those studies in which the intent is to eliminate daytime wetting by techniques that are used during the daytime and those studies in which the child is wetting at night but treatment is related to daytime behavior with the nocturnal wetting ignored.

The first class refers, of course, primarily to the work of Azrin and his colleagues, although a parallel development is to be found in the work of Van Wagenen and his colleagues (Mahoney, Van Wagenen, and Meyerson, 1971; Van Wagenen, Meyerson, Kerr, and Mahoney, 1969).

The procedures used by Azrin involve the use of various pieces of apparatus and a detailed specification of what the trainer should do or not do as a consequence of various events. With respect to apparatus, Azrin developed "wet-alarm" pants that signaled to the trainer whenever an episode of incontinence took place and a "toilet-signal" apparatus that indicated to the trainer when appropriate urination occurred in the toilet. It is important to note that these signals served a quite different purpose for Azrin than the use of the bell in the Mowrer apparatus. They were not considered to be relevant to the production of any change in the internal control system of the patient, but rather were intended solely to ensure that reinforcing or aversive consequences could be applied as close in time as possible to the occurrence of appropriate or inappropriate urination. As Azrin and Foxx (1971) put it:

the distinctive feature of this training procedure was its consideration of proper toileting as a complex and lengthy chain of responses that includes social, physical, and physiological stimuli and requires strong positive and negative operant consequences for its maintenance in that chain, rather than considering it as a simple associative muscular reflex to internal stimuli (p. 98).

It is unnecessary here to detail the program instituted by Azrin except that it involves the careful step-by-step specification of what the trainer should do and require the patient to do on the occurrence of an incontinent response and the equally detailed specification as to what should happen when appropriate elimination takes place. Nor can there be any doubt about the success of the program with exceptionally difficult cases, while the follow-up period is also satisfactory. Full details may be found in the recent manual of Foxx and Azrin (1973). The studies of Van Wagenen and his colleagues complement and support those of Azrin, but they stress one very important point that makes their contribution especially important. Their point is that normal potting by parents involves starting with the final point in the complex daytime sequence, that is, putting the child on the toilet and waiting hopefully for elimination to ocur. However, what the child has to learn in order to achieve daytime control is to perform a chain of responses that get him to the toilet, and this aspect is usually ignored in parental training. The emphasis in Van Wagenen's studies, therefore, is on detecting an instance of urination instantly, not so that it can be punished, but rather that the urination can be inhibited before it is conpleted. The child is then taken through the sequence of events that bring him into the toilet situation. The critical point is that when the child has completed this sequence, and has, as it were, adopted the urinary stance, he is very likely to urinate. There is an interesting parallel here with the use of the bell in Mowrer's technique, the purpose of which is also to inhibit urination before it is complete. The theoretical interpretation is, however, quite different.

The important point to be made, however, in relation to Azrin's work, is that he quite clearly believes that his model for eliminating daytime incontinence is equally applicable to the elimination of nocturnal incontinence in normal children. Thus the same rules are to be applied; that is, a signal is required, the sole purpose of which is to alert the attendant, who will then provide the appropriate aversive consequences, followed by institution of the training procedures used in the case of daytime incontinence—cleaning of the soiled materials, a visit to the toilet with positive reinforcement for elimination, and so on. In other words, it is the social consequences of wetting or not wetting that are regarded as the vital factors in eliminating nocturnal wetting. It is quite obvious that this conceptualization of what is going on in the change from nocturnal incontinence to control is quite different from the model provided by Mowrer. In the latter case, an attendant is considered desirable only for the purpose of ensuring that the apparatus is reset so that if the child wets again, another conditioning trial will take place, and, indeed, in Lovibond's model it is unnecessary for the child to wake at all for conditioning to take place. In Azrin's model, however, the presence of the attendant is vital, for he is a social reinforcement machine.

The importance of the issue has recently been highlighted by a second and quite different group of studies. These studies have investigated a new technique for producing *nocturnal* continence by daytime training which has become known as the Kimmel technique or procedure after its inventor. The basic technique (Kimmel and Kimmel, 1970) is absurdly simple when compared with the complexities of the methods devised by Mowrer and by Azrin. In its original form it involves reinforcing the child during the daytime for withholding urination for a specified time after he has informed the mother that he wants to go. The initial delay time may be as short as a few seconds, but Kimmel and Kimmel (1970) showed that even children as young as 3 or 4 years of age could rapidly be trained to delay urination beyond the point of expressed need for up to 45 minutes.

In the original study Kimmel and Kimmel (1970) demonstrated that in two normal females aged 4 and one psychotic female aged 10, when this daytime technique was used, nocturnal incontinence ceased within 7 days for the normal children and in 14 days in the case of the psychotic child, and did not return. Clearly, if these preliminary results could be replicated, the practical implications would be important, for no apparatus is required, the child's mother can be trained in a matter of hours to carry out the procedure, and only simple, tangible reinforcers are required.

Several attempts have been made to replicate and extend the initial findings of Kimmel and Kimmel. Miller (1973) applied the Kimmel technique to two institutionalized enuretics but incorporated three important modifications: the subjects recorded the frequency of daytime urination and nighttime wetting themselves; only social reinforcement was given for daytime control and nighttime dryness; and an A-B-A-B design was used with the reversal condition involving the subjects in discontinuing daytime delay training and increasing fluid intake. The treatment was successful in both cases, but for reasons that are discussed later Miller did not attribute the success to the social reinforcement contingency, even though the reversal condition produced some relapse. Stedman (1972) also trained a 13-year-old girl, wetting at night 4–5 times a week, to self-record her frequency of daytime urination and nighttime wettings and to delay urination during the day for up to 30 minutes. In addition, he obtained estimates from the girl of the strength of the drive to urinate during the day. In this case also, social reinforcement only was given; in addition, the girl had informational feedback from her own record keeping. Nocturnal enuresis was eliminated after a 12-week training period, and only four instances of wetting occurred during a 3-month followup. Stedman's other findings are considered later.

Two studies using the Kimmel technique or variants of it with larger numbers of subjects have recently been reported. Paschalis, Kimmel, and Kimmel (1972) divided 35 Cypriot children aged 4–13 who were severe enuretics (they had never had a dry night) into two groups. Following a 15-day baseline recording period for all children, the first group was given the Kimmel treatment that involved the child fixing his own initial duration for withholding; this was then gradually increased by 2–3 minutes per day until a 45–minute duration was achieved. It is important to note that reinforcement in the form of tokens and praise was given at the end of each withholding period and just before urination. The training period required between 15 and 20 days for criterion to be reached. During this training period, the other group of enuretic cildren was observed as an untreated control group and then switched to the Kimmel treatment. Both groups were followed up for 90 days after the end of treatment.

At the end of the training period for the first group, 9/20 of these children had been dry for at least 7 consecutive days; although it was not stated if any of the control group were dry at this point, 5/15 were dry after *their* training period to the same criterion. Additionally, seven other cildren in the two groups were dry 2–6 nights per week, and two of the failures were given further intensive training and improved. No relapses were reported over a 90-day followup period (although only parental report was available). The results compare quite well with the Mowrer technique when account is taken of the severity of the enuresis and the simplicity of the technique.

An even more recent experimental study of the Kimmel technique has been reported by Rocklin and Tilker (1973). They assigned 22 enuretics aged 3–14 to one of three treatments after 7 days of baseline recording. The subjects in the experimental group were reinforced for withholding during the day for 5 minutes initially, this period being increased by 5 minutes daily up to a maximum of 85 minutes. After 17 days the hold period was made 1 hour and dry nights were rewarded, this stage continuing for 13 days. Subjects allocated to a time-contingent control group were reinforced every 3 hours for 12 hours a day

for 17 days (thus receiving as many noncontingent reinforcements as the experimental group), after which reinforcement was
made contingent on a 1-hour delay for 17 days. Subjects allocated
to a base-rate control group simply had their daily frequency
recorded for 17 days and were then reinforced for 1-hour delays
and dry nights, but apparently without records being kept.
Rocklin and Tilker do not provide detailed results but state that
statistical analysis showed that all three groups showed an equal
increase in number of dry nights at the end of the training period.

RECENT EVIDENCE ON THE CORTICAL CONTROL MODEL

These studies have been reported in some detail because, taken
with Azrin's results, they raise important questions. Let it be
assumed that Azrin is correct in his contention that social
reinforcement procedures can be applied directly to nocturnal
enuresis with success and that Kimmel is correct in his
contention that social reinforcement techniques applied to
daytime frequence of urination will lead to nocturnal control
without any direct attempt to modify the nighttime wetting.
Leaving aside for the moment the difficulty in explaining
Kimmel's results in social reinforcement terms, the question
becomes: What implications do these studies have for Mowrer's
theoretical model from which he derived *his* treatment technique? Do these results suggest that the model of an internal
conditioning process has all along been irrelevant to the Mowrer
treatment technique and that social reinforcement (or some
alternative but essentially external process) must be postulated as
the crucial controlling variable?

Before considering this question, however, it is necessary to
refer to two other sets of studies, one of which increases the
significance of the question, the other of which leads in the
direction of a resolution of the difficulty. The first set of studies
consists of recent investigations of Mowrer's technique itself
and, more particularly, of the theoretical model proposed by

Mowrer. One group of studies (Baker, 1969; Kolvin, Taunch, Currah, Garside, Nolan, and Shaw, 1972; McConaghy, 1969) have confirmed empirically the superiority of the Mowrer technique over various alternative procedures, such as regular waking and toileting during the night and the use of drugs or placebos; whereas a second group of studies has also confirmed the increasing success rate of the Mowrer technique with increased control over the procedures involved in the use of the technique (De Leon and Sachs, 1972a; Sloop and Kennedy, 1973; Young and Morgan, 1972a, 1972b, 1973). More important is another group of studies that have examined predictions made from the Mowrer model; that is, they deal with the *processes* assumed to be operating within Mowrer's model and examine what happens when the variables controlling these processes are manipulated.

The role of the bell in Mowrer's model is assumed to be that of a US that produces two URs: awakening and inhibition of the urination that is incomplete at the time of awakening. Peterson, Wright, and Hanlon (1969) examined the effect on achieving dryness by delaying the ringing of the bell for 3 minutes after contact was made as compared with its immediate activation, arguing that delay should retard the development of conditioned awakening to detrusor muscle activity as a CS. Although it is evident that they did not have a sufficient number of conditioning trials (the duration of treatment was only 3 weeks) an increasing superiority of the no-delay over the delay group was strongly evident in their results and would almost certainly have been statistically significant had they continued training trials for a further week. Thus this study supports the validity of Mowrer's theoretical model. The deficiencies in this study were removed in a recent study by Collins (1973) in which a larger number of subjects, a much longer treatment period (8 weeks), and a follow-up period were incorporated into the design. The delay in occurrence of the bell was also increased to 5 minutes in the experimental group. The results are shown in Figure 1 and fully supported the prediction that conditioning would be retarded significantly in the delay group as compared with the nondelay

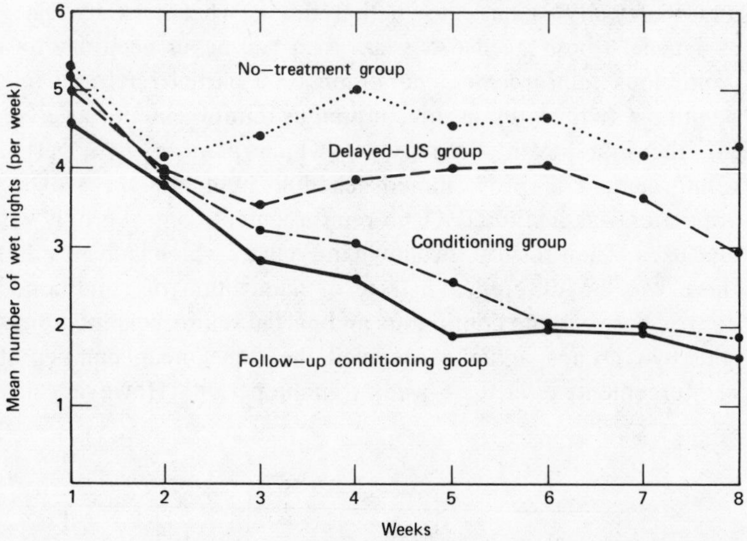

Figure 1. Mean number of wet nights a week over 8 weeks of treatment for the conditioning, delayed-UCS, no-treatment, and the follow-up conditioning group when administered a follow-up conditioning procedure. (Source: Collins, 1973.)

group. Collins, it might be added, also controlled for factors such as professional attention, "potting," parent-child cooperation, apparatus effect, and diary keeping, and he concluded that his results: "substantiated the view that the effectiveness of the conditioning treatment depends primarily upon the contiguous pairing of bladder cues with the UCS which involves sphincter contraction and/or awakening" (p. 305).

Two other important predictions from Mowrer's theoretical model have recently been tested. From what is known about partial reinforcement it would be predicted (but not confidently) that partial instead of full reinforcement during training would retard the development of control and, with more confidence, that once control has been established, relapse would be less likely following training under partial reinforcement. Thus it should be possible to reduce the relapse rate associated with use of the Mowrer technique by training under conditions of partial reinforcement. A study by Finley, Besserman, Bennett, Clapp, and Finley (1973) has shown that this is what happens. They assigned 30 boys aged 6–8 years who had never been dry to a continuous reinforcement condition or a partial reinforcement condition. In the latter group continuous reinforcement was given for the first seven wettings, at which point a 70% partial reinforcement preprogrammed schedule built into the Mowrer apparatus was instituted. A no-reinforcement control group was also used. Their results are shown in Figure 2 which indicates that there was no difference in rate of acquisition of conditioned control between the continuous and partial reinforcement groups (the two groups actually received the same mean number of reinforcements over the 6-week training period). However, only

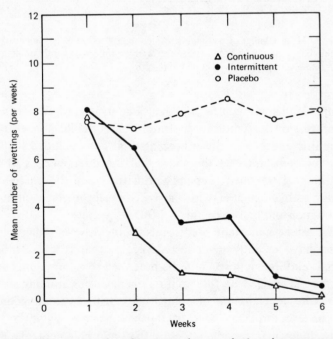

Figure 2.   Mean number of wettings per week across the 6-week treatment period for continuous, intermittent, and placebo reinforcement groups. (Source: Finley et al., 1973.)

one out of the eight partial reinforcement subjects who achieved dryness relapsed at follow-up, compared with four out of nine subjects in the continuous reinforcement group who achieved dryness. It should be noted, however, that only a single partial reinforcement schedule was used, and the optimality of this schedule for training purposes and in producing resistance to relapse is, of course, unknown.

The largest-scale study to examine the effects of partial reinforcement on acquisition and resistance to relapse is that of Turner, Young, and Rachman (1970). This study is so seriously defective in its methodology, however, that its results cannot be accepted as demonstrating anything conclusively (see Coote, 1972; Lovibond, 1972; and, for a reply, Turner, Rachman, and Young, 1972).

We now return to the problem of the explanation of the success of these various techniques that appear to demonstrate the development of internal control processes (higher cortical conditioning) on the one hand, and the controlling effects of external variables such as social reinforcement, on the other. Is one explanatory model right, and the other wrong, and if so, which? Is it possible that both are right, or even both wrong? In more general terms, what is the process by which an enuretic child achieves control over his reflex bladder voiding? Has he in fact achieved it physiologically, but is neglecting to exercise that control because he either is not reinforced socially when he does exercise it or, on the contrary, is not subject to sufficiently aversive consequences when he fails to exercise it? Is there a difference between the child who wets at night but not during the day and the child who wets during the day but not necessarily at night?

Interestingly enough, Azrin's position is very similar to that of Muellner, who was anything but operantly inclined. Muellner argued that it is in fact impossible to teach a child the mechanics of bladder control. Obviously one does not, in trying to train a child in daytime bladder control, sit him down and lecture him on the necessity of voluntarily steadiying the diaphragm, contracting the lower abdominal muscles, relaxing the pubococcygeus of the levator ani, and so forth. Muellner's argument was that the achievement of voluntary control of urination was essentially a matter of maturation. Azrin appears to accept this viewpoint and argues that the child must be taught *social* control of a skill that, physiologically, is not a matter of internal complex conditioning patterns, or, if it is, cannot be "taught." Mowrer, on the other hand, argued that achievement of control of reflex urination *does* involve conditioning and that the development of the control, even though it obviously does involve maturation, is much more than maturation and involves internal conditioning processes that his model describes and that his technique helps to develop where they are absent.

The theoretical resolution of this question is actually not very difficult, but the resolution that is proposed may not be acceptable to those who would prefer the remedial techniques of Azrin or Kimmel for nocturnal enuresis over the Mowrer technique and would account for the successes with the Mowrer technique in social reinforcement terms. In what follows, only the explanation of *nocturnal* enuresis is in question—it is not disputed that daytime wetting (and loss of continence at night in some adults, e.g., chronic schizophrenics) may often be properly explained and treated in terms of the social reinforcement model. However, it is much less certain that primary nocturnal enuresis can be accounted for in social reinforcement terms.

The argument to be developed is derived from a consideration of empirical evidence (the validity and reliability of which is not in doubt) relating to what is called functional bladder capacity. This may be measured in two ways. The first is by the water-load test in which the child, after emptying its bladder, drinks 30 ml of water per kilogram of body weight up to a maximum of 480–500 ml and is then asked to delay urination as long as possible. The larger of the first two specimens ultimately voided is measured and defines maximum functional capacity. This technique was developed by Starfield (1967). A second measure of functional capacity has been utilized by Troup and Hodgson (1971), who measured total urinary output over 24 hours and divided this by the total number of voidings to obtain an average output per voiding.

Studies using these two techniques have shown beyond doubt that the functional bladder capacity of enuretics is significantly less than that of nonenuretics. Starfield (1967), for example, compared the functional bladder capacity, by means of the water-load test, of 221 enuretics and a control group of nonenuretic siblings ranging in age from 5–13 and found the capacity of the enuretics to be significantly lower at all age levels; this finding was fully confirmed in a later study by Esperanca and Gerrard (1969). Typical results obtained by Starfield (1967) are shown in Figure 3.

The meaning of this fundamental finding has been clarified by other studies. Troup and Hodgson (1971) have confirmed the earlier observation by Vulliamy (1956) that the total urinary output of enuretics and nonenuretics over 24 hours does not differ, but that the average amount voided at each urination was

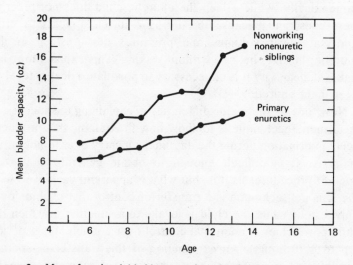

Figure 3. Mean functional bladder capacity of primary enuretics and their nonenuretic siblings at age levels 5–13. (Source: Starfield, 1967.)

significantly smaller in the case of enuretics. This in turn has clearly been shown to be a function of the fact that not only do enuretics wet more often than nonenuretics while asleep (which is, of course, what defines the enuretic) but that *they also void signigicantly more often during their waking hours.* This fact has not only been confirmed by numerous other studies (e.g. Starfield, 1972), but was shown to be the case by Paschalis et al. (1972) and by Stedman (1972), working within a different framework. Esperanca and Gerrard (1969), in fact, found the urination rate during waking hours to be nearly twice as great for enuretics as compared with nonenuretics. Cystometric studies (Hagglund, 1965; Linderholdm, 1966) have also confirmed the lower functional capacity of enuretics.

Contrary, therefore, to the opinion expressed by Azrin that day wetting is in part due to lack of physiological cues to urgency, these studies demonstrate conclusively that the nocturnal enuretic is *oversensitive* during his waking hours to detrusor muscle activity arising from low volumes and pressures within the bladder and reacts to this by urinating more frequently. Paradoxically, while asleep the enuretic child does not react to these cues, and because the detrusor muscle appears to "run wild" at lower volumes and pressures during sleep in the enuretic, he wets his bed without waking. This explanation also makes it clear why it is unnecessary to postulate a deeper level of sleep in the enuretic.

Now, one of the major difficulties in explaining the success of the Kimmel technique is to show how the training that produces delay in urination during the daytime can carry over to nocturnal enuresis. It is difficult enough to obtain generalization with operant procedures as it is, but what is apparently achieved with the Kimmel technique is a transfer of control that extends over only 1 hour while the child is awake to a situation in which the child now achieves nocturnal control over a much longer period (up to 8–10 hours). An explanation of this transfer in operant conditioning or reinforcement terms just does not make sense. If, however, what the Kimmel technique is achieving is basically training the detrusor muscle to adapt to increasing bladder pressures and the volumes (as happens in the normal child as it gains control), then the transfer becomes readily understandable. For if the detrusor muscle has been trained to adapt rather than "run wild," then it would indeed be expected that this would be reflected in a lower incidence of wetting while the child is asleep.

Paschalis et al. (1972) come close to this explanation when they conjecture that: "the reinforcement occurs at a time when the child has already reported a need to urinate, that is, when bladder distention cues are above threshhold. An inhibition of the urination response to these cues is reinforced" (p. 255). But it is unnecessary to invoke reinforcement at all in the process, and several of the studies using the Kimmel technique have shown that for success to occur, it is not necessary to provide reinforcement. Furthermore, Stedman (1972) had his patient record not only the frequency of daytime urinations and nighttime wettings but also the strength of perceived bladder distension cues immediately prior to daytime urination. He found the strong bladder cues shifted their temporal position as the delay interval lengthened so that they were always occurring just before the need to urinate became overwhelming. The point to note, however, is that the patient's daytime frequency decreased to three times which indicates that detrusor muscle activity was now adapting to less than strong bladder pressures and large volumes.

Now Stedman, like some of the other users of the Kimmel technique, did not use specific and behavior-correlated primary reinforcement but relied rather on self-recording and general verbal praise. In fact, the use of training to increase bladder capacity predates Kimmel's work by a good many years, first being suggested in the last century and seriously reintroduced by Muellner in 1962. Recent studies by Hagglund (1965) and by Starfield and Mellits (1968) have used the technique of forced drinking and delay of urination on a large scale. Starfield and Mellits (1968), for example, applied the technique to 110 enuretic children whose bladder capacity was estimated by the water-load test before and after treatment. The treatment itself extended over 6 months and involved five rules for the parents and children (the child was not, in fact, seen during treatment):

1. Unrestricted fluids during the daytime.
2. Voluntary retention to the point of discomfort at least once a day.
3. Keeping a record of the amount voided after delay.
4. Practicing interruption of the urine flow.
5. Not punishing the child for wet beds.

Starfield and Mellits found a direct relationship between bladder capacity and improvement in enuresis status. The mean increase in functional bladder capacity for "improved" children was 62.40 ml; for "unimproved" children only 11.25 ml. When 36 pairs of children with similar functional capacities at the start of treatment were compared (and when one of each pair improved while the other did not) the mean difference in bladder capacity at the end of treatment was about 90 ml.

CONCLUSION

The overall conclusion to be drawn from all of this recent work would appear to be that primary nocturnal enuresis (i.e., when the child has not been dry since birth) results from a bladder of functionally small capacity in which there is a failure of the detrusor muscle to adapt to increasing bladder volumes and pressures and in which the detrusor muscle triggers off reflex urination at low volumes and pressures. During the daytime this condition does not result in reflex wetting, because the child responds to the change in activity of the detrusor muscle from adaptation to uncontrolled contractions by experiencing urgency at low volumes and pressures and demonstrates this by a waking urination frequency that is nearly twice as great as that of the nonenuretic child. When the child is asleep, however, the bladder pressure and volume that trigger uncontrolled detrusor muscle activity, and the uncontrolled detrusor activity itself, are all below threshold, that is, are insufficiently strong even when wetting is occurring to wake the child. In the nonenuretic child, however, these stimuli will become strong enough to wake the child before wetting occurs if enough urine enters the bladder to make uncontrolled detrusor muscle activity imminent. For nocturnal enuresis to be successfully overcome, therefore, the functional capacity of the bladder must be trained to adapt to increasing volumes and pressures of urine. Essentially, this is achieved to some extent by the Kimmel technique, although it would be surprising if completely satisfactory results were obtained by this method, because it relies on a carry-over from daytime training to nighttime control. The advantage of the Mowrer technique is that it operates directly on the events occurring during sleep, producing direct inhibition of detrusor muscle activity at the moment of wetting and then relying on this inhibition to generalize to earlier stages of detrusor muscle activity. In other words, the Mowrer technique directly trains the detrusor muscle activity to induce sphincter contraction rather than sphincter relaxation, and achievement of this latter state of affairs automatically guarantees dryness. The role of reinforcement, therefore, in daytime training to control nocturnal enuresis, is seen as merely a device to produce behavior in the child that has the effect of increasing functional bladder capacity. But the reinforcement procedures are not essential to success. The Kimmel technique will work whether reinforcement is provided or not. The sole requirement is that the child refrain from urinating for longer and longer periods. Paradoxically, in the Mowrer technique, wetting is an essential part of the training, since inhibition of detrusor muscle activity and of sphincter relaxation will occur only if a training trial occurs.

REFERENCES

Azrin, N. H., Bugle, C., and O'Brien, F. Behavioral engineering: Two apparatuses for toilet training retarded children. *Journal of Applied Behavior Analysis*, 1971, **4**, 244–253.

Azrin, N. H., and Foxx, R. M. A rapid method of toilet training the institutionalized retarded. *Journal of Applied Behavior Analysis*, 1971, **4**, 89–99.

Baker, B. L. Symptom treatment and symptom substitution in enuresis. *Journal of Abnormal Psychology*, 1969, **74**, 42–49.

Collins, R. W. Importance of the bladder-cue buzzer contingency in the conditioning treatment for enuresis. *Journal of Abnormal Psychology*, 1973, **82**, 299–308.

Coote, M. A. Comment on "Treatment of nocturnal enuresis by conditioning techniques." *Behavior Research and Therapy*, 1972, **10**, 293.

DeLeon, G., and Sachs, S. Conditioning functional enuresis: A four-year follow-up. *Journal of Consulting and Clinical Psychology*, 1972, **39**, 299–300.

Ellis, N. R. Toilet training and the severely defective patient: An S-R reinforcement analysis. *American Journal of Mental Deficiency*, 1963, **68**, 98–103.

Esperanca, M., and Gerrard, D. M. Nocturnal enuresis: Studies in bladder function in normal children and enuretics. *Canadian Medical Association Journal*, 1969, **101**, 324–327.

Finley, W. W., Besserman, R. L., Bennett, F. L., Clapp, R. K., and Finley, P. K. The effect of continuous, intermittent, and "placebo" reinforcement on the effectiveness of the conditioning treatment for enuresis nocturna. *Behavior Research and Therapy*, 1973, **11**, 289–297.

Foxx, R. M. and Azrin, N. H. *Toilet training the retarded: A rapid program for day and night-time independent toileting*. Champaign, Ill.: Research Press, 1973.

Hägglund, T. B. Enuretic children treated with fluid-restriction or forced drinking. *Annales Paediatriae Fenniae*, 1965, **11**, 84–90.

Jones, H. G. The behavioral treatment of enuresis nocturna. In H. J. Eysenck (Ed.), *Behavior Therapy and the neuroses*. Oxford: Pergamon, 1960. Pp. 377–403.

Kimmel, H. D., and Kimmel, E. An instrumental conditioning method for the treatment of enuresis. *Journal of Behavior Therapy and Experimental Psychiatry*, 1970, **1**, 121–123.

Kolvin, I., Taunch, J., Currah, J., Garside, R. F., Nolan, J., and Shaw, W. B. Enuresis: A descriptive analysis and a controlled trial. *Developmental Medicine and Child Neurology*, 1972, **14**, 715–726.

Linderholm, B. E. The cystometric findings in enuresis. *Journal of Urology*, 1966, **96**, 718–722.

Lovibond, S. H. *Conditioning and enuresis*. Oxford: Pergamon, 1964.

Lovibond, S. H. Critique of Turner, Young, and Rachman's conditioning treatment of enuresis. *Behavior Research and Therapy*, 1972, **10**, 287–289.

McConaghy, N. A controlled trial of imipramine, amphetamine, pad-and-bell conditioning and random awakening in the treatment of nocturnal enuresis. *Medical Journal of Australia*, 1969, **2**, 237–239.

Mahoney, K., Van Wagenen, R. K., and Meyerson, L. Toilet training of normal and retarded children. *Journal of Applied Behavior Analysis*, 1971, **4**, 173–181.

Miller, P. M. An experimental analysis of retention control training in the treatment of nocturnal enuresis in two institutionalized adolescents. *Behavior Therapy*, 1973, **4**, 288–294.

Mowrer, O. H., and Mowrer, W. A. Enuresis: A method for its study and treatment. *American Journal of Orthopsychiatry*, 1938, **8**, 436–447.

Muellner, S. R. The voluntary control of micturition in man. *Journal of Urology*, 1958, **80**, 473–478.

Muellner, S. R. Development of urinary control in children: A new concept in cause, prevention and treatment of primary enuresis. *Journal of Urology*, 1960, **84**, 714–716.

Paschalis, A. Ph., Kimmel, H. D., and Kimmel, E. Further study of diurnal instrumental conditioning in the threatment of enuresis nocturna. *Journal of Behavior Therapy and Experimental Psychiatry*, 1972, **3**, 253–256.

Peterson, R. A., Wright, R. I. D., and Hanlon, C. C. The effects of extending the CS-UCS interval on the effectiveness of the conditioning treatment for nocturnal enuresis. *Behavior Research and Therapy*, 1969, **7**, 351–357.

Rocklin, N., and Tilker, H. Instrumental conditioning of nocturnal enuresis. *Proceedings of the 81st Annual Convention of the American Psychological Association*, 1973, 915–916.

Sloop, E. W., and Kennedy, W. H. Institutionalized retarded nocturnal enuretics treated by a conditioning technique. *American Journal of Mental Deficiency*, 1973, **77**, 717–721.

Starfield, B. Functional bladder capacity in enuretic and non-enuretic children. *Journal of Pediatrics*, 1967, **70**, 777–781.

Starfield, B. Enuresis: Its pathogenesis and management. *Clinical Pediatrics*, 1972, **11**, 343–350.

Starfield, B., and Mellits, E. D. Increase in functional bladder capacity and improvements in enuresis. *Journal of Pedriatrics*, 1968, **72**, 483–487.

Stedman, J. M. An extension of the Kimmel treatment method for enuresis to an adolescent: A case report. *Journal of Behavior Therapy and Experimental Psychiatry*, 1972, **3**, 307–309.

Troup, C. W., and Hodgson, N. B. Nocturnal functional bladder capacity in enuretic children. *Journal of Urology*, 1971, **105**, 129–132.

Turner, R. K., Rachman, S., and Young, G. Conditioning treatment of enuresis: A rejoinder to Lovibond. *Behavior Research and Therapy*, 1972, **10**, 291–292.

Turner, R. K., Young, G. C., and Rachman, S. Treatment of nocturnal enuresis by conditioning techniques. *Behavior Research and Therapy*, 1970, **8**, 367–381.

Van Wagenen, R. K., Meyerson, L., Kerr, N. J., and Mahoney, K. Field trials of a new procedure for toilet training. *Journal of Experimental Child Psychology*, 1969, **8**, 147–159.

Vulliamy, D. The day and night output of urine in enuresis. *Archives of Disease in Childhood*, 1956, **31**, 439–443.

Young, G. C., and Morgan, R. T. T. Overlearning in the conditioning treatment of enuresis. *Behavior Research and Therapy*, 1972, **10**, 147–151. (a)

Young, G. C., and Morgan, R. T. T. Overlearning in the conditioning treatment of enuresis: A long-term follow-up study. *Behavior Research and Therapy*, 1972, **10**, 419–420.

Young, G. C., and Morgan, R. T. T. Analysis of factors associated with the extinction of a conditioned response. *Behavior Research and Therapy*, 1973, **11**, 219–222.

Yates, A. J. *Behavior therapy*. New York: Wiley, 1970.

CHAPTER 4

Have We Solved the Problem of Stuttering?

Stuttering represents a particularly clear example of a dispute *within* behavior therapy, for two quite different models have been proposed to account for the genesis and maintenance of stuttering, and these models have, in turn, tended to mediate different approaches to therapy. Furthermore, these differences extend beyond stuttering to explanations of the control of normal speech. It should be stressed that what is being referred to here is not the *content* of speech but rather its *form* and *shape* (what is now coming to be called the fluency and rate characteristics of speech).

A brief recapitulation of the position as it was 5 years ago (Yates, 1970, pp. 107–131) provides a framework for the discussion of more recent work. At that time empirical studies had shown that fluency and rate in normal speakers could be significantly influenced in two main ways: by interfering with the feedback channels by means of which the speaker monitors his own voice production and by providing contingencies for speech of a positive or negative kind. Feedback control studies demonstrated how rate and fluency could be upset (mainly by the use of delayed auditory feedback), whereas contingency studies demonstrated that rate and fluency could be increased *or* decreased by the appropriate manipulation of positive and negative consequences for fluent and nonfluent speech. To account for these results, a servomechanistic model of normal speech control was formulated on the one hand; on the other, the results were explained in terms of reinforcement theory.

Similarly, empirical studies showed that stuttering could be much reduced by techniques that appeared to interfere with the feedback produced by speaking, particularly by any technique that stopped the stutterer from listening to his own voice. At the same time, stuttering could be much reduced by providing positive or negative reinforcement for not stuttering, by aversive consequences for stuttering, or by a combination of these techniques. Again, the results were interpreted, on the one hand, in terms of a servomechanical model in which stuttering was regarded as resulting from a perceptual defect; on the other hand, stuttering was regarded as an operant, even though this latter formulation was faced with the difficult task of explaining why stuttering should persist in ordinary life situations where it so obviously appeared to produce aversive social consequences. The only solution appeared to be to argue that stuttering produced reinforcing consequences for the stutterer, although it was difficult to imagine what these might be. In relation to theoretical explanations of stuttering, a third explanatory model was prominent, appearing in several different forms. This was the anxiety-reduction hypothesis which stated that stuttering was both a response to anxiety about speaking and, paradoxically, reduced the anxiety whenever a stutter occurred.

Within this framework of empirical evidence and theoretical explanation, seven therapy approaches had developed that could be regarded as alternatives to the psychodynamic approach to the therapy of stuttering which had dominated the field for so long. These seven approaches were shadowing, masking, negative practice, metronome pacing, syllable-timed speech training, the operant approach (particularly the use of delayed auditory feedback to shape speech), and the use of systematic desensitization to reduce the anxiety that was supposed to play an important role in the stuttering syndrome. Of the seven, all but two (negative practice and, very surprisingly, shadowing) are still prominent 5 years later.

Two main topics are considered in this chapter: the range and effectiveness of present treatment approaches to stuttering and the present status of some of the various theoretical models put forward to account for stuttering. No attempt is made to cover all the empirical literature that has appeared over the last 5 years, nor to consider all the theoretical models (see Ingham and Andres, 1973b for the most recent comprehensive coverage of the literature).

CURRENT TREATMENT APPROACHES

Problems of Assessment

Before considering the range and effectivenss of current treatment approaches, something should be said about the assessment of the results of therapy. This has been a much neglected matter that is only now being remedied. Andrews and Ingham (1971, 1972b) have specifically considered this problem and have pointed out that, in addition to producing change in speech, successful treatment should alter the stutterer's attitude toward his speech and, as well as making him more comfortable in speaking situations, should enable him to handle the problems that arise even for nonstutterers from time to time. Thus the stutterer should not be turned into a machine with faultless voice production, but should be able to commit the "normal" errors in speech without panicking and reverting to stuttering. Speech, in other words, should be truly normal and should also be the preferred means of communication. As indices of "normal" speech Andrews and Ingham have developed the measures of *percentage of syllables stuttered* (%SS) as an indication of fluency, and *syllables per minute* (SPM) as an indication of speech rate. These measurements should be taken in situations that at least approximate normal social situations. The other assessments required may involve self-ratings by the stutterer, ratings by observers, and the use of standardized personality tests.

Rather similar procedures for assessing final status have been developed by Brady (1971).

Behavioral Therapy of Stuttering

In examining the results of therapy, experimental studies that may throw light on the factors involved in the therapy or its validity are not considered at this point. Bearing this in mind, the use of *systematic desensitization* to reduce the anxiety supposedly involved as a causal factor in stuttering is rare. Lanyon (1969) reported success with one stutterer, but the patient's abnormality (long periods of silence before saying a word on which he anticipated he would stutter) was very atypical and the results not particularly clear.

Similarly, the use of *aversive consequences* such as shock or verbal reprimand for stuttering, on the one hand, and contingent praise or other reinforcement for fluency, on the other, do not appear to have been much used at all in therapy. Within a general operant framework, however, there have been some very interesting developments. The first of these is the use of *time-out procedures* (TO), where the TO is regarded as an aversive consequence for stuttering. The technique was introduced by Haroldson, Martin, and Starr (1968) and is very simple and adaptable to any kind of situation in which the stutterer reads or speaks. In the original study the subjects were given cards with nouns printed on them that served as prompts to help the stutterer speak continuously for a specified period. Following two base rate sessions, a TO was introduced each time the subject stuttered. A red light appeared, and the subject was required to remain silent for 10 seconds until the light disappeared and he resumed reading.

This initial study, which claimed to show that TO reduced stuttering significantly, was criticized by Adams (1970) with respect to the statistical analyses employed (see also the reply by Martin, Haroldson, and Starr, 1971), but its effectiveness has been demonstrated repeatedly since, especially when used in conjunction with other techniques, as is shortly seen. Adams and Popelka (1971) reported clinical success with its use, as did Martin and Berndt (1970). A particularly interesting, novel, and impressive use of TO was reported recently by Martin, Kuhl, and Haroldson (1972). They arranged a situation in which a child stutterer could (and did) talk to an animated puppet that responded verbally. The puppet was visible to the child but was in an illuminated box placed behind a one-way screen. Each instance of stuttering produced a 10-second TO during which the puppet became invisible and stopped talking. This technique proved particularly suitable for the TO treatment of two children aged 3½ and 4½ to whom the original procedures could not readily be applied. During the course of treatment probe sessions were conducted in which stuttering frequency was assessed for spontaneous conversation with another person in a different situation. Furthermore, after all training was completed assessments were made in the child's home in a number of different situations. The results obtained for one of the children will serve to indicate the impressiveness of the results. In the puppet situation a stuttering frequency of 40 words per 20-minute session was reduced to, and maintained at, zero, even when TO was discontinued. The changes are shown in Figure 1. Generalization to the probe situation resulted in a reduction to zero there also, as shown in Figure 2. Most importantly, the probes carried out after treatment had ended produced the following results: no words stuttered out of 481 spoken by the child while at dinner with the family, 2 stuttered words out of 664 spoken while with the family in the living room, and so on. Altogether, only 6 words were stuttered out of 2146 spoken while under observation. At an 11-month follow-up, the stuttering rate was less than 1%. Results obtained with the second child were equally striking.

The technique is based on the assumption that TO is an aversive consequence; in the case of stuttering, imposed silence is postulated as aversive, a curious form of reasoning. Adams and Popelka (1971), who used TO with stutterers, reported that their subjects, far from finding TO aversive, found it to be relaxing. Thus the explanation of the effectiveness of TO remains unclear.

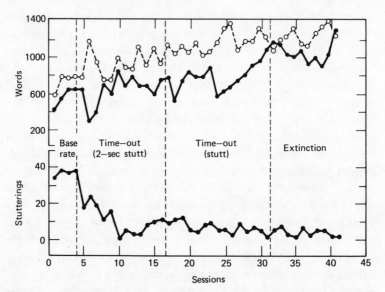

Figure 1. Numbers of words spoken by J.C. (top closed circles) and puppet (open circles), and number of stutterings by J. C. (bottom closed circles) each treatment session. (Source: Martin et al., 1972.)

The TO technique has been combined with Goldiamond's earlier technique of using delayed auditory feedback to shape the speech of stutterers to produce a composite therapy for stuttering that has been called conversational rate control therapy by Curlee and Perkins (1969). Very recently, Perkins (1973a, 1973b) has reviewed the rationale of the technique and described his clinical procedures in detail. The technique involves conversation instead of the reading Goldiamond used, and there are three stages in therapy. In the first stage, delayed auditory feedback at 250 msecs and high intensity level is used, and the subject is instructed to slow his speech down so as to restore the feedback/output time relationship of normal speech. On the assumption that this procedure eliminates the stutter and produces prolonged speech, when no stuttering has been maintained for two consecutive 15-minute periods, the 250-msec delay is reduced progressively to 0 msec by 50-msec increments.

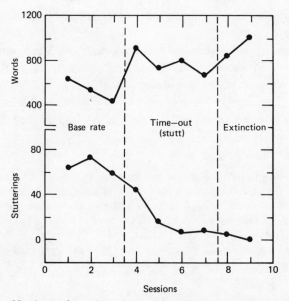

Figure 2. Numbers of words and stutterings by J. C. each probe session. (Source: Martin et al., 1972.)

If two instances of stuttering occur in any 5-minute period, the next longer delay is reinstated. When zero delay without stuttering is achieved, the second stage (TO procedure) is introduced. Whenever the stutterer now stutters more than twice in 5 minutes the room light is turned off and subject and experimenter sit in darkness and silence for 30 seconds. The third stages involves generalizing the gains made to other situations, people, family, friends, and so on and to progressively more difficult situations. Curlee and Perkins (1969) have reported results using this technique with 15 adolescent and adult stutterers. Over less than 30 hours of treatment for 1–3 hours per week, the average reduction in stuttering has been from 170 instances in 30 minutes to less than 2 instances over 30 minutes. It is claimed that there is 90–95% generalization to the real-life situation. Unfortunately, Perkins (1973a, 1973b) does not provide any further data in his most recent papers, and it is clear that the technique has become much more extended and complicated than it was originally.

The most solid therapeutic work that has been done with stutterers in recent years (and, unfortunately, also the most complex to evaluate) is undoubtedly that reported by Andrews and Ingham in Australia (Andrews and Ingham, 1972a, 1972b; Ingham and Andrews, 1971a, 1973a). As Ingham and Andrews (1971a) put it:

> The aim of the programme has been to systematically explore the changes in stuttering that occur with alterations in speech pattern produced by syllable-timed speech (Andrews and Harris, 1964), Fixed Delayed Auditory Feedback, Synchronous Auditory Feedback and graded D.A.F. (Curlee and Perkins, 1969). Concurrent with this the effects of Token Reinforcement Systems have been explored in relation to the contingency of reinforcement and the state of the token economy (p. 281).

Thus the Andrews/Ingham therapeutic approach involves the use of *syllable-timed (ST) speech training* or *conversational rate control therapy* in combination with the use of a *token system* (the term "token economy" is a little misleading here). The ST training and rate control therapy are primarily intended to eliminate the stuttering, whereas the token system is primarily designed to increase the slow rate of speech developed under DAF or ST therapy to the normal speech rate. It may be noted that the TO procedure has not been used by Andrews and Ingham, but the token system could be regarded as a substitute for it.

The details of therapy procedures reported by Andrews and Ingham are too complex to report here. They have dealt with large numbers of patients treated on both out- and in-patient bases; their procedures are extremely complex, although their treatment time tends to be relatively short and intense; they have provided data on long-term follow-up studies (although their data are confounded by the fact that maintenance therapy was continued during follow-up); and they have devised elaborate means for assessing the quantitative and qualitative results of the various kinds of treatment.

They do not make extravagant claims for their techniques. Andrews and Ingham (1972a), for example, reported that 23/56 stutterers (41%) studied did not stutter at a 9-month follow-up and that of these 23, 11 had a normal speech rate. Other studies have compared the effects of ST speech training with DAF training in which both were accompanied by the token system, to the advantage of the DAF training (Andrews and Ingham, 1972b). In another study DAF training was superior to ST training when no token system was used (Ingham and Andrews 1971a). They have also provided evidence that suggests that the token system has its greatest effect during the initial intensive treatment period and that maintenance therapy is probably not worth the great amount of time involved because little gains are made over the follow-up period. All in all, complicated though the papers describing their therapy and results are, the work of Andrews and Ingham undoubtedly represents the most important therapeutic work going on today.

The only other therapeutic technique to achieve prominence over the past 5 years is that based on the *use of a metronome* to enable the stutterer to pace his speech by matching either syllables, words, or phrases to the regular beat of a metronome. The most important work here has been done by Brady (1968, 1971). Brady stresses both the disfluencies and the anxiety in speaking situations and directs treatment at both. For eliminating disfluency Brady considers the advantages of the metronome to be that it is light and unobtrusive (it is incorporated into a hearing aid), has on-off switches that are easily manipulated, has variable volume control and beat control, and produces a complex sound rather than a tone. The treatment package involves four stages. In the first two stages an ordinary metronome is used. The next two involve the use of the miniaturized metronome:

1. The subject is shown that by using the metronome he can speak without stuttering—a demonstration is often necessary to convince the stutterers of this.

2. His speech is shaped by increasing rate and using longer speech units per beat.

3. The stutterer constructs a hierarchy of speaking situations and uses the metronome first in the least-anxiety-arousing situations, then extending its use to situations involving more anxiety (thus anxiety is simultaneously treated in the real-life situation).

4. The use of the metronome is gradually phased out if the stutterer can do this.

Brady (1971) reported on the results of metronome therapy with 26 severe, chronic stutterers, most with a long history of unsuccessful treatment. They ranged in age from 12 to 53 years and were given between 5 and 31 treatment sessions of 1-hour. The average percentage decrease in fluency when *not* wearing the metronome following treatment was 67% (a few subjects were worse than before treatment but improvement ranged up to 98%). The attrition rate was only 3/26. A significant decrease in anxiety symptoms was found; 11 subjects had been able to discard the metronome, 8 still used it occasionally, and 3 used it most of the time. An overall "success" rate of 90% was claimed by Brady.

Three recent studies provide an interesting gloss to these impressive results. Berman and Brady (1973) analyzed reports from 28 therapists (a highly selected sample) who had used the pacemaster on a total of 118 patients, mostly adolescents or young adults. Using two criteria suggesting significant clinical improvement (patients no longer used the device because it was no longer needed or used it only in difficult situations) and three criteria suggesting failure to improve (using the device all the time, dropped out of treatment, returned to stuttering), Berman and Brady found that 72% of 11 patients could be classified as improved. Further analysis suggested that chances of success would be increased if Brady's four stages were systematically followed. Adams and Hotchkiss (1973) described individual differences in reaction to the training program. One subject, having improved dramatically with the use of the metronome, was willing to wear it in public without hesitation, if necessary for the rest of his life. A second stutterer, after initial success, was unable to adjust his speech to the beat. A third was able to pace successfully but flatly refused to wear the device in public. Thus one should not assume that a successful demonstration of the elimination of stuttering with the pacer will mean a smooth journey during the rest of the treatment. Finally, Silverman and Trotter (1973) made videotapes of four stutterers speaking with and without the metronome (after only a little practice) and had judges rate them for severity of stuttering and quality of metronome-paced speech. The stuttering was invariably rated as less with the metronome, but whether the quality of the metronome-paced speech was rated satisfactory or not depended on whether the initial stutter was rated as severe or not. Thus the metronome-paced speech of a severe stutterer would be likely to be rated as an improvement whereas that of a mild stutterer might appear even more peculiar than his stutter.

It may be concluded that in spite of these difficulties metronome-paced therapy has shown promising results and merits more attention than it has so far been given.

No attention appears to have been paid in the last 5 years to *shadowing* as a therapeutic technique, although there is no doubt that stuttering can be totally inhibited by shadowing and a theoretical rationale can be provided for expecting therapeutic success with its use. Nor has the use of *masking* (the device can also be built into a hearing aid) been explored to any significant degree. The few references on the clinical use of masking are not worth reporting here.

THEORETICAL EXPLANATIONS OF STUTTERING

It is evident that in the present state of theory in relation to stuttering, with one important exception, the available new evidence does not support the *anxiety-reduction* theory. Gray and England (1972), for example, showed that systematic desensitization for speech-related and general anxiety in a group of stutterers produced a decline both in anxiety and stuttering, but there was no correlation whatsoever between the two variables as they changed. In a rather similar test Ingham and Andrews (1971b) found no change in measures of speech-related anxiety during successful therapy for stuttering, using ST speech and DAF training as well as a token system. Adams and Moore (1972) also found no change in anxiety in conditions in which white noise significantly reduced stuttering.

However, a recent study by Ickes and Pierce (1973) has presented a very different picture. They required stutterers and nonstutterers to view 50 words in succession for 30 seconds each (approach period), then speak the word (4 seconds allowed) and then rest for 30 seconds (recovery period). While they were doing this vasoconstriction (digital blood volume) was measured continuously from the second finger of the left hand. Amplitude was measured via a pen recording for seven periods (three approach, one during enunciation of the word, and three recovery) for 10 words from each control subject, and for 10 fluent and 10 nonfluent words for each stutterer.

This well-designed study demonstrated that the stutterers showed a significant increase in vasoconstriction on approach to stuttered words as compared with the controls, but there was no difference between the groups on words that were not stuttered. Of course, it follows that the stutterers showed more vasoconstriction on approach to words they stuttered than on approach to words on which they did not stutter. If it is a reasonable assumption that changes in digital blood volume reflect anxiety about approach to a word with which the stutterer knows he is likely to have difficulty, then this study demonstrates three things very clearly. First, that it is not stumbling over the word itself that causes anxiety (vasoconstriction declined during the recovery period for stuttered words). Second, that stutterers can anticipate accurately words on which they are going to stutter. Third, support is afforded for the proposition that stuttering does reduce anxiety.

Mention should be made at this point of Bloodstein's anticipatory hypothesis, which states: "that a person stutters because he believes in the difficulty of speech, anticipates failure, and struggles to avoid it. His very efforts to avoid difficulty are his stutterings, or lead directly to them. Having stuttered, he is vindicated in his expectation of speech difficulty and so the cycle continues" (Bloodstein, 1972, p. 487).

Bloodstein (1972) has recently reviewed the impact on his hypothesis of evidence originating from studies with the metronome, with DAF, with white noise, and from adaptation and punishment studies; he has attempted to show that this evidence does not contradict his hypothesis. Here it may merely be noted that in the majority of those studies that have attempted to test his hypothesis directly the results have generally not supported its validity. Berecz (1973) has indeed devised what he calls *cognitive arousal and punishment therapy*, in which the stutterer vividly imagines (but not just visually—he conjures up all the correlates of the stuttering moment) the approach to stuttering and then shocks himself, the intent being to disrupt the anticipatory pattern. However, Berecz has not provided any hard data on the efficacy of this type of therapy. On the other hand, Curlee and Perkins (1968) shocked stutterers at the moment they signaled an expectancy of stuttering and found a significant reduction in stuttering as compared to a yoked control group given noncontingent shocks (neither group was shocked for stuttering) and a control group given no shock. However, Harris, Martin, and Haroldson (1971) found that TO for anticipation of stuttering in some instances reduced expectancy frequency *or* stuttering, but there was no correlation between the two. Since the anticipatory struggle hypothesis presumably involves anticipatory anxiety, the work of Ickes and Pierce (1973) is relevant to the theory.

The theory that stuttering is under operant control has definitely been seriously weakened in the last 5 years. The original study by Flanagan, Goldiamond, and Azrin (1958), which claimed to demonstrate that stuttering would decline significantly if it produced a blast of high-intensity white noise, was replicated with additional controls by Biggs and Sheehan (1969). They showed that stuttering would be reduced to an equal extent whether the stuttering turned white noise on, turned it off, or was presented noncontingently. They attributed the effect of white noise to a distraction effect, but an examination of their procedures shows that the decrease in stuttering could have been an adaptation effect. In any event, the results of the study cast serious doubt on the validity of the aversive control theory, a doubt that is strengthened by the results of several other studies. Thus Moore and Ritterman (1973) showed that punishment (shock) reduced stuttering whether it coincided with or followed stuttering. Cooper, Cady, and Robbins (1970) found that positive, negative, or neutral verbal consequences for stuttering produced the same amount of decline, whereas Siegel and Hanson (1972) interpreted the changes in fluency in normal subjects under contingency control in terms of cues, a point made recently by Brookshire (1973) who noted the distinction between the incentive and the information aspects of contingencies, a distinction that might well explain the success of Shriberg (1971) in apparently aconditioning fundamental frequency by providing differential contingencies for maintaining a predetermined pitch level in speaking. Similarly, the finding of Siegel, Lenske, and Broen (1969) that response cost reduces disfluency may be explicable in cue rather than motivational terms. Siegel (1970) has provided a very thorough review of all the studies on operant control of fluency.

We now turn to studies that are relevant to the closed-loop *servomechanical model* of speech in general and stuttering in particular. It is necessary, to put this in proper perspective, to recall that it has been shown conclusively that stuttering may be totally eliminated by a variety of techniques, all of which stop the stutterer from listening to his own voice via the air and/or bone-conduction channels. Thus stutterers do not stutter when they shadow another speaker (their attention necessarily being directed away from their own voice by the amount of attention involved in following the speaker), if high-intensity white noise is fed into their auditory system via headphones so the air and bone-conducted feedback is no longer heard, and by rhythmic speaking in time to a metronome (the suggestion here being that the output-feedback relationship is altered so as to abolish overlap, which makes it equivalent to speaking under white-noise conditions). Finally, it has been shown that DAF may abolish stuttering, especially if the appropriate individual delay for each stutterer is found (the assumption here being that the discrepant feedback channels—ear and bone are brought into phase, as it were). Most significantly, it has been shown that stutterers will continue to stutter as long as they can hear the low-frequency components (mainly bone conducted) of their own voice, but will not stutter if these are selectively filtered out. The conclusion from all this work was that stuttering is essentially a defect arising from a faulty feedback control system, with the locus of the fault being tentatively placed in the bone-conduction channel. The contribution of learning to the final form of the stutter was not denied by this explanation, since the stutterer learns various ways of attempting to overcome his basic difficulty—but the basic difficulty was regarded as a faulty servomechanism present from birth (Yates, 1970,pp. 116–119)

The present status of this model may be assessed by considering the recent experimental work on masking and metronome studies, followed by a look at some other experimental work and a reformulation of the closed-loop model.

Most of the experimental work on the use of the metronome to abolish stuttering has not, in fact, been directly concerned with its relevance to the servomechanical model, but rather with the question whether distraction can explain the results. Brady (1969) carried out four experimental studies to examine four alleged effects of metronome pacing on the speech of stutterers. The first showed that the reduction in stuttering was not necessarily accompanied by a slower rate of speech, although this has been shown to occur unless the metronome is set at a rate equal to that of unaided reading (Silverman, 1971). The second produced evidence that the effect is not due to distraction, by showing that disfluency was reduced more by reading in time with a metronome than by writing down numbers presented intermittently while the stutterer reads. The third study showed that the effect was not an auditory effect, because equivalent reduction in disfluency was produced when reading was paced by visual, auditory, or tactile beats. The fourth study showed that disfluency was reduced more by a rhythmic metronome beat than by an arhythmic one. These latter two results have been independently confirmed by Azrin, Jones, and Flye (1968) and by Jones and Azrin (1969), whose detailed studies of the use of a vibrotactile stiumlator suggest that the portable instrument developed by them might have advantages over the portable auditory stimulus. The only contrary evidence to these results comes from the study of Greenberg (1970) who found that with a conversation rather than a reading task stuttering was reduced to an equal extent when the metronome was beating at 98 beats per minute, whether the stutterer was instructed to speak in time with it or not. She concluded that the presence of a rhythmic stimulus was the important factor, not its synchronization with the stutterer's speech. However, Greenberg reports that some of her stutterers "fell into" rhythm with the metronome even though not instructed to do so, and her study was criticized on other grounds by Yates (1971; see also Greenberg, 1971, for a reply).

The recent evidence from masking studies is more directly relevant to the closed-loop feedback hypothesis. As pointed out earlier, the demonstration that stuttering can be totally abolished by the use of high-intensity filtered white noise that prevents the stutterer from hearing the low-frequency components of his own speech feedback has been regarded as the most significant evidence in favor of this hypothesis, especially because the effect has been replicated since many times (Yates, 1970, p. 117). Three recent experimental studies appear to support this interpretation of the masking effect, whereas two others throw quite serious doubt on its validity.

The confirmatory studies are those by Burke (1969), Murray

(1969), and Adams and Moore (1972). Burke (1969) had stutterers read long prose pasages for 2 minutes under each of five masking conditions that involved continuous masking noise at high intensity for 120, 90, 60, or 30 seconds of the 2-minute period (in the fifth, control condition, there was no masking). He found that correct word rate and percentage of words stuttered decreased, whereas number of words read increased, as a function of the percentage of auditory feedback that was masked. Murray (1969) also had stutterers read prose passages under each of five conditions: no masking noise, no ear-phones; a constant masking noise, the level of which was described as sufficiently high to prevent the stutterer from hearing his own voice; repeated 1 second bursts of masking noise occurring randomly at intervals of from 0 to 9 seconds; 1-second bursts of masking noise applied by the stutterer during the moment of stuttering; and 1-second bursts of masking noise applied by the experimenter during the moment of stuttering. Murray found that the constant masking noise produced a significantly greater reduction in stuttering than any of the other conditions. Adams and Moore (1972) also confirmed that masking noise significantly reduced stuttering, but they did not interpret their results in terms of the feedback control model.

In the first of the two studies that throw doubt on the feedback model, Webster and Dorman (1970) had several stutterers read lists of 120 words individually with a 1-second pause between each word under four conditions: continuous white noise, white noise triggered by the onset of speaking a word and remaining on for the duration of the word, white-noise cessation triggered by the onset of a spoken word and remaining off while the word was spoken, and a no-noise-control condition. Webster and Dorman found that an average of 77 words were stuttered under the no-noise-control condition and that this dropped to an average of 34–36 words in each of the experimental conditions. On the face of it these results suggest that the explanation given for the dramatic effects of white noise on stuttering in terms of preventing the stutterer from hearing his own feedback is untenable because white noise presented during periods of silence was as effective in reducing stuttering as white noise presented during periods of phonation. It should be noted that Webster and Dorman do not mention the differential effect found on stuttering of filtered white noise, nor that the reduction in stuttering found in their three experimental conditions was by no means as great as can be achieved. In this connection it is worth recalling that white noise totally abolishes stuttering only when it is presented at an intensity (120–130 dB) close the pain threshold whereas Webster and Dorman used a very much lower intensity (90 dB). A possible explanation of the results obtained by Webster and Dorman that would maintain the original model would postulate that the continuous white noise prevents the stutterer physiologically from hearing his own voice; whereas the contingent white noise, operating in a situation that actually involved *continuous* responding (the interval between successive phonations was only 1 second), effectively prevented the stutterer from *listening* to his own voice. The shadowing technique shows conclusively that a stutterer will not stutter if his attention is directed away from the sound of his own feedback, but this is *not* a distraction effect in the sense in which that term is usually used. This alternative account can be applied to both the contingent noise conditions and could readily be tested by increasing the interval between each spoken word.

In the second study, Barr and Carmel (1969) carried out Carhart tone decay tests for the frequency range 2–6 kHz and SISI tests for the frequencies 0.25, 1, 2, and 4 kHz on 10 male stutterers who then read passages under each of three conditions: normal reading conditions, continuous narrow-band masking noise presented monaurally to that ear and at that frequency which had shown the greatest amount of decay on the tone decay test, and continuous narrow-band masking noise presented similarly at one other frequency (4 or 6 kHz). It should be noted that in the experimental conditions high-frequency narrow-band masking noise was used at a relatively low intensity level (50 dB) and presented monaurally so that the stutterer could always hear the sound of his own voice. The results showed that the condition in which the masking was at the frequency to which the greatest adaptation occurred in the tone decay test produced a dramatic decrease in stuttering as compared to the control condition. This result, if valid, throws serious doubt on the previous explanations of the masking effect. However, it should be pointed out that although Barr and Carmel present only tabulated data, it is quite clear that their other experimental conditions also produced a dramatic reduction in stuttering.

It should be emphasized that the authors of these two studies do not reject the feedback-control model of stuttering—only the explanation of the effects of masking white noise in terms of preventing the stutterer from hearing the sound of his own voice. Webster and Dorman (1970), in fact, account for their results in terms of the effect of sudden noise onset or offset on the middle ear muscle contractions that are known to occur 65–100 msecs before vocal emission and that may be faulty in stutterers under normal speech conditions. Thus they argue that delayed or unstable contractions of the middle ear muscles during speech initiation may produce stuttered speech. Barr and Carmel (1969), on the other hand, put forward two possible alternative explanations for their data: either the stutterer's ability to monitor his own speech at those frequencies to which he shows adaption in the tone decay test is impaired, or his difficulty arises from the interaural phase difference that leads to monitoring difficulties which are alleviated by masking because it shifts the monitoring emphasis to the other ear. The closed-loop servome-chanical model has recently received closer attention in engineering terms by Sklar (1969). He has pointed out that:

Oscillation in a closed-loop system is manifested by an output signal without a causative input signal. It starts with a transient perturbation at the system input which is then amplified at the output. If enough of the output signal is fed back to the input, in phase with the original perturbation, the output signal continues in a self-sustained fashion and the system is described as oscillatory. The original perturbation that gave rise to the output is no longer required to sustain it. The system now "feeds upon itself" and supplies its own input from the fed-back portion of its sustained output (Sklar, 1969, p. 228).

Using the mathematics of feedback, Sklar has shown that what is called the closed-loop transfer function (K) will show a gain that is a function of $A/1-A\beta$ where A represents a forward transfer function and β a feedback transfer function. Because the transfer function for an oscillatory closed-loop system is infinite and because K approaches infinity as the product $A\beta$ approaches unity, oscillation may only be reduced by decreasing the closed-loop gain (K), and this may be accomplished by reducing the open-loop gain ($A\beta$) from unity or by reducing the forward transfer function (A). Because the latter is very difficult to achieve, the former possibility is to be preferred, and, as Sklar points out, there is much evidence that reducing amplitude of the speech output in stutterers does reduce stuttering. The masking effect itself may, of course, be used to reduce the speech output.

Sklar's paper is important because it shows clearly for the first time that, provided the initial perturbation can be explained, the properties of the postulated closed-loop system can be logically stated from a consideration of closed-loop systems that "run wild" in engineering. Further, it enables clear deductions as to where and how to intervene in the system to reduce the oscillation What it does not explain, of course, is the initial perturbation. Two approaches to this aspect of the problem have recently been suggested. Webster and Lubker (1968) have proposed an auditory interference theory involving interference between the air-conducted and bone-conducted feedback channels. Their model is very similar to earlier closed-loop models in that they postulate that returning auditory feedback blocks the output signals of the neurological mechanism responsible for speech output control. This situation, they argue, may arise because of a distortion in phase relationships between air-conducted and bone-conducted feedback in stutterers. Stromsta (1972) has been the main proponent of this viewpoint. In a recent study he took advantage of the well-known fact that: "through appropriate methods, movements of the basilar membrane caused by bone-conducted vibrations can be compensated by equal and opposite air-conducted vibrations to produce a cessation of preceived sounds" (Stromsta, 1972, p.773). In his experiment,

"the subjects, stutterers and non-stutterers, cancelled the binaural auditory sensation evoked by bone-conducted sinusoidal signals. They accomplished this by appropriate phase and amplitude adjustments of simultaneously-presented binaural air-conducted signals of the same frequency. The phase angle between the two air-conducted signals at the point of cancellation served as the criterion measure of interaural phase disparity (Stromsta, 1972, p.773).

In his study the bone-conduction signal was applied to the superior medial incisors with a force of 560 g by means of a plexiglass cone cemented to the driving end of a crystal stack transducer. Two air-conducted signals were driven by a single generator (and therefore identical in characteristics). For seven frequencies (150, 300, 600, 900, 1200, 1800, and 2400 Hz) detection threshold values were established for each of the three channels (one bone and two air conducted). A signal was then introduced simultaneously in all three channels at 25 dB. By means of a continuously variable 360°, phase shifter and an amplitude alternator, the right and left airborne channels were adjusted till points of least sensation were obtained in the right and left ears; these signals were then more finely adjusted until no signal was perceived in either ear. When steady-state cancellation of the bone-conducted signal was achieved the phase angle between the two air-conducted signals was read off the phase angle meter, as well as the relative amplitude values from the attenuators. Stromsta found that in stutterers the phase angle differences were significantly greater at all frequencies, the differences being especially marked at 150 and 300 Hz, a result of particular interest in view of the finding that masking out frequencies below 500 Hz eliminates stuttering. Stromsta concluded from his results that:

stutterers differ from nonstutterers in terms of interaural phase disparity suggesting that the stutterers as a group possessed greater asymmetry than did the nonstutterers with regard to anatomical or physiological influences or the propagation of energy to or via the auditory receptors. . . . (Stromsta, 1972, p. 778).

The implication of these studies seems to be that interaural phase disparities arising from bone and air-conducted feedback from the stutterer's own speech are involved in stuttering. If these findings are combined with the oscillatory model of Sklar (1969), a reasonable explanation can be given of how the oscillation gets started, how it is maintained, and how it may be interrupted. Thus in spite of criticisms of the model (e.g., Wingate, 1969, 1970) and in spite of awkward evidence that, for example, stutterers do not stutter when talking aloud to themselves in isolation (Svab, Gross, and Langova, 1972), the feedback control model is still viable.

The interaction between theory and practice in stuttering therapy and research undoubtedly represents the most advanced and sophisticated example of the importance of theory to clinical practice to be found in behavior therapy. The fact that what 5 years ago appeared to be a virtually solved problem has turned out to be even more complex than it was thought to be does not in any way lessen the importance of this continuing interaction; this fact should serve as an object-lesson for other areas of behavior therapy, especially perhaps those in which thus far, in spite of great effort, little progress has been made, such as smoking and weight reduction.

REFERENCES

Adams, M. R. Some comments on "time-out as punishment for stuttering." *Journal of Speech and Hearing Research*, 1970, **13**, 218–220.

Adams, M. R., and Hotchkiss, J. Some reactions and responses of stutterers to a miniaturized metronome and metronome-conditioning therapy: Three case reports. *Behavior Therapy*, 1973, **4**, 565–569.

Adams, M. R., and Moore, W. H. The effects of auditory masking on the anxiety level, frequency of dysfluency, and selected vocal characteristics of stutterers. *Journal of Speech and Hearing Research*, 1972, **15** , 572–578.

Adams, M. R., and Popelka, G. The influence of "time-out" on stutterers and their dysfluency. *Behavior Therapy*, 1971, **2** , 334–339.

Andrews, G., and Ingham, R. J. Stuttering: Considerations in the evaluation of treatment. *British Journal of Disorders of Communication*, 1971, **6**, 129–138.

Andrews, G., and Ingham, R. J. Stuttering: An evaluation of follow-up procedures for syllable-timed speech/token system therapy. *Journal of Communication Disorders*, 1972, **5** , 307–319. (a)

Andrews, G., and Ingham, R. J. An approach to the evaluation of stuttering therapy. *Journal of Speech and Hearing Research*, 1972, **15**, 296–302. (b)

Azrin, N. H., Jones, R. J., and Flye, B. A synchronization effect and its application to stuttering by a portable apparatus. *Journal of Applied Behavior Analysis*, 1968, **1** , 283–295.

Barr, D. F., and Carmel, N. R. Stuttering inhibition with high frequency narrow band masking noise. *Journal of Auditory Research*, 1969, **9**, 40–44.

Berecz, J. M. The treatment of stuttering through precision punishment and cognitive arousal. *Journal of Speech and Hearing Disorders*, 1973, **38**, 256–267.

Berman, P. A., and Brady, J. P. Miniaturized metronomes in the treatment of stuttering: A survey of clinicians' experience. *Journal of Behavior Therapy and Experimental Psychiatry*, 1973, **4**, 117–119.

Biggs, B., and Sheehan, J. Punishment or distraction? Operant stuttering revisited. *Journal of Abnormal Psychology*, 1969, **74**, 256–262.

Bloodstein, O. The anticipatory struggle hypothesis: Implications of research on the variability of stuttering. *Journal of Speech and Hearing Research*, 1972, **15**, 487–499.

Brady, J. P. A behavioral approach to the treatment of stuttering. *American Journal of Psychiatry*, 1968, **125**, 843–848.

Brady, J. P. Studies on the metronome effect on stuttering. *Behavior Research and Therapy*, 1969, **7**, 197–204.

Brady, J. P. Metronome-conditioned speech retraining for stuttering. *Behavior Therapy*, 1971, **2** , 129–150.

Brookshire, R. H. The use of consequences in speech pathology: Incentive and feedback functions. *Journal of Communication Disorders*, 1973, **6**, 88–92.

Burke, B. D. Reduced auditory feedback and stuttering. *Behavior Research and Therapy*, 1969, **7**, 303–308.

Cooper, E. B., Cady, B. B., and Robbins, C. J. The effect of the verbal stimulus words "wrong," "right" and "tree" on the disfluency rates of stutterers and nonstutterers. *Journal of Speech and Hearing Research*, 1970, **13**, 239–244.

Curlee, R. F., and Perkins, W. H. The effect of punishment of expectancy to stutter on the frequencies of subsequent expectancies and stuttering. *Journal of Speech and Hearing Research*, 1968, **11**, 787–795.

Curlee, R. F., and Perkins, W. H. Conversational rate control therapy for stuttering. *Journal of Speech and Hearing Disorders*, 1969, **34**, 245–250.

Flanagan, B., Goldiamond, I., and Azrin, N. Operant stuttering: The control of stuttering behavior through response-contingent consequences. *Journal of the Experimental Analysis of Behavior*, 1958, **1**, 173-177.

Gray, B. B., and England, G. Some effects of anxiety deconditioning upon stuttering frequency. *Journal of Speech and Hearing Research*, 1972, **15**, 114–122.

Greenberg, Janet B. The effect of a metronome on the speech of young stutterers. *Behavior Therapy*, 1970, **1**, 240–244.

Greenberg, Janet B. The effect of a metronome on the speech of young stutterers: A rejoinder to Yates. *Behavior Therapy*, 1971, **2**, 604–605.

Haroldson, S. K., Martin, R. R. and Starr, C. D. Time-out as a punishment for stuttering. *Journal of Speech and Hearing Research*, 1968, **11**, 550–566.

Harris, C. M., Martin, R. R. and Haroldson, S. K. Punishment of expectancy responses by stutterers. *Journal of Speech and Hearing Research*, 1971, **14**, 710–717.

Ickes, W. K., and Pierce, S. The stuttering moment: A plethysmographic study. *Journal of Communication Disorders*, 1973, **6**, 155–164.

Ingham, R. J., and Andrews, G. Stuttering: The quality of fluency after treatment *Journal of Communication Disorders*, 1971, **4**, 279–288. (a).

Ingham, R. J., and Andrews, G. The relation between anxiety reduction and treatment. *Journal of Communication Disorders*, 1971, **4**, 289–301. (b)

Ingham, R. J., and Andrews, G. An analysis of a token economy in stuttering therapy. *Journal of Applied Behavior Analysis*, 1973, **6**, 219–229. (a)

Ingham, R. J., and Andrews, G. Behavior therapy and stuttering: A review *Journal of Speech and Hearing Disorders*, 1973, **38**, 405–441. (b)

Jones, R. J., and Azrin, N. H. Behavioral engineering: Stuttering as a function of stimulus duration speech synchronization. *Journal of Applied Behavior Analysis*, 1969, **2**, , 223–229.

Lanyon, R. I. Behavior change in stuttering through systematic desensitization. *Journal of Speech and Hearing Disorders*, 1969, **34**, 253–260.

Martin, R., and Berndt, L. A. The effects of time-out on stuttering in a 12 year old boy. *Exceptional Children*, 1970, **37**, 303–304.

Martin, R. R., Haroldson, S. K., and Starr, C. D. Time-out as punishment for stuttering: A reply to Martin Adams. *Journal of Speech and Hearing Research*, 1971, **14**, 220–222.

Martin, R. R., Kuhl, P., and Haroldson, S. An experimental treatment with two preschool stuttering children. *Journal of Speech and Hearing Research*, 1972, **15**, 743–752.

Moore, W. H., and Ritterman, S. I. The effects of response contingent reinforcement and response contingent punishment upon the frequency of stuttered verbal behavior. *Behavior Research and Therapy*, 1973, **11**, 43–48.

Murray, F. P. An investigation of variably induced white noise upon moments of stuttering. *Journal of Communication Disorders*, 1969, **2**, 109–114.

Perkins, W. H. Replacement of stuttering with normal speech: I. Rationale. *Journal of Speech and Hearing Disorders*, 1973, **38**, 283-294. (a)

Perkins, W. H. Replacement of stutttering with normal speech: II. Clinical procedures. *Journal of Speech and Hearing Disorders*, 1973, **38**, 295–303. (b)

Shriberg, L. D. A system for monitoring and conditioning modal fundamental frequency of speech. *Journal of Applied Behavior Analysis.* 1971, **4**, 337–339.

Siegel, G. M. Punishment, stuttering, and disfluency. *Journal of Speech and Hearing Research*, 1970, **13** , 677–714.

Siegel, G. M. and Hanson, B. The effect of response-contingent neutral stimuli on normal speech disfluency. *Journal of Speech and Hearing Research*, 1972, **15**, 123–133.

Siegel, G. M., Lenske, J., and Broen, P. Suppression of normal speech disfluences through response cost. *Journal of Applied Behavior Analysis*, 1969, **2**, , 265–267.

Silverman, F. H. The effect of rhythmic auditory stimulation on the disfluency of nonstutterers. *Journal of Speech and Hearing Research*, 1971, **14**, 350–355.

Silverman, F. H., and Trotter, W. D. Impact of pacing speech with a miniature electronic metronome upon the manner in which a stutterer is perceived. *Behavior Therapy*, 1973, **4**, 414–419.

Sklar, B. A feedback model of the stuttering problem—an engineer's view. *Journal of Speech and Hearing Disorders*, 1969, **34**, 226–230.

Stromsta, C. Interaural phase disparity of stutterers and nonstutterers. *Journal of Speech and Hearing Research*, 1972, **15**, 771–780.

Svab, L., Gross, J., and Langova, J. Stuttering and social isolation: Effect of social isolation with different levels of monitoring on stuttering frequency. (A pilot study). *Journal of Nervous and Mental Disease*, 1972, **155**, 1–5.

Webster, R. L., and Dorman, M. F. Decreases in stuttering frequency as a function of continuous and contingent forms of auditory masking. *Journal of Speech and Hearing Research*, 1970, **13**, 82–86.

Webster, R. L., and Lubker, B. B. Interrelationships among fluency producing variables in stuttered speech. *Journal of Speech and Hearing Research*, 1968, **11**, 754–766.

Wingate, M. E. Sound and pattern in "artificial" fluency. *Journal of Speech and Hearing Research*, 1969, **12**, 677–686.

Wingate, M. E. Effect on stuttering of changes in audition. *Journal of Speech and Hearing Research*, 1970, **13**, , 861–873.

Yates, A. J., *Behavior Therapy*, New York: Wiley, 1970.

Yates, A. J., The effect of a metronome on the speech of young stutterers: A comment on Greenberg's paper. *Behavior Therapy*, 1971, **2**, 602–603.

CHAPTER 5

When Behavior Therapy Fails: I. Smoking

By the end of 1968 interest in the application of behavior therapy techniques to eliminate or reduce smoking behavior (especially cigarette smoking) was increasing rapidly, and the past 5 years have witnessed a concerted effort in this area. The incidence of positive results has scarcely been commensurate, however, with the effort involved. The point has been made that although behavior therapists have had little success in bringing smoking under control, millions of people *have* succeeded in quitting smoking *without* professional help. One author has drawn the implication that voluntary unaided quitters probably use techniques that behavior therapists have not used (Premack, 1970). The approaches by behavior therapists have been largely technological and have tended to neglect theory, although whether this is the reason for the relative lack of success in this area remains to be seen.

An outline is first given of the principal techniques that have been used; the main results are then considered; and theoretical approaches to the problem of smoking are looked at.

TREATMENT TECHNIQUES

Treatment techniques may be rather arbitrarily divided into seven main categories. In the first category fall those techniques that arrange *aversive consequences*, either for the smoking act itself or for imagining or thinking about smoking. Thus the smoking act itself has been accompanied or followed by electric shock (Berecz, 1972a, 1972b; Best and Steffy, 1971), as has imagining smoking (Berecz, 1972a, 1972b; Ober, 1968). In some cases, the shock is administered by the smoker himself. A second kind of aversive stimulation involves the use of hot, smoky air, which produces a nauseous state in the smoker (Grimaldi and Lichtenstein, 1969; Lichtenstein, Harris, Birchler, Wahl and Schmahl, 1973; Schmahl, Lichtenstein and Harris, 1972). Even more popular than hot, smoky air has been the use of satiation, in which the smoker is required to smoke several cigarettes rapidly in succession (Lichtenstein et al., 1973; Marrone, Merksamer and Salzberg, 1970; Marston and McFall, 1971; Resnick, 1968; Sushinsky, 1972). Covert sensitization, in which the smoker imagines the nauseous consequences that may accompany excessive smoking, has also been tried (Lawson and May, 1970; Sachs, Bean and Morrow, 1970; Wagner and Bragg, 1970), as has what might be called overt sensitization in which a pill is used to produce, in combination with smoking, a foul-tasting sensation in the mouth (Marston and McFall, 1971; Whitman, 1972). Certainly, there has been no lack of effort in attempts to make the smoker feel uncomfortable when he smokes or even contemplates smoking.

A second class of techniques involves attempts to produce a reduction in smoking frequency by techniques that may be labeled *smoking on cue*. Typical of these approaches is the study by Azrin and Powell (1968) in which heavy smokers were required to use a specially designed cigarette case that remained locked for a specified time after a cigarette was removed from it. The time period between cigarettes could be increased but not decreased by the smoker. Bernard and Efran (1972) used a similar device and programmed it either to eliminate smoking entirely or to reduce smoking to eight cigarettes per day over a period of 28 days. Levinson, Shapiro, Schwartz and Tursky (1971) also used a gradual reduction procedure, involving either a randomly programmed signalling device not under the smoker's control or a simple counter on which the smoker recorded each instance of smoking. The latter technique was regarded by Shapiro, Tursky, Schwartz and Schnidman (1971) as involving the attachment of smoking to a neutral cue, and in this latter study the smoker smoked every time an auditory cue sounded. A study by Miller and Gimpl (1971) in which the smoker instructed himself to smoke less each week as a percentage of his previous week's smoking rate, could be regarded as falling into the category of smoking on cue.

The use of *contingency and contractual management* has not proved to be as popular as might have been expected. Bernstein (1970) required smokers to commit themselves to quitting in a social group situation; Elliott and Tighe (1968) required a substantial deposit that was returnable in installments if the smoker refrained but was forfeited if he did not; Lawson and May (1970) made use of both contingencies (the Premack principle was used) and contractual management; Roberts (1969) used the method of smoking only in very inconvenient places in an attempt to eliminate his own smoking; and Winett (1973) has recently reported a comprehensive study of the use of deposit contracts in which he contrasted two groups. One group knew that the deposit would be returned only if they reduced smoking; the deposit of the other group was returnable whether they reduced smoking or not.

The fourth kind of approach has involved what might be termed *self-treatment* training programs. In such programs, the smoker is given instructions of a varying degree of complexity and sophistication and then left to get on with it. Such a program has been described by Harris and Rothberg (1972), although no data are provided. McFall and Hammen (1971) abstracted what they believed to be the common characteristics of all smoking treatment programs and utilized self-monitoring of daily consumption together with positive, negative or no contingencies in the form of points. Ober (1968) trained one of his groups of smokers in the the principles of operant self-control and required them to try to apply these principles, whereas Sachs et al. (1970)

also trained smokers in self-control by getting them to tabulate the discriminative stimuli for their smoking. Whitman (1969) taught his smokers techniques for unlearning smoking behavior by developing patterns of behavior incompatible with smoking.

Systematic desensitization has not been a popular technique for smoking reduction. Marston and Mcfall (1971) utilized what they termed hierarchical reduction, in which smokers divided their day into four periods, ranked in terms of the difficulty of controlling smoking during each period, and an attempt was then made to eliminate smoking progressively, starting with the easiest period. Wagner and Bragg (1970) used systematic desensitization in standard fashion, as did Morganstern and Ratliffe (1969).

Emotional role-playing (in which the smoker may play the part of a patient with cancer facing an operation or the role of a doctor having to tell a smoker he has cancer) has received little attention apart from a study by Lichtenstein, Keutzer and Himes (1969), which failed to replicate the original study by Janis and Mann (1965).

The final category of treatment techniques involves the use of more than one method simultaneously. Indeed, it is doubtful whether there are more than a few studies in which several independent variables are not manipulated simultaneously. In several instances, however, a combination of techniques has been used as a single treatment technique. Thus within the aversive class of approaches, shock has been utilized, but with the possibility that the subject could escape or avoid the shock by not lighting or by stubbing out a cigarette (Steffy, Meichenbaum and Best, 1970; Gendreau and Dodwell, 1968). Whitman (1969) combined quinine on the tongue with shock, whereas Lichtenstein et al. (1973) combined rapid smoking (satiation) with warm, smoky air in one of their conditions to determine whether there was an additive effect of aversive stimuli. Wagner and Bragg (1970) used covert sensitization to attack the cigarette smoking habit itself, while simultaneously using systematic desensitization to cope with the anxiety supposedly underlying the smoking— again the intent was to compare the effects of the combined treatment with those of either treatment used alone. A similar approach was used by Gerson and Lanyon (1972). Chapman, Smith and Layden (1971) combined shock with training in alternative activities.

Thus it may be concluded that there has indeed been no lack of variety in techniques for treating smoking behavior and this is even more apparent when to all these behavioral techniques are added the many control conditions that have been employed.

RESULTS

With reference to the results obtained with behavior modification techniques, it is necessary to make a clear distinction between the immediate effects of treatment, and the maintenance of effects obtained over the follow-up period. The follow-up period has varied from a matter of only weeks to as long as 4–6 months, but has rarely exceeded this period. Several clear-cut statements may be made with respect to the immediate effects of treatment.

There is no doubt that specific techniques do lead to a significant decline in cigarette consumption over a relatively short period of treatment time. The range of techniques that can produce such a decline is very wide and at least ten can be identified:

1. Progressive reduction of consumption by means of timer-control or other regulatory devices (Azrin and Powell, 1968; Bernard and Efran, 1972; Levinson et al., 1971; Shapiro et al., 1971).

2. Administration of shock while the subject is actually smoking (Berecz, 1972a, 1972b; Best and Steffy, 1971; Chapman et al., 1971; Gendreau and Dodwell, 1968; Steffy et al., 1970; Whitman, 1969).

3. Administration of shock while the subject is imagining smoking or verbalizing about it (Berecz, 1972a, 1972b; Ober, 1968; Steffy et al., 1970).

4. Administration of hot, smoky air while the subject is smoking (Grimaldi and Lichtenstein, 1969; Lichtenstein et al., 1973; Schmahl et al., 1972).

5. Satiation produced by rapid smoking (Lichtenstein et al., 1973; Marrone et al., 1970; Marston and McFall, 1971; Resnick, 1968; Sushinsky, 1972).

6. Overt sensitization (Gerson and Lanyon, 1972; Lawson and May, 1970; Sachs et al., 1970; Wagner and Bragg, 1970).

7. Administration of a pill that combined with smoking produces an unpleasant sensation (Marston and McFall, 1971; Whitman, 1972).

8. Contingency or contractual management (Bernstein, 1970; Elliott and Tighe, 1968; Lawson and May, 1970; Winett, 1973).

9. Systematic desensitization or variants of it (Marston and McFall, 1971; Morganstern and Ratliffe, 1969; Wagner and Bragg, 1970).

10. Training in self-control, including monitoring of behavior and progressive reduction of consumption without the use of timing devices (Miller and Gimpl, 1971; Ober, 1968; Sachs et al., 1970; Whitman, 1969).

There is also no doubt that the reduction achieved by these techniques at the end of the training period is significantly greater than that found in a number of control conditions. Such control groups have included the usual no-treatment groups (whose base rate and end-of-treatment rates are assessed but who are given no treatment), as well as more specialized control groups. These special control groups have included:

1. Minimal contact and wait groups.

2. Effort control groups in which the subject is urged to stop smoking by his own efforts, with or without the expectation of treatment at some future time.

3. Subjects given subliminal shocks while smoking (Gendreau and Dodwell, 1968) or imagining smoking (Berecz, 1972a, 1972b).

4. General attention and encouragement groups.

5. A group lodging a deposit, but return of the deposit not contingent on reduction in smoking (Winett, 1973).

However, the significance of these differential results is considerably reduced, if not abolished altogether, by the repeated demonstration that conditions used explicitly by experimenters as control conditions have frequently produced as great a reduction in smoking as the experimental techniques themselves. This has occasionally happened even with no-treatment control groups (Grimaldi and Lichtenstein, 1969; Marston and McFall, 1971; Whitman, 1972). More commonly, however, the control condition has involved attempts to estimate the contribution of nonspecific factors such as minimal attention, encouragement or discussion (Bernstein, 1970; Lawson and May, 1970; Lichtenstein et al., 1973; Sushinsky, 1972; Whitman, 1969). Gerson and Lanyon (1972) found that covert sensitization followed by nonspecific group discussion were as effective as covert sensitization followed by systematic desensitization, although this of course, could have been due to the effect of covert sensitization alone. Ober (1968) found that transactional analysis produced the same results as self-administered shock for craving, whereas Steffy et al. (1970) and Wagner and Bragg (1970) found that insight and counseling control groups produced as much change as their experimental treatment groups. Other investigators (e.g., Bernard and Efran, 1972; Best and Steffy, 1971) have also found their control conditions as effective as their experimental conditions. These results led McFall and Hammen (1971) to design a study in which as many specific factors as possible were eliminated from treatment, leaving only the nonspecific factors as treatment variables. They defined the common nonspecific factors as volunteeer subjects expressing strong motivation to stop smoking, the treatment to consist of instructions to follow a structured program for a fixed period of time with the expectation induced that the procedure would lead to the cessation of smoking by the end of that time, and the subject to monitor and record his smoking rate. McFall and Hammen varied the kind of instructions they gave to each group of smokers and showed that an equal reduction in smoking was found in each of their groups. They concluded that the results attributed to *specific* techniques could be accounted for in terms of more general factors commonly found in all therapy programs.

Although it is true that both experimental treatments and control conditions for nonspecific factors often produce the same results, there is some sparse but important evidence of significant differences *between* specific experimental conditions that should be noted. Berecz (1972a, 1972b) demonstrated that self-administered shock while imagining the smoking sequence not only produced greater decrement in smoking behavior than did various control conditions, but also produced significantly greater decrement than did self-administered shock while actually smoking—although this result applied only to male heavy smokers. For male moderate smokers, both shock techniques were equally effective, whereas quite indeterminate results for shock and control conditions were obtained for female smokers (possibly because females tended to administer less severe shocks to themselves than did the males). Marrone et al. (1970) found a differential effectiveness of satiation as a function of the length of time the satiation program was in effect. Whitman (1972) showed that the effectiveness of the aversive pill technique differed significantly according to whether the pill was taken in a group situation or individually. These findings suggest, of course, that negative or nondifferential results may, in part, be a function of such variables as how long a treatment technique is persisted with or how strongly it is applied, as well as suggesting that a combination of techniques may be superior to the use of a single technique. As is seen shortly, however, this possibility does not always hold.

With one major exception the follow-up results are always the same. Provided the follow-up period is sufficiently long (i.e., at least 4 months) a significant degree of relapse will have occurred, irrespective of treatment technique, so that at the end of the follow-up period, recovery to about 60–80% of base-rate smoking will be apparent. This finding is so universal that it does not need to be documented. The appropriate analyses have been carried out and graphical evidence presented by McFall and Hammen

(1971). More recently Hunt and Matarazzo (1973) have analyzed the results of a large number of studies and presented a composite curve which is reproduced in Figure 1, which also shows the similar results obtained for heroin and alcohol addiction. It will be evident from the graph, however, that the relapse rate is not 100% which appears to arise from the fact that in most studies considerable individual differences in relapse rate are found. Whether this relapse rate arises from a bimodal distribution in which one group of smokers relapses completely to its original level (provided the follow-up period is long enough) whereas a much smaller group achieves total abstinence or whether there is a continuous distribution is unclear. It should also be pointed out that although the curve remains asymptotic even at 12 months, the data available for a follow-up period longer than 6 months are relatively sparse, and more adequate

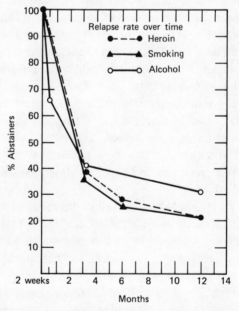

Figure 1. Relapse rate over time for heroin, smoking, and alcohol. (Source: Hunt and Matarazzo, 1973.)

data for the 6–12-month follow-up period (and beyond to, say, 3 years) might well reveal an even greater relapse rate.

There are two studies, however, that reveal a quite different result from this dismal follow-up picture. Lichtenstein et al. (1973) used warm, smoky air combined with rapid smoking; warm, smoky air with normal smoking; and rapid smoking alone. They found that 39/40 subjects in these three groups had stopped smoking completely at the end of treatment (each of the treatments was thus equally effective, and no additive effect for the two aversive conditions was found). At a 6-month follow-up, 60% of the experimental subjects were still *abstinent*, and again no difference was found *between treatment groups* (Figure 2). Because a similar result was found in an earlier, less-well-controlled study (Schmahl et al., 1971), Lichtenstein concluded that

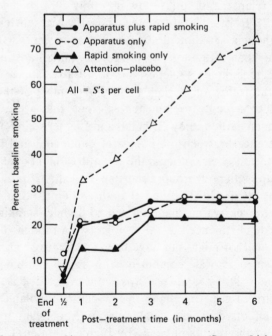

Figure 2. Follow-up smoking rates by treatment groups. (Source: Lichtenstein et al., 1973.)

either treatment technique could be used successfully with a high expectation that relapse would not take place. A possibly vital factor leading to this positive result was the continuation of the treatment on an individual basis until the smoker refused to smoke another cigarette in the experimental situation. Some caution, however, must be exercised in accepting these results as a definitive demonstration of the effectiveness of satiation and/or warm, smoky air as a treatment for smoking. First, the failure of other, similar treatments to produce resistance to relapse makes it imperative that these results be replicated by independent workers (even though Lichtenstein made every attempt in his second study to control for experimenter bias and involvement). Second, Lichtenstein et al. (1973) found an equal and total abstinence rate at the end of treatment in the attention-placebo control group. This group did, however, show a significantly greater relapse rate on follow-up, only 30% being abstinent (Figure 2). It was, therefore, necessary for Lichtenstein to argue that although satiation and/or hot, smoky air was no more effective than attention in producing initial abstinence, the aversive techniques somehow produced a resistance to relapse during the follow-up period, even though most of the smokers refused to accept the booster sessions that were available. Third, in an earlier study Grimaldi and Lichtenstein (1969) found no difference between the effects of contingent and noncontingent hot, smoky air, either at the end of treatment or at a 1-month follow-up, with both groups relapsing. Fourth, in the earlier study Schmahl et al. (1972) found that the administration of warm, smoky air *or* warm, mentholated air while smoking rapidly produced abstinence in all subjects. Although the warm, mentholated air might not have been an effective variable in this study (since it was combined with rapid smoking that the subsequent study showed *was* effective), it has not been demonstrated experimentally that warm, mentholated air would not be effective. These comments are not meant to deny the validity of the results obtained by Lichtenstein et al. (1973), but they are so out of line with those generally obtaining in this area that judgment about a major breakthrough should be reserved at this time.

THEORIES ABOUT SMOKING

The relative failure of behavior modification techniques in relation to smoking has led to much heart searching. Hunt and Matarazzo (1973) made four suggestions for improving current treatment programs:

1. The utilization of more effective stimulus conditions. In providing as examples the use of hot, smoky air and satiation, on the one hand (which they consider more realistic than the use of electric shock) and in recommending the application of the techniques to covert processes rather than the act of smoking itself, on the other hand, they anticipated the most recent results obtained by Lichtenstein et al. (1973) and Berecz (1972a, 1972b), which strongly support these suggestions.

2. The use of multiple treatment techniques.

3. More stress to be laid on the maintenance of initial decrements by the use of overlearning techniques, booster sessions, and so on.

4. More extensive use of ancillary support programs, such as training in recreational and social activities.

It is somewhat ironical that this opening paper (Hunt and Matarazzo, 1973) of a symposium devoted to the problem of smoking is followed by seven papers that are oriented primarily toward theory (some of them exclusively so). These contributors clearly did not believe that the answer to the control of smoking problem would be found along the lines suggested by Hunt and Matarazzo. When an empirical impasse is reached, theories, rightly or wrongly, proliferate. A brief consideration of the various theoretical viewpoints that have been put forward recently can show that adoption of any one of the theoretical viewpoints would be very likely to influence quite profoundly the empirical approach to the control of smoking.

These theoretical approaches may be broadly classified into four types. The first may be called the physiological addiction theory. This theory takes two forms, both of which involve the nicotine content of tobacco. In its most specific form, the theory argues that smoking serves the purpose of bringing high concentrations of nicotine—the main alkaloid of tobacco—to the brain in the most efficient way. Jarvik (1970) has reviewed the literature relating to this theory and summarized direct evidence that, for example, the injection of nicotine is experienced as pleasant by smokers, but as unpleasant by nonsmokers and that high dosages of nicotine injections reduce smoking frequency (Lucchesi, Schuster, and Emley, 1967). In its more general form, the theory originally postulated that nicotine ingested as a result of inhalation had an arousal effect. Thus Armitage, Hall and Morrison (1968) showed that when rats are injected with nicotine they show EEG changes that are indicative of cortical arousal, whereas Fuller and Forrest (1973) provided some evidence that if high arousal is experimentally induced in heavy smokers they will tend to smoke less. There is now evidence, however, that the ingestion of nicotine may have an arousing effect if it is taken small doses, whereas larger doses will produce a state of tranquillization (Frith, 1971) and that smokers will vary their smoking habits according to whether the situation requires arousal or relaxation; that is, they will optimize their arousal level (Ashton and Watson, 1970).

A rather different theoretical framework of a very general kind has been advanced by Solomon and Corbit (1973) in their *opponent-process theory of motivation*. In effect, this is another modern version of homeostasis, but with learned components forming an essential part of the structure of the theory, it is very much more sophisticated. Basically, Solomon and Corbit argue that there are feedback control systems in the brain designed to suppress or reduce excursions from hedonic neutrality. Thus the appearance of a strong affective state will activate an opponent process, tending to counteract the initial state, which will become apparent mainly after the input producing the initial state has terminated. The opponent process itself will gradually subside, and the normal state of hedonic neutrality supervene. However, repeated evocation of the initial state will lead to changes both in that state and in the opponent-process state, together with a link between them such that the reinstatement of the first state will become necessary to control the second state. In this way a self-perpetuating cycle will be set up represented in cigarette smoking, for example, by the craving for cigarettes, a craving that is reduced by smoking and that will not, in fact, occur in the established smoker as long as he smokes frequently enough. It is not possible here to describe the model of Solomon and Corbit in detail—suffice it to point out that they show clearly that their model has implications for how *not* to treat the smoker as well as how to treat him.

The second major theoretical position is that which regards *smoking as a habit* that in most smokers has been subjected to massive overlearning and that is very much under the control of external stimuli which bombard the smoker on all sides (presence of cigarettes in almost every shop, advertising, etc.). As Hunt and Matarazzo (1970) put it, smoking may be regarded as: "a fixed behavior pattern overlearned to the point of becoming automatic and marked by decreasing awareness and increasing dependence on secondary rather than primary reinforcement" (p. 78). One implication that Hunt and Matarazzo draw with respect to therapy is that awareness may be a more critical factor to take into account in designing remedial programs as compared with personality factors, drives, or reinforcement; that is, it is possible that the crucial stimulus for lighting up a cigarette is *stimulus change*. Almost any change in the smoker's environment may become a cue for smoking without the smoker being consciusly aware of the cue. Smoking may be regarded as a skill like walking that is exercised automatically until the ground becomes uneven. This line of argument provides a link between habit theories of smoking and the *cognitive conditioning* model of Berecz (1972a,

1972b). Berecz has postulated what he calls "amplifier elements," which are the cognitive precursors of smoking behavior. In light or moderate smokers these amplifier elements are still active, whereas in heavy smokers they have dropped out. Thus shock for smoking does not work with heavy smokers but does work for moderate smokers because in the former case the amplifier elements are absent, whereas in the latter they are present and the shock modifies the amplifier elements. In the case of heavy smokers, therefore, the amplifier elements must be reinstated by retraining the smoker to activate them.

Logan (1970, 1973) and Premack (1970; Premack and Anglin, 1973) have also presented detailed theories about smoking within the habit-forming framework. Logan (1970), for example, stresses the importance of both internal and external stimuli as elicitors of smoking responses, especially of nonsmoking, response-produced stimuli that occur simultaneously with the smoking response. He distinguishes between the drive and incentive aspects of motivation in relation to the genesis of smoking behavior; thus, a teenager may initially smoke to gain approval (the drive aspect) and may then be rewarded by the approval of his peers (the incentive aspect). Premack (1970) is particularly critical of aversive techniques that involve laboratory control because of the ease with which the smoker discriminates the laboratory from the real-life situation, and he lines up with Berecz in recommending more attention be paid to the cognitive antecedents of smoking:

> Although smoking is conditioned to virtually everything, thinking about smoking is probably conditioned to very little; in the inveterate smoker thinking about smoking is a rare event. But if the thought of smoking can be intruded at critical points, the act of smoking can either be stopped before it starts or aborted at some early point in the sequence (Premack, 1970, p. 117).

Finally, brief mention should be made of two other theoretical approaches. One is the theory that there are smoking types (Coan, 1973; Ikard and Tomkins, 1973); the other that a whole lifestyle is involved in smoking (Sarbin and Nucci, 1973; Mausner, 1973; Mausner and Platt, 1971). In relation to smoking types, such a demonstration would appear to have little practical significance, at least at the present time; in relation to life-styles, such all-embracing concepts would appear to be too general to be likely to have much influence on therapeutic techniques

REFERENCES

Armitage, A. K., Hall, G. H., and Morrison, C. F. Pharmacological basis for the tobacco smoking habit. *Nature*, 1968, **217**, 331–334

Ashton, H., and Watson, D. W. Puffing frequency and nicotine intake in cigarette smokers. *British Medical Journal*, 1970, **3**, 679–681.

Azrin, N. H., and Powell, J. Behavioral engineering: The reduction of smoking behavior by a conditioning apparatus and procedure. *Journal of Applied Behavior Analysis*, 1968, **1**, 193–200.

Berecz, J. Modification of smoking behavior through self-administered punishment of imagined behavior: A new approach to aversion therapy. *Journal of Consulting and Clinical Psychology*, 1972, **38**, 244–250. (a)

Berecz, J. Reduction of cigarette smoking through self-administered aversive conditioning: A new treatment model with implications for public health. *Social Science and Medicine*, 1972, **6**, 57–66, (b)

Bernard, H. S., and Efran, J. S. eliminating versus reducing smoking using pocket timers. *Behavior Research and Therapy*, 1972, **10**, 399–401.

Bernstein, D. A. The modification of smoking behavior: a search for effective variables. *Behavior Research and Therapy*, 1970, **8**, 133–146.

Best, J. A., and Steffy, R. A. Smoking modification procedures tailored to subject characteristics. *Behavior Therapy*, 1971, **2**, 177–191.

Chapman, R. F., Smith, J. W., and Layden, T. A. Elimination of cigarette smoking by punishment and self-management training. *Behavior Research and Therapy*, 1971, **9**, 255–264.

Coan, R. W. Personality variables associated with cigarette smoking. *Journal of Personality and Social Psychology*, 1973, **26**, 86–104.

Elliott, R., and Tighe, T. Breaking the cigarette habit: Effects of a technique involving threatened loss of money. *Psychological Record*, 1968, **18**, 503–513.

Frith, C. D. Smoking behavior and its relation to the smoker's immediate experience. *British Journal of Social and Clinical Psychology*, 1971, **10**, 73–78.

Fuller, R. G. C., and Forrest, D. W. Behavioral aspects of cigarette smoking in relation to arousal level. *Psychological Reports*, 1973, **33**, 115–121.

Gendreau, P. E., and Dodwell, P. C. An aversive treatment for addicted cigarette smokers: Preliminary report. *Canadian Psychologist*, 1968, 9, 28–34.

Gerson, P., and Lanyon, R. I. Modification of smoking behavior with an aversion-desensitization procedure. *Journal of Consulting and Clinical Psychology*, 1972, 38, 399–402.

Grimaldi, K. E., and Lichtenstein, E. Hot, smoky air as an aversive stimulus in the treatment of smoking. *Behavior Research and Therapy*, 1969, 7, 275–282.

Harris, M. B., and Rothberg, C. A self-control approach to reducing smoking. *Psychological Reports*, 1972, 31, 165–166.

Hunt, W. A., and Matarazzo, J. D. Habit mechanisms in smoking. In W. A. Hunt (Ed.). *Learning mechanisms in smoking*. Chicago: Aldine, 1970. Pp. 65–90.

Hunt, W. A., and Matarazzo, J. D. Three years later: Recent developments in the experimental modification of smoking behavior. *Journal of Abnormal Psychology*, 1973, 81, 107–114.

Ikard, F. F., and Tomkins, S. The experience of affect as a determinant of smoking behavior: A series of validity studies. *Journal of Abnormal Psychology*, 1973, 81, 172–181.

Janis, I. L., and Mann, L. Effectiveness of emotional role-playing in modifying habits and attitudes. *Journal of Experimental Research in Personality*, 1965, 1, 84–90.

Jarvik, M. E. The role of nicotine in the smoking habit. In W. A. Hunt (Ed.), *Learning mechanisms in smoking*. Chicago: Aldine, 1970. Pp. 155–190.

Lawson, D. M., and May, R. B. Three procedures for the extinction of smoking behavior. *Psychological Record*, 1970, 20, 151–157.

Levinson, B. L., Shapiro, D., Schwartz, G. E., and Tursky, B. Smoking elimination by gradual reduction. *Behavior Therapy*, 1971, 2, 477–487.

Lichtenstein, E., Harris, D. E., Birchler, G. R., Wahl, J. M., and Schmahl, D. P. Comparison of rapid smoking, warm smoky air, and attention placebo in the modification of smoking behavior. *Journal of Consulting and Clinical Psychology*, 1973, 40, 92–98.

Lichtenstein, E., Keutzer, C. S., and Himes, K. H. "Emotional" role-playing and changes in smoking attitudes and behavior. *Psychological Reports*, 1969, 25, 379–387.

Logan, F. A. The smoking habit. In W. A. Hunt (Ed.), *Learning mechanisms in smoking*. Chicago: Aldine 1970. (Pp. 131–145).

Logan, F. A. Self-control as habit, drive, and incentive. *Journal of Abnormal Psychology*, 1973, 81, 127–136.

Lucchesi, B. R., Schuster, C. R., and Emley, G. S. The role of nicotine as a determinant of cigarette smoking frequency in man with observations of certain cardiovascular effects associated with the tobacco alkaloid. *Clinical Pharmacology and Therapeutics*, 19 67, 8, 789–796.

McFall, R. M., and Hammen, C. L. Motivation structure and self-monitoring:

The role of nonspecific factors in smoking reduction. *Journal of Consulting and Clinical Psychology*, 1971, **37**, 80–86.

Marrone, R. L., Merksamer, M. A., and Salzberg, P. M. A short duration group treatment of smoking behavior by stimulus saturation. *Behavior Research and Therapy*, 1970, **8**, 347–352. ·

Marston, A. R., and McFall, R. M. Comparison of behavior modification approaches to smoking reduction. *Journal of Consulting and Clinical Psychology*, 1971, **36**, 153–162.

Mausner, B. An ecological view of cigarette smoking. *Journal of Abnormal Psychology*, 1973, **81**, 115–126.

Mausner, B., and Platt, E. S. *Smoking: A behavioral analysis*. New York: Pergamon, 1971.

Miller, A., and Gimpl, M. Operant conditioning and self-control of smoking and studying. *Journal of Genetic Psychology*, 1971, **119**, 181–186.

Morganstern, K. P., and Ratliff, R. G. Systematic desensitization as a technique for treating smoking behavior: A preliminary report. *Behavior Research and Therapy*, 1969, **7**, 397–398.

Ober, D. C. Modification of smoking behavior. *Journal of Consulting and Clinical Psychology*, 1968, **32**, 543–549.

Premack, D. Mechanisms of self-control. In W. A. Hunt (Ed.), *Learning mechanisms in smoking*. Chicago: Aldine, 1970. Pp. 107–123.

Premack, D., and Anglin, B. On the possibilities of self-control in man and animals. *Journal of Abnormal Psychology*, 1973, **81**, 137–151.

Resnick, J. H. Effects of stimulus satiation on the overlearned maladaptive response of cigarette smoking. *Journal of Consulting and Clinical Psychology*, 1968, **32**, 501–505.

Roberts, A. H. Self-control procedures in modification of smoking Behavior: Replication. *Psychological Reports*, 1969, **24**, 675–676.

Sachs, L. B., Bean, H., and Morrow, J. E. Comparison of smoking treatments. *Behavior Therapy*, 1970, **1**, 465–472.

Sarbin, T. R., and Nucci, L. P. Self-reconstitution processes: A proposal for reorganizing the conduct of confirmed smokers. *Journal of Abnormal Psychology*, 1973, **81**, 182–195.

Schmahl, D. P., Lichtenstein, E., and Harris, D. E. Successful treatment of habitual smokers with warm, smoky air and rapid smoking. *Journal of Consulting and Clinical Psychology*, 1972, **38**, 105–111.

Shapiro, D., Tursky, B., Schwartz, G. E., and Schnidman, S. R. Smoking on cue: A behavioral approach to smoking reduction. *Journal of Health and Social Behavior*, 1971, **12**, 108–115.

Solomon, R. L, and Corbit, J. D. An opponent-process theory of Motivation: II. Cigarette addiction. *Journal of Abnormal Psychology*, 1973, **81**, 158–171.

Steffy, R. A., Meichenbaum, D., and Best, J. A. Aversive and cognitive factors in the modification of smoking behavior. *Behavior Research and Therapy*, 1970, **8**, 115–125.

Sushinsky, L. W. Expectation of future treatment, stimulus satiation, and smoking. *Journal of Consulting and Clinical Psychology*, 1972, **29**, 343.

Wagner, M. K., and Bragg, R. A. Comparing behavior modification approaches to habit decrement—smoking. *Journal of Consulting and Clinical Psychology*, 1970, **34**, 258–263.

Whitman, T. L., Modification of chronic smoking behavior: A comparison of three approaches. *Behavior Research and Therapy*, 1969, **7**, 257–263.

Whitman, T. L., Aversive control of smoking behavior in a group context. *Behavior Research and Therapy*, 1972, **10**, 97–104.

Winett, R. A. Parameters of deposit contracts in the modification of smoking. *Psychological Record*, 1973, **23**, 49–60.

CHAPTER 6

When Behavior Therapy Fails:
II. Obesity

In 1959 Stunkard and McLaren-Hume reviewed the literature relating to the treatment of obesity, noting that it was generally believed that such programs are effective and harmless. They pointed out, however, that the treatment programs might in fact have some undesirable side-effects, such as depression. In their review of the effectiveness of such programs, they could find only eight studies that met even the most lenient of design criteria, and in each of these programs the results could only be described as dismal. As if to stress their objectivity, they then reported the results of their own recent treatment of 100 patients (97 of them female) who were all at least 20% overweight and who were given instruction in the use of balanced diets. Even using as criterion the lowest weight loss achieved during a 2½ year follow-up, the results were found to be less successful than those of the eight studies they had found to be ineffective.

Behavior therapists are not reluctant to step in where angels fear to tread; like smoking, weight reduction is an attractive problem to behavior therapists, in part because the criterion of success is relatively clear-cut and assessable in quantitative terms. Although only a few studies were available for inclusion in *Behavior Therapy*, there has been a rapid increase in studies over the past 5 years; the results parallel those obtained with smoking to a remarkable degree. It is unnecessary here to review the background to this research, as this task has been admirably carried out by Stuart and Davis (1972). The same plan is carried out as in the review of smoking: the principal techniques used are described; the results obtained with these techniques are considered; and the recent intriguing theories of obesity that have been formulated are examined.

The treatment techniques used in attempts to obtain weight reduction are very similar to those used in attempts to control smoking behavior, although there are some interesting variations, and some of the techniques have been elaborated to a degree of sophistication not yet achieved with smoking. This is largely because the behaviors that produce obesity are more readily identifiable than the behaviors that maintain smoking behavior.

Not unexpectedly, *aversive techniques* have been widely utilized, although the use of shock for eating (Wijesinghe, 1973) or punishment for weight gain (Harmatz and Lapuc, 1968; Penick, Filion, Fox, and Stunkard, 1971) is relatively rare. *Covert sensitization*, or variations of it, has proved to be by far the commonest of the aversive techniques. The standard procedures for covert sensitization were used by Manno and Marston (1972) and by Murray and Harrington (1972). Sachs and Ingram (1972), in what was an experimental rather than a therapeutic endeavor, compared the effects of visualizing favorite foods and then imagining aversive consequences with the effects of imagining the aversive consequences of eating first, followed by visualization of favorite foods. Harris (1969) used covert sensitization as a follow-up procedure to training in self-control of eating, whereas Janda and Rimm (1972), although they state they used covert sensitization by itself, actually combined it with imagining weight-reducing foods with pleasure and imagining resisting weight-increasing foods with pleasurable consequences. A variant of covert sensitization was used by Foreyt and Kennedy (1971) in which the subject both handled favorite foods and imagined eating them (without actually eating them). While this was going on they were subjected to one of several extremely noxious odors on an intermittent schedule basis. Similarly, Maletzky (1973) combined covert sensitization with the use of valeric acid, which produces a particularly revolting odor when smelled. One other aversive technique can be mentioned: Tyler and Straughan (1970) used an aversion-relief technique in which the subject imagined being tempted by food, then held his breath until he felt uncomfortable The rationale for this technique is unclear, but the reinforcement associated with releasing one's breath may become associated with stopping thinking about food.

The use of *positive contingencies* for weight reduction, except as part of more complex programs, is relatively rare, although both Bernard (1968) and Penick et al. (1971) provided reinforcement for weight loss; Manno and Marston (1972) had their subjects imagine an attractive food, reject it, and reward themselves by imagining their ideal self-image.

Most of the techniques used by behavior therapists in this area, however, have been derived from the pioneering study of Ferster, Nurnberger, and Levitt (1962), who stressed the need to *control the environment* of the obese person and train him to become an active participant in altering his habitual behavior patterns in such a way as to make eating responses fewer. Partly because it was published in an obscure and short-lived journal, Ferster's paper attracted little notice for several years, but it has proved a rich mine of suggestions for the treatment of obesity in more recent studies. Closely allied to this approach is the use of *contractual and contingency management* which have also been very popular in the treatment of smoking behavior.

Contractual management has been used by Hall (1972) and by Harris and Bruner (1971). Hall required her subjects to put on lay-by a desired object having a substantial monetary value ($20); they were then given $5 toward payment for it (sampling the reinforcer). If the specified weight loss was achieved, the remaining money required was provided. Harris and Bruner (1971) simply required their subjects to put down a deposit that was refunded gradually as weight was lost or forfeited if the contract terms were broken. A much more complicated contractual system was used by Mann (1972). In his study each subject surrendered a large number of genuine valuables at the beginning of treatment. These valuables could be "bought back" or "lost forever" depending on specified weight gains or losses over specified periods. The contract was signed by both subject and therapist in front of witnesses and specified the minimal weight loss to be achieved cumulatively over each 2-week treatment period, as well as terminal weight requirement. Three sets of contingencies were also specified: *immediate*, in which the subject received one valuable back or lost it irrevocably for each 2-lb gain or loss of weight occurring at *any time* during the treatment; *2-week*, in which the same result could occur if the specified loss required during that period was achieved; and *terminal*, in which a group of valuables was set aside for return (or loss) only when the terminal weight loss was achieved (or not achieved).

Contingency management, making use of the Premack principle, has not been used frequently on its own, but Horan and Johnson (1971) had their subjects think of negative-positive coverant pairs ("shortened life span"-"clothes fitting better") and made high probability behaviors (e.g., sitting in a chair, reading the newspaper) contingent on thinking of a negative-positive coverant pair)

Training in *self-control techniques* has been developed to a high degree of complexity and sophistication, but the use of a package program makes it impossible to sort out the respective contribution of each factor. As pointed out earlier, this approach is essentially based on the detailed analysis of the control of eating behavior provided by Ferster et al. (1962). Using a self-control training approach which she called focal therapy, Wollersheim (1970) first of all informed her subjects that,

their eating practices were learned patterns of behavior. Just as they had learned inappropriate eating patterns, they could, by application of appropriate principles, learn appropriate eating practices which would promote weight loss and make effective maintenance of the loss possible (p. 465).

In subsequent training sessions the therapist's main task was perceived as being "to help each S specifically identify discriminative, reinforcing and eliciting stimuli related to overeating and to implement self-control techniques in the circumstances arising in her individual mode of living" (p. 466). The comprehensiveness of the training program can be seen from a list of the techniques to be used by the subject which were introduced progressively in succeeding sessions:

1. Building positive associations concerning eating control.
2. Developing appropriate stimulus control of eating behavior and manipulation of deprivation and satiation by shaping and fading.
3. Rewarding oneself for developing self-control in eating and developing and using personally meaningful ultimate aversive consequences of overeating.
4. Obtaining reinforcers from areas of life other than eating and establishing alternative behaviors incompatible with eating.
5. Utilization of chaining.
6. Supplementary techniques involving aversive imagery.

These subjects were also trained in relaxation; were presented with factual information pertaining to obesity, health, nutrition, and weight reduction; and were urged to decrease their caloric intake to between 1000 and 1500 calories daily (they were provided with lists of foods and their caloric value). The target weight loss was 2 lb per week.

Similar programs involving training in self-control of eating behavior have been described (Hall, 1972; Harris, 1969; Harris and Bruner, 1971; Martin and Sachs, 1973) of which the most comprehensively developed is undoubtedly that of Stuart and his colleagues (Stuart, 1971; Stuart and Davis, 1972). In addition to the kind of training described by Wollersheim (1970), Stuart lays great stress (as did Ferster) on the subject learning a great deal about nutrition and diet and the specification of individualized dietary programs. Stuart adds, as a third important area, programs of physical exercise. Thus the manipulation of environmental control, the manipulation of energy balance, and the regulation of exercise are seen as the vital keys to weight control, though Stuart plays down the importance of self-control, by which he means attention to internal feedback cues, not the kind of self-control to which Wollersheim is referring and which Stuart himself stresses. As is seen later, the soft-pedaling of "internal awareness" by Stuart is derived from the work of Schachter and his colleagues.

Finally, mention should be made of the *induced-anxiety technique* used by Bornstein and Sipprelle (1973b). This technique involves the elicitation of stimuli associated with anxiety while in a state of relaxation. The stimuli elicited are internal "feelings" (small motor movements, muscular tensions, respiratory irregularities) but not necessarily those connected with eating. The assumption underlying this technique is that overeating is indulged in to reduce anxiety and that, therefore, the reduction of anxiety by this training will reduce eating frequency. The technique is a variant of systematic desensitization, which otherwise does not appear to have been used in this area, at least with normal subjects.

Results

Turning now to the results obtained with the use of these various techniques, it may be noted first that although some striking results have occasionally been obtained in single-case studies carried out in a clinical setting (Bernard, 1968; Bornstein and Sipprelle, 1973a; Maletzky, 1973; Martin and Sachs, 1973) the majority of studies have involved group comparative designs. As with smoking, there is no doubt that the use of these techniques commonly produces more weight reduction at termination of treatment as compared with no treatment, effort control, supportive therapy, and other kinds of control conditions. Furthermore, unlike smoking, the differences are not infrequently maintained at follow-up, although once again it is apparent that the follow-up period is often insufficient. The treatment period, of course, needs to be much longer in the case of weight reduction than smoking because it is possible to reduce rate of smoking very rapidly if not immediately to close to zero, but loss of weight is a much slower process. The basic question once again, therefore, becomes the maintenance of the loss achieved by the experimental groups, and a substantial follow-up period becomes very important in determining the success of behavior therapy techniques in view of the well-established very high rate of relapse when the follow-up period is sufficiently long.

Considering *covert sensitization* first, Foreyt and Kennedy (1971) found a significantly different weight loss at the end of treatment for covert sensitization as compared with a control group that attended weight-reducing classes. This difference was maintained at a 48-week follow-up point. Significant differences were obtained at the end of treatment between experimental and control groups by Horan and Johnson (1971), Janda and Rimm (1972), and Manno and Marston (1972), although in these studies either no follow-up was reported or it was far too short.

Contractual and contingency managements have also been reported to produce significant differences between experimental and control groups at the end of treatment, but follow-up data have again been inadequate (Harmatz and Lapuc, 1968; Penick et al., 1971). Harris and Bruner (1971) did have a reasonably adequate follow-up period of 10 months and found that differences at the end of treatment between the experimental and control groups were not maintained. Two studies are worthy of special mention. The control used by Hall (1972) was a 16-week baseline record of weight, the assumption being that in the absence of treatment weight that was stable over that period of time would not have changed. She found that contracting produced a significant decline compared with baseline level, and the weight loss was maintained at a follow-up point that, unfortunately, was only 4 weeks.[1] Mann (1972), using the complex contract procedure described earlier, tried a within-sub-

---

[1] However, in a subsequent follow-up study, the results were described as disappointing (Hall, 1973).

ject reversal design to test the effect of his experimental variable and was able to demonstrate both loss and recovery of weight as a function of the stage of treatment in force.

With respect to *training in self-control*, Harris (1969), Harris and Bruner (1971), and Wollersheim (1970) all found that this technique produced significant weight changes as compared with control groups given no treatment or nonspecific forms of treatment. The results obtained by Wollersheim (1970), using a large sample of overweight women, are shown in Figure 1. At a very short follow-up period of 8 weeks, however, the difference between the focal therapy group and the nonspecific therapy

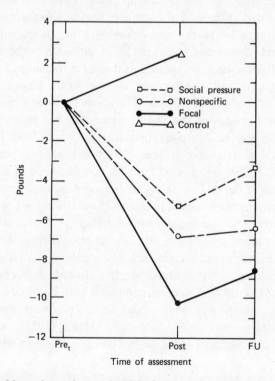

Figure 1. Mean change in actual weight from pre-treatment to post-treatment and follow-up. (Source: Wollersheim, 1970.)

group, although still significant, was very small in absolute weight terms, whereas in the study of Harris and Bruner (1971) the difference had disappeared at a 10-month follow-up. Harris (1969) followed her subjects up rather casually at 6 months and maintained there was some evidence that weight loss was maintained.

Perhaps the most striking positive results so far obtained were those of Stuart (1971) for two small groups of overweight women. One group was treated over a period of 15 weeks, using Stuart's three-dimensional program described earlier; during this time the control group was trained in diet-control and exercising, but was not instructed in food-management techniques. At the end of this period the control group was then placed on the full training program, whereas the experimental group continued with the full program, a further 15 weeks of training being involved in each case. The results at the end of a 6-month follow-up period (i.e., approximately 1 year after training commenced) are shown in Figure 2. The results are striking, although the follow-up period remains inadequate.

There are a few studies that indicate, as was the case with smoking, that nonspecific factors may sometimes produce as much weight loss as specific techniques. Harmatz and Lapuc (1968) found that group therapy produced the same amount of weight loss as a combination of positive reinforcement for weight loss and punishment for weight gain at the end of treatment. Horan and Johnson (1971) found no difference between the effects of two forms of coverant treatment and a placebo therapy involving information about dieting and provision of a 1000 calorie diet, again at the end of treatment. Tyler and Straughan (1970) found that relaxation training (used as a control condition), coverant control, and breath holding were all equally effective in producing weight loss.

Several studies have compared the effects of different behavioral treatments. Two studies (Hall, 1972; Harris and Bruner, 1971) presented evidence suggesting that behavioral contracting was superior to self-control training as far as status at

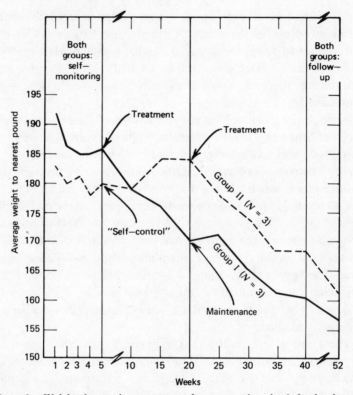

Figure 2. Weight changes in two groups of women undergoing behavior therapy for overeating. (Source: Stuart, 1971.)

the end of treatment was concerned. Hall's finding that the difference in effectiveness was maintained at a 4-week follow-up is counter-balanced by the failure of Harris and Bruner to find a difference at a longer follow-up of 10 months. Horan and Johnson (1971) showed that the success of covariant treatment, using the Premack principle, was apparently not dependent on the presence or absence of reinforcement. Similarly, Manno and Marston (1972) could find no additional benefit when they added positive covert reinforcement as a technique to covert sensitization; Sachs and Ingram (1972) found that it made no difference to the success of covert sensitization whether visualization of food preceded or followed the aversive imagining. In a recently reported study Harris and Hallbauer (1973) found that a package program involving a contract, training in self-control, and exercise produced the same results at termination of treatment as a program involving only a contract and training in self-control, but that the former program resulted in better retention of the weight reduction at a follow-up after 7 months. The absolute differences were once again, however, quite small.

In summary, there is fairly cogent evidence that a variety of behavioral techniques do succeed in producing weight reduction and in maintaining it for periods up to 10 months after the end of treatment. But the results are not particularly impressive given the time and effort involved (especially in the contracting and self-control techniques), and the studies are plagued frequently by high attrition rates and inadequate follow-up.

THEORIES OF OBESITY

As in the case of smoking, there is no shortage of theories about obesity. In the latter case, however, the theories have been derived from a consideration of empirical data to a much greater degree and are, consequently, more important and relevant to the problem of therapy. Three major theories have been advanced. The most influential of these is that of Schachter (1971) who pointed out some parallels between the behavior of obese humans and obese rats, all of which are supported by empirical data in both cases:

1. Obese rats and humans will eat more of a good-tasting food than nonobese rats and humans, but will eat less of a bad-tasting food.

2. In an ad-lib situation, the obese will eat slightly but not excessively more food, provided the food is close at hand (i.e., both visible and attainable with little expenditure of effort).

3. The obese will eat a higher number of meals per day and will

eat a greater amount of food at any meal; they will also eat faster.

4. The obese will show greater emotional reactivity and are more lethargic (they will not work to obtain food, even if hungry—e.g., they will eat more peanuts than the nonobese, but not if they have to shell the peanuts).

These empirical facts assume importance when taken in conjunction with certain other facts that contradict common conceptions about why the obese eat so much. Stunkard and Koch (1964) had shown that obese subjective reports of feeling hungry do not correlate with hunger contractions, objectively measured by passing a balloon into the stomach. Schachter, Goldman, and Gordon (1968) found that when biscuits are made available on an ad-lib basis the obese will consume the same amount whether they have been prefed or not, whereas nonobese persons will eat less if they have been prefed. Nisbett (1968) showed that the obese would eat *less* than the nonobese if food was made difficult to obtain (e.g., by placing it in a refrigerator) even though lunch had been missed.

Schachter's explanation of these and many other empirical observations is that the eating behavior of the obese person is based on external stimulus control and not on internal feedback factors arising from change in physiological state (e.g., hunger stimuli). If an external stimulus cue for eating is present, the obese person will eat; if it is absent, he will not eat; he will eat or not eat irrespective of his immediate past history of eating. However, Schachter goes further than this and argues that the obese person is more generally controlled by external stimulation than just in relation to his eating. Thus Schachter presents evidence to show that the obese person has faster complex reaction time, is more affected by distracting stimuli, and will work less hard for "distant" food, but more hard for "near" food. In summary, the obese are stimulus bound, and because food cues (and the availability of food) are omnipresent, his eating behavior is constantly being activated.

Schachter's hypothesis that the obese are more influenced by external stimulus conditions than are the nonobese has recently been subjected to careful experimental test by Pliner (1973a, 1973b) with generally supportive results. Pliner has suggested one modification of Schachter's cue-saliency theory, namely, that the obese are more sensitive to external stimuli, provided they have high visibility—the reverse may be the case if the stimuli have low saliency. To test the generality of Schachter's theory, Pliner (1973a) presented obese and nonobese subjects with tape-recordings of varying length (4–8 minutes) that contained either relatively few (40) or many (80) auditory stimuli (100 msecs tone pulses of 500 Hz) and that varied in saliency (presented at 45-db or 90-db level). The study was disguised as an investigation of physiological and cognitive reactions to a visual stimulus (TAT card) that the subject was required to view while the tape was played. Subsequently, the subject was asked to estimate the duration of the tapes played, the estimates being part of a more general questionnaire. The rationale of the study was as follows: it had been shown in earlier studies that estimates of the duration of a time interval were greater when that interval was filled by many stimuli than when it was filled by few stimuli. Because obese persons are more sensitive, by hypothesis, to external stimuli (in this case the auditory stimuli) they will perceive the more salient stimuli more readily than nonobese persons and hence will overestimate the duration of the interval. Pliner found that this indeed did happen. The obese subjects rated the intervals as longer than did the nonobese when the saliency of the stimuli was high and perceived the intervals as shorter when the saliency of the stimuli was low. In a second study Pliner (1973b) had obese and nonobese subjects perform a task that involved submerging their hand in ice-cold water and indicating when pain was experienced. While doing this they were asked to think about a presented scene (external cue present) or about a scene presented before a trial began (cue absent) or when there was no cue at all. The effect of these variables was examined in relation to the length of time the subject subsequently reported he thought about the assigned topics and the point at which the subject reported the sensation of pain. Pliner argued that if there were no topic-relevant external cues present, obese subjects would report having spent less time thinking about the assigned topic than nonobese subjects, whereas the reverse would be the case if topic-relevant cues were present during performance of the task. She also predicted that, if topic-relevant cues were absent, obese subjects would report pain sooner than nonobese subjects and that the reverse would hold if topic-related cues were present. The predictions were all confirmed, and Pliner also presented evidence that obese subjects tended to think more about environmentally generated topics than about self-generated topics, whereas the reverse was the case for nonobese subjects.

In formulating his external control theory Schachter (1971) had relied in part on the work of Nisbett. It is somewhat disconcerting to find Nisbett (1972) appearing as the champion of the ventromedial hypothalamus hypothesis about obesity. Starting from the same observations as Schachter, Nisbett concluded that: "some individuals have no choice but to be fat . . . they are biologically programmed to be fat. . . ." (Nisbett, 1972, p. 433). His basic hypothesis is that obesity does not produce but rather results from an elevated baseline of adipose tissue stores. His rather complicated line of reasoning, which is based on experimental evidence, is as follows:

1. Body fat in the form of esterified fatty acids is stored in specialized fat cells called adipocytes or lipocytes.

2. The quantity of fat in a subject is a function of the number and size of his adipocytes.

3. Adiposity of obese humans is determined primarily by the *number* (not the size) of fat cells.

4. Obese subjects have been found to have as high as 3 times as many fat cells as a normal weight group.

5. The number of fat cells in a person is essentially fixed and stable. Severe starvation in rats does not reduce the number of fat cells, and the same has been found in humans. Similarly, overeating does not increase the *number* of fat cells in humans (though it may increase the size).

6. Adiposity has a strong genetic basis but may also be determined or permanently changed by *early* nutritional experiences, effects that will be irreversible.

7. The central nervous system, via the hypothalamus, adjusts food intake so as to maintain fat stores at the base line. Damage to the ventromedial nucleus elevates the adipose tissue level and leads to increased weight,[2] whereas damage to the lateral hypothalamus produces the opposite effect. Thus the ventromedial hypothalamus prevents excess fat from being added; the lateral hypothalamus prevents fat from being lost.

8. The appropriate level of adipose tissue would then depend on individual body size and bone structure, and what might represent obesity in one person would represent normal weight in another person even though, according to standard weight tables, he is grossly overweight. To force or persuade such a person to reduce his weight would be like trying to persuade a normal weight person (according to the usual standards) to reduce. Nisbett points out that, in some persons, starvation leads to emotional depression, apathy, and loss of sex drive. Obese persons may show similar behaviors, especially those in the upper social classes, where they may be pressured into reducing below their physiologically ideal weight in order to meet a socially determined criterion.

Nisbett's argument, on the face of it, appears to be the direct opposite of Schachter's, but this is not necessarily so. Indeed, Schachter, in the paper in which he propounds his stimulus-bound theory of obesity, and after apparently rejecting ventromedial arguments, concludes finally that "one may guess that the obesity of rats and men has a common physiological locus in the ventromedial hypothalamus" (Schachter, 1971, p. 143). Presumably, resolution lies in the possibility that the obese person has a physiological drive that sensitizes him to cues relating to food,

[2]Gold (1973) has produced evidence to show that there is no precise correlation between lesioning of the ventromedial nucleus and hypothalamic obesity. This does not refute Nisbett's argument, but extends the brain area, damage to which will lead to obesity in rats.

hence there is eventually a learned component that makes him genuinely stimulus bound. Presumably also the physiological drive, being located in the hypothalamus, does not function through hunger cues but, as indicated above, by sensitizing the individual directly to external cues relating to food.

Schachter's hypothesis has come under attack recently by Singh (1973) who points out several facts that the stimulus-binding theory has difficulty in explaining (e.g., how an obese person stops eating in the presence of food). Rather, he argues that obesity represents a deficit in response inhibition and reports the results of several experiments that support this hypothesis. In his first experiment obese and nonobese subjects were first trained, within the guise of a taste task, to remove crackers from a spiral ring in one direction and were then required to repeat the task in either the same (response compatible) or opposite (response incompatible) direction. The results indicated that when the second response was incompatible with the first, obese subjects consumed fewer crackers, whereas the opposite effect was obtained when the second response was compatible with the first. Analogously to Schachter's generalization of the stimulus control of obese persons to all situations, Singh then showed that obese persons manifest greater interference effects to prior habits on subsequent task behavior than do nonobese subjects.

Singh does not consider his results as disproving Schachter's hypothesis, but rather considers that both response-inhibition *and* stimulus-control factors may be important in obesity. Although Schachter would presumably accept this conclusion and would presumably accept Nisbett's thesis as not incompatible with his own, the three theories are important because there is no doubt that whether or not internal or external factors are important, and their comparative importance, could significantly affect therapeutic orientation toward obesity. If Nisbett's arguments are valid, then it may well be futile, if not positively dangerous, to attempt to induce weight reduction in some obese persons. On the other hand, if all three formulations are valid (i.e., not incompatible), then it is clear that is it not really

surprising that behavior therapists have had little success with the
problem of obesity as yet on a long-term basis and that there will
have to be some radical rethinking of the approaches thus far
adopted.

REFERENCES

Bernard, J. L. Rapid treatment of gross obesity by operant techniques. *Psychological Reports*, 1968, **23**, 663–666.

Bornstein, P. H., and Sipprelle, C. N. Induced anxiety in the treatment of obesity: A preliminary case report. *Behavior Therapy*, 1973, **4**, 141–143. (a)

Bornstein, P. H., and Sipprelle, C. N. Group treatment of obesity by induced anxiety. *Behavior Research and Therapy*, 1973, **11**, 339–341. (6)

Ferster, C. B., Nurnberger, J. I., and Levitt, E. E. The control of eating. *Journal of Mathetics*, 1962, **1**, 87–109.

Foreyt, J. P., and Kennedy, W. A. Treatment of overweight by aversion therapy. *Behavior Research and Therapy*, 1971, **9**, 29–34.

Gold, R. M. Hypothalamic obesity: The myth of the ventromedial nucleus. *Science*, 1973, **182**, 488–489.

Hall, S. M. Self-control and therapist control in the behavioral treatment of overweight women. *Behavior Research and Therapy*, 1972, **10**, 59–68.

Hall, S. M. Behavioral treatment of obesity: A two-year follow-up. *Behavior Research and Therapy*, 1973, **11**, 647–648.

Harmatz, M. G., and Lapuc, P. Behavior modification of overeating in a psychiatric population. *Journal of Consulting and Clinical Psychology*, 1968, **32**, 583–587.

Harris, M. B. Self-directed program for weight control: A pilot study. *Journal of Abnormal Psychology*, 1969, **74**, 263–270.

Harris, M. B., and Bruner, C. G. A comparison of a self-control and a contract procedure for weight control. *Behavior Research and Therapy*, 1971, **9**, 347–354.

Harris, M. B., and Hallbauer, E. S. Self-directed weight control through eating and exercise. *Behavior Research and Therapy*, 1973, **11**, 523–529.

Horan, J. J., and Johnson, R. G. Coverant conditioning through a self-management application of the Premack principle: Its effect on weight reduction. *Journal of Behavior Therapy and Experimental Psychiatry*, 1971, **2**, 243–249.

Janda, L. H., and Rimm, D. C. Covert sensitization in the treatment obesity. *Journal of Abnormal Psychology*, 1972, **80**, 37–42.

Maletzky, B. M. "Assisted" covert sensitization: A preliminary report. *Behavior Therapy*, 1973, **4**, 117–119.

Mann, R. A. The behavior-therapeutic use of contingency contracting to control an adult behavior problem: Weight control. *Journal of Applied Behavior Analysis*, 1972, **5**, 99–109.

Manno, B., and Marston, A. R. Weight reduction as a function of negative covert reinforcement (sensitization) versus positive covert reinforcement. *Behavior Research and Therapy*, 1972 **10**, 201–207.

Martin, J.E., and Sachs, D. A. The effects of a self-control weight loss program on a obese woman. *Journal of Behavior Therapy and Experimental Psychiatry*, 1973, **4**, 155–159.

Murray, D. C., and Harrington, L. G. Covert aversive sensitization in the treatment of obesity. *Psychological Reports*, 1972, **30**, 560.

Nisbett, R. E. Determinants of food intake in human obesity. *Science*, 1968, **159**, 1254–1255.

Nisbett, R. E. Hunger, obesity, and the ventromedial hypothesis. *Psychological Review*, 1972, **79**, 433–453.

Penick, S. B., Filion, R., Fox, S., and Stunkard, A. J. Behavior modification in the treatment of obesity. *Psychosomatic Medicine*, 1971, **33**, 49–55.

Pliner, P. L. Effects of cue salience on the behavior of obese and normal subjects. *Journal of Abnormal Psychology*, 1973, **82**, 226–232. (a)

Pliner, P. L. effect of external cues on the thinking behavior of obese and normal subjects. *Journal of Abnormal Psychology*, 1973 **82**, 233–238.

Sachs, L. B., and Ingram, G. L. Covert sensitization as a treatment for weight control. *Psychological Reports*, 1972 **30**, 971–974.

Schachter, S. Some extraordinary facts about obese humans and rats. *American Psychologist*, 1971, **26**, 129–144.

Schachter, S., Goldman, R., and Gordon, A. Effects of fear, food deprivation and obesity on eating. *Journal of Personality and Social Psychology*, 1968, **10**, 91–97.

Singh, D. Role of response habits and cognitive factors in determination of behavior of obese humans. *Journal of Personality and Social Psychology*, 1973 **27**, 220–238.

Stuart, R. B. A three-dimensional program for the treatment of obesity. *Behavior Research and Therapy*, 1971, **9**, 177–186.

Stuart, R. B., and Davis, B. *Slim chance in a fat world*. Champaign, Ill.: Research Press Co., 1972.

Stunkard, A. J. The management of obesity. *New York State Journal of Medicine*, 1958, **58**, 79–87.

Stunkard, A. J., and Koch, C. The interpretation of gastric motility: I. Apparent bias in the reports of hunger by obese persons. *Archives of General Psychiatry*, 1964, **11**, 74–82.

Stunkard, A.J., and McLaren-Hume, M. The results of treatment for obesity: A review of the literature and report of a series. *Archives of Internal Medicine*, 1959, **103**, 79–85.

Tyler, V. O., and Straughan, J. H. Coverant control and breath-holding as techniques for the treatment of obesity. *Psychological Record*, 1970, **20**, 473–478.

Wijesinghe, B. Massed electrical aversion treatment of compulsive eating. *Journal of Behavior Therapy and Experimental Psychiatry*, 1973, **4**, 133–135.

Wollersheim, J. P. Effectiveness of group therapy based upon learning principles in the treatment of overweight women. *Journal of Abnormal Psychology*, 1970, **76**, 462–474.

CHAPTER 7

The Birth, Life, and Death of
Systematic Desensitization

The experiments of the behaviorists have shown that there is not only a process of conditioning or building taking place constantly from birth to death but that there is also a process of *unconditioning* taking place as well. A simple experiment of the type described below best illustrates it. A conditioned negative response was set up in a 1½ year old child—that of drawing back or running away from a bowl containing goldfish. We quote from a recent experiment:

The child, the moment he sees the fish bowl, says "bite." No matter how rapid his walk, he checks his step the moment he comes within seven or eight feet of the fish bowl. If I lift him by force and place him in front of the bowl, he cries and tries to break away and run. No psychoanalyst, no matter how skillful, can remove this fear by analysis. No advocate of reasoning can remove it by telling the child all about beautiful fishes, how they move and live and have their being. As long as the fish is not present, you can by this verbal organization get the child to say, "Nice fish, fish won't bite"; but show him the fish and the old reaction returns. Try another method. Let his brother, aged 4, who has no fear of fish, come up to the bowl and catch the fish. No amount of watching a fearless child play with these harmless animals will remove the fear from the toddler. Try shaming him, making a scapegoat of him. Your methods are equally futile. Let us, however, try this simple method. Get a table 10 to 12 feet long. At one end of the table place the child at meal time, move the fish bowl to the extreme other end of the table and cover it. Just as soon as the meal is placed in front of him, remove the cover from the bowl. If disturbance occurs, extend your table and put the bowl still farther away, so far away that no disturbance occurs. Eating takes place normally, nor is digestion interfered with. The next day repeat the procedure but move the bowl a little nearer. In four

152

or five such sessions the bowl can be brought close to the food tray without causing the slightest bit of disturbance.

(From an article on 'Behaviorism' by John Broadus Watson in *The Encyclopaedia Britannica*, 13th Edition, Supplementary Volume I, 1926, p. 346)

Although the quotation shows clearly that desensitization as a therapeutic procedure has been around for a long time, there can be no doubt that the particular version of it propounded by Wolpe (1958) in his book *Psychotherapy by Reciprocal Inhibition* and now known as systematic desensitization has preempted the field. The purpose of this chapter is not to provide a review of the work on systematic desensitization (a task that would require a book in itself) but to show the interaction of theory and technique in systematic desensitization and how a consideration of recent psychophysiological work related to systematic desensitization leads naturally into the final topic, biofeedback. It should be stressed, however, that the work discussed did not, in fact, play any part in the development of biofeedback.

In light of subsequent developments perhaps the most striking feature of systematic desensitization as it was developed by Wolpe is that it is *not* an example of a behavior therapy technology but rather an example of a technique developed out of a specific theoretical model. As a result of its theoretical attachment, the rules governing the use of the technique were very precisely laid down by Wolpe, and dire warnings were issued as to the undesirable effects of violating these rules.

THE TECHNIQUE OF SYSTEMATIC DESENSITIZATION

There are three basic stages in the original specifications of the technique:

1. Training in progressive muscular relaxation, with or without the use of hypnosis or drugs.
2. The construction of one or more individualized hierarchies.
3. Systematic desensitization proper.

Progressive muscular relaxation training is carried out right from the beginning of therapy while a detailed case history is taken, and, subsequently, one or more fear hierarchies are constructed. Thus by the time systematic desensitization itself begins, relaxation training is well advanced. The relaxation training, although extending over a number of sessions and involving progressively finer and finer control, is by no means as prolonged a procedure as advocated, for example, by Jacobson. The construction of hierarchies is regarded by Wolpe as being, of course, of the greatest importance because systematic desensitization involves working on individual items in the hierarchy. It is hierarchy construction that makes case-history taking so important for Wolpe as, without a detailed knowledge of the patient, the hierarchies may be trivial or misleading or the distance between items in the hierarchy in terms of their anxiety-arousing potential may not be equal.

When hierarchy construction is complete and relaxation training sufficiently well advanced, systematic desensitization itself may begin. Basically, this involves the presentation of an item from the lower end of the hierarchy while the patient is in a state of relaxation. Thus the item will arouse minimal anxiety and will be able to be tolerated by the patient, whereas the relaxation state itself will be antagonistic to anxiety arousal. Thus the anxiety will be reciprocally inhibited, and after several presentations the patient will have been desensitized to that particular item. The item next in the hierarchy will then be presented, the procedure repeated, and so on up the hierarchy until all items have been desensitized. At each stage the patient signals (verbally or, more usually, by raising his finger) any excessive increase in anxiety. When this happens the item is withdrawn while the patient relaxes. The item may then be represented, or an earlier item (to which the patient has been desensitized) substituted.

Now, in his original description of the technique of systematic desensitization Wolpe laid great stress on the importance of following the specified procedures carefully and exactly. For example, he asserted that systematic desensitization should begin with the item lowest in the hierarchy, that the anxiety aroused by this item should be completely reduced before passing on to the next item, that at the least sign of anxiety in relation to an item, visualization of the item should be stopped and the patient relaxed, and that hierarchies should be individualized (i.e., each hierarchy should be unique for a given patient). These and many other "rules of procedure" for systematic desensitization were laid down by Wolpe, and deviation from them was regarded as highly undesirable. The reason for these highly controlled specifications was simple: they appeared to be demanded by the theory from which the technique was derived. As stated by Wolpe: "If a response antagonistic to anxiety can be made to occur in the presence of anxiety-evoking stimuli, so that it is accompanied by a complete or partial suppression of the anxiety responses, the bond between those stimuli and the anxiety responses will be weakened" (Wolpe, 1958, p. 71).

It should be noted that Wolpe has subsequently made it very clear that by anxiety he means autonomic over-reactivity. Any response that produces, or is accompanied by, a reduction in autonomic reactivity may be regarded as reciprocally inhibiting the anxiety. Thus muscular relaxation is only one way in which reciprocal inhibition of anxiety (autonomic reactivity) may be achieved; the same result may be obtained by assertive responses, sexual responses, and so on. This argument is an unfortunate one, for it makes Wolpe's theory of reciprocal inhibition almost as slippery as a psychoanalytical proposition. However, although one implication is that relaxation may not be a *necessary* condition for reciprocal inhibition of anxiety, it would appear to follow from the theory that relaxation should be a *sufficient* condition and to that extent the validity of the theory is readily determinable.

There are, therefore, two basic questions that can be put concerning Wolpe's technique of systematic desensitization: first, assuming that the technique "works," what aspects of the technique are essential to its success? and second, is Wolpe's theoretical account of systematic desensitization valid?

As has already been pointed out, Wolpe has argued that the technique has three essential components: training in relaxation, construction of individualized hierarchies, and progression through the hierarchies in a systematic manner. Should these components turn out not to be vital to the success of systematic desensitization, then grave doubt would be thrown on the reasons for the success of the technique.

The Role of Relaxation

Early studies on the role of relaxation (summarized in Yates, 1970, pp. 64–72) appeared to support Wolpe's contention that relaxation training significantly enhanced desensitization therapy (even though, as has been pointed out, it is not a necessary condition of successful therapy). Subsequent research, however, enables the following paragraphs to be written with considerable confidence:

Systematic desensitization is effective in reducing phobic anxiety, whether relaxation training is part of the program or not (Cooke, 1968; Crowder and Thornton, 1970; Freeling and Shemberg, 1970; Waters, McDonald, and Koresko, 1972). This statement has been most recently demonstrated in a carefully controlled study by Craighead (1973) and has been shown to be true even for clinical cases (Agras, Leitenberg, Barlow, Curtis, Edwards, and Wright, 1971). There are suggestions that relaxation training may facilitate desensitization (e.g., Nawas, Welsch, and Fishman, 1970), but on the whole its presence or absence appears to have little effect on the results achieved.

Similar results are obtained with systematic desensitization whether the subject is required to relax *or* tense his muscles (Grim, 1971; Sue, 1972; Vodde and Gilner, 1971). An important qualification to this finding was made by Farmer and Wright (1971). They measured physiological reactivity (indirectly by way of Fisher and Cleveland's Barrier Score) and found that for Hi Barrier subjects (who *tense* muscles under stress) desensitization with relaxation produced a significant reduction in snake avoidance, whereas desensitization with muscle tensing did not; for Lo Barrier subjects (who tense their muscles less under stress) the two desensitization techniques (relaxation or tensing of muscles) were equally effective. This is one of the few studies that hint at the possibility that training in muscular relaxation may be appropriate for some, but not all, subjects.

Desensitization with muscular relaxation is no more effective than desensitization with mental or cognitive relaxation (Bellack, 1973; Marshall, Strawbridge, and Keltner, 1972) or a combination of both (Marshall et al., 1972).

In addition to the general findings referred to above, more specific experimental studies have cast doubt on the role played by relaxation in systematic desensitization. Thus Aponte and Aponte (1971) showed that it was not necessary to pair relaxation with imagery during desensitization; Benjamin, Marks and Huson (1972) in a study of clinical phobias found that it made no difference whether patients were allowed to relax or not between hierarchy items; Linder and McGlynn (1971) demonstrated that it was not necessary to make the subject repeat parts of the relaxation procedure if he was not sufficiently relaxed. McGlynn (1973) showed that the pairing of relaxation with graded imagination was unnecessary to the success of desensitization.

The Role of Hierarchy Construction

The role assigned to relaxation in systematic desensitization was as important as that assigned to hierarchy construction and the rules for progressing through the hierarchy. Recent research has shown that all these rules can be broken without impairing the effectiveness of desensitization:

Standard, as opposed to individualized hierarchies have been used successfully (Cotler, 1970; Donner and Guerney, 1969). When group (standard) hierarchies have been compared with individualized hierarchies the former have usually been shown to be as effective as the latter (Ihli and Garlington, 1969; McGlynn, 1971a), and this is so even when the items in the group hierarchy are essentially random (McGlynn, Wilson, and Linder, 1970). One exception is the finding of Lutker, Tasto, and Jorgensen (1972) that individualized hierarchies were more effective than group hierarchies. Other rule violations do not appear to make any significant difference. Most importantly, desensitization is as effective when only high-anxiety items from the hierarchy are presented as compared with progressing through the hierarchy from low to high-anxiety items (Cohen, 1969; Suinn, Edie and Spinelli, 1970). Edelman (1971) has shown directly that repeated presentation of high-fear stimuli does reduce autonomic nervous system reactivity. Krapfl and Nawas (1970) found that it made no difference whether hierarchy items are presented in ascending order of anxiety-arousing properties, in descending order, or in random order, whereas Miller and Nawas (1970) showed that it was unnecessary to reduce the anxiety associated with a particular hierarchy item before proceeding to the next. As in the case of relaxation, however, occasional studies can be found that support the rules. MacDonough, Adams, and Tesser (1973) found that subjects who were allowed to control the rate of progression through the hierarchy did better in therapy than subjects who were denied such control. Although Grossberg (1973) could find no support for the requirement that reduction of anxiety to one item in the hierarchy should generalize to adjacent items, Lomont and Brock (1971b) did find such generalization. Some of these discrepancies were resolved by Ross and Proctor (1973), who showed that repetition frequency of an item and duration of its exposure were both important factors in hierarchy presentation. On the whole, however, it seems that neither individualized hierarchies nor any special way of presenting the hierarchies are critical to the success of desensitization.

Massing and Spacing of Systematic Desensitization

This conclusion is supported by the demonstration that yet another presumed crucial procedure in desensitization is, in fact, unnecessarily restrictive. Wolpe had stressed the need not only to proceed cautiously through the hierarchies, but to proceed cautiously with systematic desensitization as a whole. Several studies have provided convincing evidence that this is not so. Robinson and Suinn (1969), for example, found that they could successfully program five 1-hour sessions of desensitization in a single day, and comparative studies of massing versus spacing of the desensitization package have shown equal effectiveness. Thus Hall and Hinckle (1972) compared two 4-hour sessions with ten 45-minute sessions; Suinn and Hall (1970) compared eleven 1-hour sessions completed in 1 day with three 1-hour sessions per week until eleven sessions had been completed; Lanyon, Manosevitz and Imber (1968) compared two trials per day with two per week. In all three studies the results were the same in indicating massed desensitization to be as effective as spaced desensitization. Suinn et al. (1970) went even further and compared the effects of massing with accelerated massing. In the former case there were five treatment blocks over 4 hours, and movement up through the hierarchy was carried out in the usual way. In the latter case there was only one 2-hour period, and only the most anxiety-provoking items were used. Again, no difference in effectiveness of the two procedures was found.

Of course, the most convincing evidence against the need for relaxation and the need to progress through the hierarchy from bottom to top comes from the studies of "flooding" or implosive therapy in which the subject is placed in the most frightening situation (rather than the least anxiety-arousing) and held there for long periods of time. Within Wolpe's theoretical structure, of course, the use of such an approach would be rejected because of the danger (indeed the apparent certainty) of producing a panic attack in the patient, and both Wolpe and Lazarus pointed out on several occasions that weeks of painful progress could be lost through inadvertent resensitization, as a result of progressing too quickly through the hierarchy. Yet implosive therapy shows quite clearly that, practically speaking, doing the exact opposite of what was recommended by Wolpe and Lazarus could produce results as least as good, if not better than, those obtained by systematic desensitization carried out strictly within the set of rules specified by Wolpe.

Automated Systematic Desensitization

Although Wolpe had laid great stress on the important role of the therapist in systematic desensitization (not, of course, in a transference role but in that of an expert in desensitization procedures) he was one of the first to explore the possibilities of automating desensitization (see Yates, 1970, p. 72) and a good deal of attention has been paid to this matter since.

The extent to which automation of systematic desensitization has progressed may be seen by reference to two studies. Dealing with snake and spider phobias in students, Cotler (1970) has described his automated technique as follows:

> Desensitization was conducted using a Stenorette dictating machine (Embassy model) and a series of standardized tapes which dealt with various aspects of the desensitization procedure. The S controlled the operation of the Stenorette by pressing one of five buttons located by the S's hand. The first button stopped the recorder so that the S could visualize a scene or concentrate on relaxation. The other four buttons corresponded to different subjective levels of anxiety which the S reported after visualizing a particular scene. The second and third buttons restarted the recorder and moved it forward; the fourth and fifth buttons restarted the recorder but recycled the tape to previously given relaxation instructions. The length of time that the tapes recycled could be adjusted through the use of two Lafayette timers. An event recorder was used to record which button was pressed (Cotler, 1970, p. 275).

In Cotler's study the relaxation instructions were similarly recorded on tape, and the subject, having listened to these instructions, practiced relaxation on his own at home, having been given a list of the muscles to be relaxed and the order in which to practice them. Further, a standard 16-item hierarchy was used, divided into four segments and presented over four sessions together with an additional session in which the last five hierarchy items were reviewed. Not only was the whole procedure automated, but the therapist was eliminated. Although technical considerations made it necessary for the desensitization procedure itself to be carried out under supervision it is obvious that, in principle the entire apparatus could be "rented" to the subject who could, with suitable additional taped instructions, carry out the therapy entirely on his own. Cotler's results indicated that this kind of automated desensitization produced results comparable to those obtained with the "personalized" Wolpe technique. Lang (1969) has described a more sophisticated computer-controlled desensitization technique with individual rather than standard hierarchies, and his results also indicate that this high degree of automation does not reduce the effectiveness of systematic desensitization (Lang, Melamed, and Hart, 1970).

Many other studies have investigated various possibilities in the automating of one or more aspects of systematic desensitization. T. K. H. Beck (1972) has described the use of videotaped material, based on the earlier work of Woody and Schauble (1969a, 1969b), and Lautch (1970) has described an ingenious and original use of a similar technique. Lautch's patient was a 40-year old man who was unable to look at his own face and thus avoided mirrors. A television film was made of the patient's face while he was being interviewed. The resultant film was first shown to him in a blurred form, then the image was gradually sharpened. After 18 sessions the patient was able to look at his own sharply focused face. A technique such as this could undoubtedly be applied to the hierarchical presentation of items more generally. In general the results of studies using automated desensitization have been favorable (e.g., Donner and Guerney, 1969; Donner, 1970; Kahn and Baker, 1968; Krapfl and Nawas, 1969; Martin, 1970; Nawas, Fishman, and Pucel, 1970; Nawas, 1971), although Paul and Trimble (1970) found that live relaxation instructions were superior to recorded instructions. (Riddick and Meyer, 1973, however, have recently shown that the difference was abolished if appropriate feedback about progress was provided as part of the automated relaxation training.) Most of these studies were, of course, analog studies involving students and specific fears. McGlynn, Williamson, and Davis (1973) found that automated desensitization was unsuccessful with really fearful subjects, and it is therefore quite possible that automated desensitization would be much less successful with clinical phobias.

Other Modifications of Systematic Desensitization

Other recent significant modifications of systematic desensitization that have occurred include the successful use of vicarious systematic desensitization in which the fearful subject watches someone else behaving fearfully and then gradually losing his fears (Hall and Hinckle, 1972; Mann and Rosenthal, 1969; Woody and Schauble, 1969b); the demonstration that group desensitization is as effective as individualized desensitization (Ihli and Garlington, 1969; Mann and Rosenthal, 1969), although individualized hierarchies are feasible in a group situation (Taylor, 1971) and group interaction may facilitate desensitization as compared with the individuals in the group not interacting (Cohen, 1969); and the demonstration that self-administration of systematic desensitization is feasible in many circumstances (Baker, Cohen, and Saunders, 1973; Clark, 1973; Rardin, 1969; Shrauger and Katkin, 1970).

Conclusions

The original technique of systematic desensitization was precisely, if complexly, specified. Over the years, however, each and every one of the components of systematic desensitization have been shown to be neither necessary nor sufficient—like the Cheshire cat left with only its smile, systematic desensitization seems to work, but there seem to be no component parts that cannot be removed, and the technique will then fail or be significantly reduced in its efficiency. Does this matter? If it works, does it matter if it is impossible to specify how it works? Let the question be put another way. If relaxation is unnecessary, if hierarchies can be worked equally well through from top to bottom as the reverse, if only the most feared items need to be presented, if the rate of progressing through the hierarchies is unimportant, if the process can be massed or spaced with equivalent results, if the process can be completely automated, can we then continue to accept that we are dealing with a form of therapy that can be meaningfully called systematic desensitization, as Wolpe originally used the term? Can we meaningfully continue to refer to the Cheshire cat when only its smile is left? Even from a purely technological viewpoint, this would have to be regarded as an unsatisfactory situation. When it is realized that the procedures laid down by Wolpe were laid down in that form because his underlying theory demanded that form, then the situation with respect to systematic desensitization can fairly be described as catastrophic. When it is further realized that the theoretical underpinnings of systematic desensitization have been subjected to severe assault over the past 5 years, then a major reappraisal would appear to be required.

THE THEORY OF SYSTEMATIC DESENSITIZATION

Reciprocal Inhibition, Counterconditioning, Habituation, or Extinction?

Wolpe's original theory involved the postulation of reciprocal inhibition as the explanation of the effects produced by systematic desensitization. Subsequently, three other explanatory constructs have been put forward: counterconditioning, extinction, and habituation. As Davison (1968) pointed out, there are strong affinities between a reciprocal inhibition and a counterconditioning explanation, the former constituting the neurological equivalent of the latter, which is at a behavioral level. This equivalence is, however, somewhat misleading. Wolpe (1969) has made it clear that his view "has always been that the effort of relaxing skeletal muscles carries with it autonomic responses opposite in direction to those characteristic of anxiety. These autonomic responses are seen as concomitants, not consequences, of muscle relaxation (Wolpe, 1969, p. 219). Thus for Wolpe reciprocal inhibition involves antagonistic autonomic neural events that may occur in conjunction with several kinds of behavioral events including relaxation, assertive responses, and sexual responses. Neither the original anxiety responses nor the relaxation responses are the autonomic events. A counterconditioning explanation, however, appears to imply that a particular kind of behavioral response (e.g., relaxation) is incompatible with another particular kind of of behavioral response (e.g., anxiety), whatever may be the neurological underpinnings. It has been pointed out on numerous occasions (Evans and Wilson, 1968; Lader and Mathews, 1968; Yates, 1970, pp, 64–65; Evans, 1973) that considerable confusion exists over the terminology used in systematic desensitization. The extinction theory of systematic desensitization, for example, may refer to the elimination or reduction of the anxiety response, or it may refer to the replacement of the anxiety response by an incompatible response, such as relaxation. Indeed, Wolpe's own definition of reciprocal inhibition appears to refer to extinction of the anxiety at the neurological level without its replacement by a reciprocal state, although it is clear that he did not intend this interpretation. Also, there appear to be similarities between the extinction and habituation theories.

The most important attempt both to resolve these difficulties and to test the alternative theories is the work of Van Egeren and his colleagues (Van Egeren, 1970, 1971; Van Egeren, Feather, and Hein, 1971). Van Egeren (1971) pointed out that the term reciprocal inhibition originally referred to the momentary and easily reversible inhibition of one nerve process by another, such as the reciprocal inhibition of antagonistic skeletal muscles. Habituation refers to the temporary and reversible diminuation of a response following its repeated evocation by a repetitive stimulus, especially one of low strength. Extinction refers to the more long-lasting and possibly permanent diminuation of a response by its repeated evocation under conditions of nonreinforcement (where previously the response had been reinforced). Counterconditioning refers to the elimination of a stimulus-response connection by the attachment of an alternative response to the stimulus, the new response being of greater strength than the original response (which therefore, in principle, remains available, should the new response itself be extinguished or otherwise unavailable). As a result of these considerations, Van Egeren (1971) postulated a two-dimensional system involving the presence or absence of antagonistic inhibition and the occurrence of short-term versus long-term effects of response change which is illustrated in Figure 1.

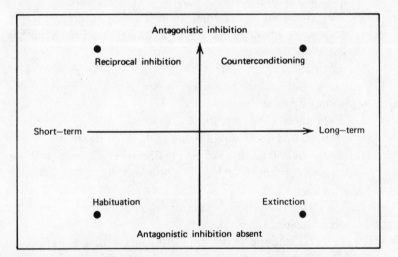

Figure 1. Autonomic change surface. Four types of autonomic response plasticity (reciprocal inhibition, habituation, counterconditioning, and extinction) are represented as extrema on two dimensions (permanence of change and antagonistic inhibition). (Source : Van Egeren, 1971.)

In this model the four processes of reciprocal inhibition, counterconditioning, habituation, and extinction are seen as not necesarily being competing explanations but rather as separate processes, each occurring under specifiable conditions.

With these considerations in mind, Van Egeren (1971) and Van Egeren, Feather, and Hein (1971) proceeded to examine the evidence bearing on physiological implications of desensitization theory in general and Wolpe's theory in particular. They derived twelve reasonably firm hypotheses that should receive empirical support if the kind of theorizing applied to desensitization is at all valid:

H1: Threatening stimuli will produce sympathetic activation.

H2: Sympathetic responses will be greater to threatening stimuli than to neutral stimuli.

H3: Sympathetic responses will be directly proportional to the degree of threat attached to threatening stimuli.

H4: Muscle relaxation will reduce sympathetic response to threatening stimuli (reciprocal-inhibition hypothesis).

H5: Repetition of threatening stimuli will result in stable reductions in sympathetic responses (extinction hypothesis).

H6: Extinction of sympathetic responses will be greater under muscle relaxation than under nonrelaxation (counterconditioning hypothesis).

H7: Extinction of sympathetic responses will be inversely proportional to the threat value of threatening stimuli.

H8: Counterconditioning of sympathetic responses will be inversely proportional to the threat value of threatening stimuli.

H9: Extinction of sympathetic responses will manifest stimulus generalization.

H10: Generalization of extinction of sympathetic responses will be greater under relaxation than nonrelaxation.

H11: The magnitude of sympathetic responses will be a function of the order of presentation of threatening stimuli.

H12: The reduction in sympathetic responses will be accompanied by a reduction in reported anxiety.

Van Egeren (1971) reviewed the evidence relating to the validity of each of these hypotheses, and Van Egeren et al. (1971) carried out a complex experiment involving the measurement of respiration rate, digital pulse amplitude, heart rate and skin conductance frequency and magnitude in subjects with public-speaking phobias under conditions of relaxation or no-relaxation training and who were presented with threatening or neutral scenes. They found very strong support for the first hypothesis (that threatening stimuli produce sympathetic activation); less strong support for hypotheses 2 and 3; weak support for hypotheses 4, 5, 6, and 9; and no support for hypotheses 7, 8, 10, 11, and 12, as shown in Table 1.

In another study, Van Egeren (1970) tested the habituation model of Lader and Mathews (1968) and found no evidence to support it. As Van Egeren points out, the habituation model is inconsistent with Wolpe's whole position, which stresses the permanent nature of the changes produced by systematic desensitization, whereas habituation is essentially a temporary change in behavior. However, support for the habituation model has been demonstrated by Watts (1971), who argued that the speed of desensitization should be greatest when low anxiety stimuli are presented for a short period of time. This prediction is demanded by the habituation model, but Watts went further and argued that for both low- and high-anxiety arousing items, long presentation time should lead to greater intersession anxiety reduction. Both of these predictions received support from his empirical study.

It is clear that, with respect to physiological measures, Wolpe's theory has not yet received any strong support; when these findings are combined with the empirical evidence relating to the components of the technique itself, it is evident that systematic desensitization is in very poor shape indeed.

The Role of Cognitive Factors in Systematic Desensitization

Given this situation, it is not surprising that alternative interpretations of what is happening in systematic desensitization

Table 1. Validity of Twelve Hypotheses Derived from Systematic Desensitization Theory

Hypo-thesis	Description	Con-firmed	Nature of Result
H1	Phobic stimulus	yes	Vasoconstriction, cardiac and respiratory acceleration, and elevated skin conductance during imagery.
H2	Phobic—neutral stimuli	yes	Larger cardiac and respiratory responses, number of skin conductance responses, and vasocontriction to phobic stimuli than to neutral stimuli.
H3	Stimulus intensity	yes	Vasomotor responses and number and size of skin conductance responses a positive linear function of affective intensity of phobic stimulus.
H4	Reciprocal inhibition	yes[a]	Fewer and smaller skin conductance responses to moderately intense phobic stimuli under relaxation.
H5	Extinction	yes[a]	Vasomotor responses a negative linear function of stimulus presentation in non-relaxed Ss; no inter-session recovery of autonomic responses.
H6	Counterconditioning	yes[a]	Faster extinction of vasomotor and skin conductance responses in relaxed Ss than in non-relaxed Ss.
H7	Extinction—stimulus intensity	no	Extinction of number of skin conductance responses a positive linear function of affective intensity of phobic stimulus.
H8	Counterconditioning — stimulus intensity	no	Counterconditioning of vasomotor responses and size of skin conductance responses a positive linear function of affective intensity of phobic stimulus.

168

Table 1.   Validity of Twelve Hypotheses Derived from Systematic Desensitization Theory (Cont.)

Hypothesis	Description	Confirmed	Nature of Result
H9	Stimulus generalization	yes[a]	Reduction of number of skin conductance responses generalized forward in phobic stimulus series.
H10	Stimulus generalization—relaxation	no	Stimulus generalization of extinction unrelated to relaxation.
H11	Stimulus order	no	Autonomic responses to phobic stimuli unrelated to order of stimulus presentation.
H12	Anxiety—stimulus repetition	no	Reported anxiety did not decrease when phobic scenes were repeated.

[a]Confirmed for some responses but not for autonomic system as a whole; multivariate F test not significant.

(Source: Van Egeren et al., 1971)

have been advanced. The possible role of cognitive factors in systematic desensitization has received a good deal of attention in recent years. The general background (which, of course, is not restricted to systematic desensitization) may be found in papers by A.T. Beck (1970a, 1970b), which were criticized by Bergin (1970) and Nawas (1970). The relevance of the empirical evidence to this issue is reflected in a spirited debate between Wilkins (1971, 1972) and Davison and Wilson (1972, 1973), who provide quite different interpretations of the empirical evidence relating to the role of cognitive factors in systematic desensitization. The expectancy model of systematic desensitization manifests itself in several different ways that are to be dealt with briefly. First, it has been argued that successful desensitization depends on the effect of the verbal instructions given to the subject, which in effect exert a demand pull by implying that the therapy will be successful, that is, by inducing a positive expectancy of outcome. Attempts to demonstrate that expectancy of outcome is a significant variable in systematic desensitization are equivocal, however. Borkovec (1937b) concluded that nine studies supported the expectancy hypothesis whereas ten did not. An independent analysis made by the present writer before consulting Borkovec's paper revealed substantially the same picture with, however, minor disagreements in the allocation of studies to the confirming or disconfirming category.[1] Wilson and Thomas (1973), however, obtained equivocal results in that the expectancy hypothesis was supported when self-report measures were considered, but not when behavioral approach measures were in question. Borkovec (1973a, 1973b) has suggested that whether expectancy may operate as a significant factor in systematic desensitization will depend on subject characteristics relating to physiological reactivity type. Powell and Watts (1973) have pointed out that it may not be legitimate to infer that outcome instructions (positive or negative) will be so perceived by the subject, and Borkovec and Nau (1972) have provided experimental evidence that control conditions involving expect-

[1]Studies classified as disconfirming the expectancy hypothesis by the present writer are Howlett and Nawas (1971); Lomont and Brock (1971a); McGlynn (1971b, 1972); McGlynn, Gaynor, and Puhr (1972); McGlynn and Mapp (1970); McGlynn, Mealiea, and Nawas (1969); McGlynn, Reynolds, and Linder (1971a, 1971b); McGlynn and Williams (1970); Maleski (1971); Miller (1972); and Woy and Efran (1972). The studies that support the expectancy hypothesis are Borkovec (1972); Leitenberg, Agras, Barlow, and Oliveau (1969); Marcia, Rubin, and Efran (1969); Oliveau, Agras, Leitenberg, Moore, and Wright (1969); Parrino (1971); Persely and Leventhal (1972); and Rappaport (1972). Borkovec (1973b) classified the study of Miller (1972) as supporting the expectancy model, but Miller found no difference between positive and neutral expectancy instruction, although both were superior to misleading instructions. In the Leitenberg et al. (1969) study, expectancy instructions were confounded with reinforcement, but this confounding was removed in the Oliveau et al. (1969) study. Borkovec's (1972) results were equivocal.

ancy of outcome may not be as credible as the systematic desensitization procedure itself, from which it follows that failure to find an expectancy effect does not necessarily rule out their operation in systematic desensitization itself. The situation with respect to the effects of expectancy thus remains indeterminate.

Three other aspects of the cognitive approach to systematic desensitization may be briefly mentioned. Clearly, imagery plays an important role in the technique. Recent studies have revealed serious difficulties with this part of the technique. Danaher and Thoresen (1972), for example, showed that self-report and behavioral measures of imagery do not correlate with each other. Davis, McLemore, and London (1970) found that an imagery scale score did not correlate with change scores, following treatment, on a behavioral avoidance test. In a variant of systematic desensitization called semantic desensitization Hekmat (1972) found that verbalization but not imagery was necessary for successful desensitization. McLemore (1972) could not demonstrate any correlation between changes produced by systematic desensitization and several kinds of imagery measures, and Mylar and Clement (1972) found that the subjective units of disturbance (SUDS) measure devised by Wolpe did not predict behavioral changes. Rehm (1973) also failed to find significant correlations between different imagery measures. Secondly, Hekmat (1972; Hekmat and Vanian, 1971) has argued that phobias may involve semantic conditioning rather than conditioning via direct experience and may therefore be desensitized in the same way. Hekmat's approach involves presenting a word representing a phobic object (e.g., "Snake") and pairing it with words having high loadings on the positive evaluation dimension of the semantic differential (the control condition involves pairing the phobic word with words that are evaluatively neutral for the subject). Hekmat's technique is confounded with Wolpe's, for the subject is required to visualize the pleasant or neutral association, and further control conditions in which the phobic, pleasant, and neutral words are presented alone are clearly required. Finally, mention should be made of those studies that stem from the famous experiment of Valins and Ray (1967) that claimed to show the effects of cognitive expectations on phobic behavior. Most subsequent studies, using misleading or false feedback information, have failed to confirm the original findings of Valins and Ray (1967) or have reinterpreted the results in noncognitive terms (Gaupp, Stern, and Galbraith, 1972; Kent, Wilson, and Nelson, 1972,; Rosen, Rosen, and Reid, 1972; Sushinsky and Bootzin, 1970; Wilson, 1973).

On balance it seems clear that the conclusion of Davison and Wilson (1973—that a cognitive interpretation of systematic desensitization has not received strong empirical support—is correct, even though, as they are willing to admit, cognitive factors may play some role.

The Role of Social Reinforcement Factors in Systematic Desensitization

An examination of the technique of systematic desensitization, at least in its nonautomated form, indicates quite clearly that social reinforcement factors may play a significant role, that is, that the procedures may gradually shape the subject's behavior away from avoidance and in the direction of approach to the feared object by means of selective reinforcement (Sherman and Baer, 1969). The selective-reinforcement approach to systematic desensitization takes two forms. First, the attempt to show that the explicit use of operant shaping procedures will reduce fear as effectively as, if not more effectively than, systematic desensitization itself. Second, the attempt to demonstrate that selective reinforcement operates in the classical desensitization technique itself. There seems to be no doubt that selective positive (verbal) reinforcement of approach behavior to a feared object will significantly increase approach behavior, and there is now sound evidence that it will result in more approach behavior than the usual form of systematic desensitization. Barlow, Agras, Leitenberg, and Wincze (1970) found this result when they compared systematic desensitization in imagination (with the addition of verbal praise) with selective verbal reinforcement of approach behavior to the feared object. Suinn, Jorgensen, Stewart, and McGuirk (1971) have suggested that fears be regarded as attitudes, a position that enables them to apply all the knowledge of the social psychology of attitudes to the therapy of fears, including knowledge of the effects of reinforcement on attitudes. In their study they found that subjects who were reinforced for reading positive instead of negative statements about feared snakes showed a significant decrease in behaviorally expressed fear (though not in questionnaire-rated fear). Positive results for the effects of reinforcement were also found by Vodde and Gilner (1971), who concluded that: "any contingency which provides an incentive for the subject to remain in the presence of a fear-arousing stimulus, and to attend to it, will facilitate extinction of the avoidance response to that stimulus, in the absence of real aversive consequences" (p. 173).

Negative results were, however, obtained by Anthony and Duerfeldt (1970) in a very complex study, involving the use of tangible rewards for approach behavior to the feared object, and by Rimm and Mahoney (1969), who compared the effects of contingent and noncontingent tokens for approach behavior. Thus although reinforcement may indeed play a role in systematic desensitization, it does not seem that it can wholly account for the positive results obtained, any more than the expectancy-of-outcome variable can.

Conclusions

There has been no intention here to review exhaustively the present status of either the technique or the theory of systematic desensitization. Rather, the intention has been to show that although systematic desensitization apparently "works," the critical factors involved remain unclear and the theoretical explanations conflicting and indecisive. Given this unsatisfactory position, the question naturally arises: Where do we go from here? The answer to this question comes from all the foregoing considerations, taken together with one other matter that must be briefly noted.

As was pointed out earlier, the technique of systematic desensitization originally involved the presentation of anxiety-arousing items, beginning with items arousing but little anxiety, reducing the anxiety associated with these items by presenting them while the subject was in a relaxed state, and proceeding to the next item only when the subject indicated no anxiety to the currently presented item. Now, the technique required the subject to indicate the occurrence of anxiety by raising his finger (occasionally, by other means such as verbal report). Further-more, the training in relaxation utilized a subjective criterion (subject report) to indicate both tensing of muscles and their subsequent relaxation. Apart from the subject's report and casual observations of indices of tension such as sweating and agitated movement, there was little employment of independent objective indices of tension and relaxation. However, eventually, attempts were made to correlate these verbal, subjective reports of anxiety or relaxation with physiological indices. Two studies by Paul (1969a, 1969b) attempted to remedy the deficiency. Paul (1969a) compared heart rate, respiratory rate, tonic muscle tension, and skin conductance of female subjects while imagining neutral or stressful stimuli (the latter chosen on the basis of responses to the fear survey schedule) while in a relaxed state (physiological reactivity during a pretest adaptation period served as a baseline control). Paul (1969a) found that relaxation did, indeed, reduce physiological activity and that the amount of induced relaxation correlated significantly with the physiological changes. Many subsequent studies have confirmed and extended these intitial findings (e.g., Lader and Mathews, 1970; Marks and Huson, 1973; Marks, Marset, Boulougouris, and Huson, 1971; Mathews and Gelder, 1969; Lehrer, 1972; Van Egeren, 1970; Van Egeren et al., 1971), although some inconclusive findings have been reported (Edelman, 1970, 1971, 1972). However, the crucial point to be made here is that in none of these studies were the subjects *shown* their physiological activity. The important question which then arises is: what would be the effect of displaying the subject's physiological behavior to him directly and determining whether or not he could thereby come to control that activity? It is precisely this kind of question that constitutes the essence of biofeedback, which must now be considered.

REFERENCES

Agras, W. S., Leitenberg, H., Barlow, D. H., Curtis, N-A., Edwards, J., , and Wright, D. Relaxation in systematic desensitization. *Archives of General Psychiatry*, 1971, **25**, 511–514.

Anthony, R. M., and Duerfeldt, P. H. The effect of tension level and contingent reinforcement on fear reduction. *Behavior Therapy*, 1970, **1**, 445–464.

Aponte, J. F., and Aponte, C. E. Group preprogrammed systematic desensitization without the simultaneous presentation of aversive scenes with relaxation training. *Behavior Research and Therapy*, 1971, **9**, 337–346.

Baker, B. L., Cohen, D. C., and Saunders, J. T. Self-directed desensitization for acrophobia. *Behavior Research and Therapy*, 1973, **11**, 79–89.

Barlow, D. H., Agras, W. S., Leitenberg, H., and Wincze, J. P. An experimental analysis of the effectiveness of "shaping" in reducing maladaptive avoidance behavior: An anologue study. *Behavior Research and Therapy*, 1970, **8**, 165–173.

Beck, A. T. Cognitive Therapy: Nature and relation to behavior therapy. *Behavior Therapy*, 1970, **1**, 184–200. (a.).

Beck, A. T. Role of fantasies in psychotherapy and psychopathology. *Journal of Nervous and Mental Disease*, 1970, **150**, 3–17. (b).

Beck, T. K. H. Videotaped scenes for desensitization of test anxiety. *Journal of Behavior Therapy and Experimental Psychiatry*, 1972, **3**, 195–197.

Bellack, A. Reciprocal inhibition of a laboratory conditioned fear. *Behavior Research and Therapy*, 1973, **11**, 11–18.

Benjamin, S., Marks, I. M. and Huson, J. Active muscular relaxation in desensitization of phobic patients. *Psychological Medicine*, 1972, **2**, 381–390.

Bergin, A. E. Cognitive therapy and behavior therapy: Foci for a multidimensional approach to treatment. *Behavior Therapy*, 1970, **1**, 205–212.

Borkovec, T. D. The effects of instructional suggestion and physiological cues on analogue fear. *Behavior Therapy*, 1973, **4**, 185–192. (a)

Borkovec, T. D. The role of expectancy and physiological feedback in fear research: A review with special reference to subject characteristics. *Behavior Therapy*, 1973, 4, 491–505. (b)

Borkovec, T. D. Effects of expectancy on the outcome of systematic desensitization and implosive treatments for analogue anxiety. *Behavior Therapy*, 1972, 3, 29–40.

Borkovec, T. D., and Nau, S. D. Credibility of analogue therapy rationales. *Journal of Behavior Therapy and Experimental Psychiatry*, 1972, 3, 257–260.

Clark, F. Self-administered desensitization. *Behavior Research and Therapy*, 1973, 11, 335–338.

Cohen, R. The effects of group interaction and progressive hierarchy presentation on desensitization of test anxiety. *Behavior Research and Therapy*, 1969, 7, 15–26.

Cooke, G. Evaluation of the efficacy of the components of reciprocal inhibition psychotherapy. *Journal of Abnormal Psychology*, 1968, 73, 464–467.

Cotler, S. B. Sex differences and generalization of anxiety reduction with automated desensitization and minimal therapist interaction. *Behavior Research and Therapy*, 1970, 8, 273–285.

Craighead, W. E. The role of muscular relaxation in systematic desensitization. In R. D. Rubin, J. P. Brady, and J. D. Henderson (Eds.). *Advances in Behavior Therapy*, Vol. 4. New York: Academic Press, 1973. Pp. 177–197.

Crowder, J. E., and Thornton, D. W. Effects of systematic desensitization, programmed fantasy and bibliotherapy on a specific fear. *Behavior Research and Therapy*, 1970, 8, 35–41.

Danaher, B. G., and Thoresen, C. E. Imagery assessment by self-report and behavioral measures. *Behavior Research and Therapy*, 1972, 10, 131–138.

Davis, D., McLemore, C. W., and London, P. The role of visual imagery in desensitization. *Behavior Research and Therapy*, 1970, 8, 11–13.

Davison, G. C. Systematic desensitization as a counter-conditioning process. *Journal of Abnormal Psychology*, 1968, 73, 91–99.

Davison, G. C. And Wilson, G. T. Critique of "Desensitization: social and cognitive factors underlying the effectiveness of Wolpe's procedure." *Psychological Bulletin*, 1972, 78, 28–31.

Davison, G. C., and Wilson, G. T. Processes of fear-reduction in systematic desensitization: Cognitive and social reinforcement factors in humans. *Behavior Therapy*, 1973, 4, 1–21.

Donner, L. Automated group desensitization—a follow-up report. *Behavior Research and Therapy*, 1970, 8, 241–247.

Donner, L., and Guerney, B. G. Automated group desensitization for test anxiety. *Behavior Research and Therapy*, 1969, 7, 1–13.

Edelman, R. I. Effects of progressive relaxation on autonomic processes. *Journal of Clinical Psychology*, 1970, 26, 421–425.

Edelman, R. I. Desensitization and physiological arousal. *Journal of Personality and Social Psychology*, 1971, **17**, 259–266.

Edelman, R. I. Vicarious fear induction and avowed autonomic stereotypy. *Behavior Research and Therapy*, 1972, **10**, 105–110.

Evans, I. M. The logical requirements for explanations of systematic desensitization. *Behavior Therapy*, 1973, **4**, 506–514.

Evans, I., and Wilson, T. Note on the terminological confusion surrounding systematic desensitization. *Psychological Reports*, 1968, **22**, 187–191.

Farmer, R. G., and Wright, J. M. C. Muscular reactivity and systematic desensitization. *Behavior Therapy*, 1971, **2**, 1–10.

Freeling, N. W., and Shemberg, K. M. The alleviation of test anxiety by systematic desensitization. *Behavior Research and Therapy*, 1970, **8**, 293–299.

Gaupp, L. A., Stern, R. M., and Galbraith, G. G. False heart-rate feedback and reciprocal inhibition by aversion relief in the treatment of snake avoidance behavior. *Behavior Therapy*, 1972, **3**, 7–20.

Grim, P. F. Anxiety change produced by self-induced muscle-tension and by relaxation with respiration feedback. *Behavior Therapy*, 1971, **2**, 11–17.

Grossberg, J. M. Generalization of extinction effects in fear scene hierarchies. *Behavior Research and Therapy*, 1973, **11**, 343–345.

Hall, R. A., and Hinkle, J. E. Vicarious desensitization of test anxiety. *Behavior Research and Therapy*, 1972, **10**, 407–410.

Hekmat, H. The role of imagination in semantic desensitization. *Behavior Therapy*, 1972, **3**, 223–231.

Hekmat, H., and Vanian, D. Behavior modification through covert semantic desensitization. *Journal of Consulting and Clinical Psychology*, 1971, **36**, 248–251.

Howlett, S. C., and Nawas, M. M. Exposure to aversive imagery and suggestion in systematic desensitization. In R. D. Rubin, H. Fensterheim, A. A. Lazarus, and C. M. Franks (Eds.), *Advances in behavior therapy.* New York: Academic Press, 1971. Pp. 123–135.

Ihli, K. L., and Garlington, W. K. A comparison of group vs. individual desensitization of test anxiety. *Behavior Research and Therapy*, 1969, **7**, 207–209.

Kahn, M. and Baker, B. Desensitization with minimal therapist contact. *Journal of Abnormal Psychology*, 1968, **73**, 198–200.

Kent, R. N., Wilson, G. T., and Nelson, R. Effects of false heart-rate feed-back on avoidance behavior: an investigation of "cognitive desensitization." *Behavior Therapy*, 1972, **3**, 1–6.

Krapfl, J. E., and Nawas, M. M. Client-therapist relationship factor in systematic desensitization. *Journal of Consulting and Clinical Psychology*, 1969, **33**, 435–439.

Krapfl, J. E., and Nawas, M. M. Differential ordering of stimulus presentation in systematic desensitization. *Journal of Abnormal Psychology*, 1970, **75**, 333–337.

Lader, M. H. and Mathews, A. M. A physiological model of phobic anxiety and desensitization. *Behavior Research and Therapy*, 1968, **6**, 411–421.

Lader, M. H., and Mathews, A. M. Comparison of methods of relaxation using physiological measures. *Behavior Research and Therapy*, 1970, **8**, 331–337.

Lang, P. J. The on-line computer in behavior therapy research. *American Psychologist*, 1969, **24**, 236–239.

Lang, P. J., Melamed, B. G., and Hart, J. A psychophysiological analysis of fear modification using an automated desensitization procedure. *Journal of Abnormal Psychology*, 1970, **76**, 220–234.

Lanyon, R. I., Manosevitz, M., and Imber, R. R. Systematic desensitization: Distribution of practice and symptom substitution. *Behavior Research and Therapy*, 1968, **6**, 323–329.

Lautch, H. Video-tape recording as an aid to behavior therapy. *British Journal of Psychiatry*, 1970, **117**, 207–208.

Lehrer, P. M. Physiological effects of relaxation in a double-blind analog of desensitization. *Behavior Therapy*, 1972, **3**, 193–208.

Leitenberg, H., Agras, W. S., Barlow, D.H., and Oliveau, D. C. Contribution of selective positive reinforcement and therapeutic instructions to systematic desensitization therapy. *Journal of Abnormal Psychology*, 1969, **74**, 113–118.

Linder, L. H., and McGlynn, F. D. Experimental desensitization of mouse-avoidance following two schedules of semi-automated relaxation training. *Behavior Research and Therapy*, 1971, **9**, 131–136.

Lomont, J. F. and Brock, L. Cognitive factors in systematic desensitization. *Behavior Research and Therapy*, 1971, **9**, 187–195. (a)

Lomont, J. F. and Brock, L. Stimulus hierarchy generalization in systematic desensitization. *Behavior Research and Therapy*, 1971, **9**, 197–208. (b)

Lutker, E. R., Tasto, D.L., and Jorgensen, G. A brief note on multi-hierarchy desensitization. *Behavior Therapy*, 1972, **3**, 619–621.

MacDonough, T. S., Adams, H. E., and Tesser, A. The effects of choice in systematic desensitization. *Psychological Record*, 1973, **23**, 397–404.

McGlynn, F. D. Individual versus standardized hierarchies in the systematic desensitization of snake-avoidance. *Behavior Research and Therapy*, 1971, **9**, 1–5. (a)

McGlynn, F. D. Experimental desensitization following three types of instructions. *Behavior Research and Therapy*, 1971, **9**, 367–369. (b)

McGlynn, F. D. Systematic desensitization under two conditions of induced expectancy. *Behavior Research and Therapy*, 1972, **10**, 229–234.

McGlynn, F. D. Graded imagination and relaxation as components of experimental desensitization. *Journal of Nervous and Mental Disease*, 1973, **156**, 377–385.

McGlynn, F. D., Gaynor, R., and Puhr, J. Experimental desensitization of snake-avoidance after an instructional manipulation. *Journal of Clinical Psychology*, 1972, **28**, 224–227.

McGlynn, F. D. and Mapp, R. H. Systematic desensitization of snake-avoidance following three types of suggestion. *Behavior Research and Therapy*, 1970, **8**, 197–201.

McGlynn, F.D., Mealiea, W. L., and Nawas, M. M. SD of snake avoidance under two conditions of suggestion. *Psychological Reports*, 1961, **25**, 220–222.

McGlynn, F. D., Reynolds, E. J. and Linder, L. H. Experimental desensitization following therapeutically oriented and physiologically oriented instructions. *Journal of Behavior Therapy and Experimental Psychiatry*, 1971, **2**, 13–18. (a)

McGlynn, F. D., Reynolds, E. J., and Linder, L. H. Systematic desensitization with pre-treatment and intra-treatment therapeutic instructions. *Behavior Research and Therapy*, 1971, **9**, 57–63. (b)

McGlynn, F. D., and Williams, C. W. Systematic desensitization of snake-avoidance under three conditions of suggestion. *Journal of Behavior Therapy and Experimental Psychiatry*, 1970, **1**, 97–101.

McGlynn, F. D. Williamson, L. M., and Davis, D. J. Semi-automated desensitization as a treatment for genuinely fearful subjects. *Behavior Research and Therapy*, 1973, **11**, 313–315.

McGlynn, F. D., Wilson, A. L., and Linder, L. H. Systematic desensitization of snake-avoidance with individualized and non-individualized hierarchies. *Journal of Behavior Therapy and Experimental Psychiatry*, 1970, **1**, 201–204.

McLemore, C. W. Imagery in desensitization. *Behavior Research and Therapy*, 1972, **10**, 51–57.

Maleski, E. F. Effects of contingency awareness and suggestion on systematic desensitization: unplanned therapist differences. *Journal of Consulting and Clinical Psychology*, 1971, **37**, 446.

Mann, J. and Rosenthal, T. L. Vicarious and direct counterconditioning of test anxiety through individual and group desentization. *Behavior Research and Therapy*, 1969, **7**, 359–367.

Marcia, J. E., Rubin, B. M., and Efram, J. S. Systematic desensitization: Expectancy change or counterconditioning? *Journal of Abnormal Psychology*, 1969, **74**, 382–387.

Marks, I. M. and Huson, J. Physiological aspects of neutral and phobic imagery. *British Journal of Psychiatry*, 1973, **122**, 567–572.

Marks, I. M., Marset, D., Boulougouris, J., and Huson, J. Physiological accompaniments of neutral and phobic imagery. *Psychological Medicine*, 1971, **1**, 299–307.

Marshall, W. L., Strawbridge, H., and Keltner, A. The role of mental relaxation in experimental desensitization. *Behavior Research and Therapy*, 1972, **10**, 355–366.

Martin, I. C. A., Progressive relaxation facilitated. *Behavior Research and*

Therapy, 1970, **8**, 217–218.

Mathews, A. M., and Gelder, M. G. Psychophysiological investigations of brief relaxation training. *Journal of Psychosomatic Research*, 1969, **13**, 1–12.

Miller, H. R., and Nawas, M. M. Control of aversive stimulus termination in systematic desensitization. *Behavior Research and Therapy*, 1970, **8**, 57–61.

Miller, S. B. The contribution of therapeutic instructions to systematic desensitization. *Behavior Research and Therapy*, 1972, **10**, 159–169.

Mylar, J. L., and Clement, P. W. Prediction and comparison of outcome in systematic desensitization and implosion. *Behavior Research and Therapy*, 1972, **10**, 235–246.

Nawas, M.M. Wherefore cognitive therapy?: A critical scrutiny of three papers by Beck, Bergin, and Ullmann. *Behavior Therapy*, 1970, **1**, 359–370.

Nawas, M. M. Standardized scheduled desensitization: Some unstable results and an improved program. *Behavior Research and Therapy*, 1971, **9**, 35–38.

Nawas, M. M., Fishman, S. T., and Pucel, J. C. A standardized desensitization program applicable to group and individual treatments. *Behavior Research and Therapy*, 1970, **8**, 49–56.

Nawas, M. M., Welsch, W. V., and Fishman, S. T. The comparative effectiveness of pairing aversive imagery with relaxation, neutral tasks and muscular tension in reducing snake phobia. *Behavior Research and Therapy*, 1970, **8**, 63–68.

Oliveau, D. C., Agras, W. S., Leitenberg, H., Moore, R. C., and Wright, D. E. Systematic desensitization, therapeutically oriented instructions and selective positive reinforcement. *Behavior Research and Therapy*, 1969, **7**, 27–33.

Parrino, J. J. Effect of pretherapy information on learning in psychotherapy. *Journal of Abnormal Psychology*, 1971, **77**, 17–24.

Paul, G. L. Inhibition of physiological response to stressful imagery by relaxation training and hypnotically suggested relaxation. *Behavior Research and Therapy*, 1969, **7**, 249–256. (a)

Paul, G. L. Physiological effects of relaxation training and hypnotic suggestion. *Journal of Abnormal Psychology*, 1969, **74**, 425–437. (b)

Paul, G. L., and Trimble, R. W. Recorded vs. "live" relaxation training and hypnotic suggestion: Comparative effectiveness for reducing physiological arousal and inhibiting stress response. *Behavior Therapy*, 1970, **1**, 285–302.

Persely, G., and Leventhal, D. B. The effects of therapeutically oriented instructions and of the pairing of anxiety imagery and relaxation in systematic desensitization. *Behavior Therapy*, 1972, **3**, 417–424.

Powell, G. E. and Watts, F. N. Determinants of expectation in imaginal desensitization. *Perceptual and Motor Skills*, 1973, **37**, 246.

Rappaport, H. The modification of avoidance behavior: Expectancy, autonomic reactivity, and verbal report. *Journal of Consulting and Clinical Psychology*, 1972, **39**, 404–414.

Rardin, M. W., Treatment of a phobia by partial desensitization. *Journal of Consulting and Clinical Psychology*, 1969, **33**, 125–126.

Rehm, L. P. Relationships among measures of visual imagery. *Behavior Research and Therapy*, 1973, **11**, 265–270.

Riddick, C., and Meyer, R. G. The efficacy of automated relaxation training with response contingent feedback. *Behavior Therapy*, 1973, **4**, 331–337.

Rimm, D. C., and Mahoney, M. J. The application of reinforcement and participant modeling procedures in the treatment of snake-phobic behavior. *Behavior Research and Therapy*, 1969, **7**, 369–376.

Robinson, C., and Suinn, R. M. Group desensitization of a phobia in massed sessions. *Behavior Research and Therapy*, 1969, **7**, 319–321.

Rosen, G. M., Rosen, E., and Reid, J. B. Cognitive desensitization and avoidance behavior: A re-evaluation. *Journal of Abnormal Psychology*, 1972, **80**, 176–182.

Ross, S. M., and Proctor, S. Frequency and duration of hierarchy item exposure in a systematic desensitization analogue. *Behavior Research and Therapy*, 1973, **11**, 303–312.

Sherman, J. A., and Baer, D. M. Appraisal of operant therapy techniques with children and adults. In C. M. Franks (Ed.), *Behavior therapy: Appraisal and status*. New York: McGraw-Hill, 1969. PP 192–219.

Shrauger, J. S., and Katkin, E. S. The use of nonspecific underlying motivational factors in the systematic desensitization of specific marital and interpersonal fears: A case study. *Journal of Abnormal Psychology*, 1970, **75**, 221–226.

Sue, D. The role of relaxation in systematic desensitization. *Behavior Research and therapy*, 1972, **10**, 153–158.

Suinn, R. M., Edie, C. A., and Spinelli, P. R. Accelerated massed desensitivation: Innovation in short-term treatment. *Behavior Therapy*, 1970, **1**, 303–311.

Suinn, R. M. and Hall, R. Marathon desensitization groups: An innovative technique. *Behavior Research and Therapy*, 1970, **8**, 97–98.

Suinn, R. M., Jorgensen, G. T., Stewart, S. T., and McGuirk, F. D. Fears as attitudes: Experimental reduction of fear through reinforcement. *Journal of Abnormal Psychology*, 1971, **78**, 272–279.

Sushinsky, L. W. and Bootzin, R. R. Cognitive desensitization as a model of systematic desensitization. *Behavior Research and Therapy*, 1970, **8**, 29–33.

Taylor, D. W. A comparison of group desensitization with two control procedures in the treatment of test anxiety. *Behavior Research and Therapy*, 1971, **9**, 281–284.

Valins, S., and Ray, A. A. Effects of cognitive desensitization on avoidance behavior. *Journal of Personality and Social Psychology*, 1967, **7**, 345–350.

Van Egeren, L. F. Psychophysiology of systematic desensitization: The habituation model. *Journal of Behavior Therapy and Experimental Psychiatry*, 1970, **1**, 249–255.

Van Egeren, L. F. Psychophysiological aspects of systematic desensitization: Some outstanding issues. *Behavior Research and Therapy*, 1971, **9**, 65–77.

Van Egeren, L. F., Feather, B. W., and Hein, P. L. Desensitization of phobias: Some psychophysiological propositions. *Psychophysiology*, 1971, **8**, 213–228.

Vodde, T. W., and Gilner, F. H. The effects of exposure to fear stimuli on fear reduction. *Behavior Research and Therapy*, 1971, **9**, 169–175.

Waters, W. F., McDonald, D. G., and Koresko, R. L. Psychophysiological responses during analogue systematic desensitization and nonrelaxation control procedures. *Behavior Research and Therapy*, 1972, **10**, 381–393.

Watts, F. Desensitization as an habituation phenomenon: I. Stimulus intensity as determinant of the effects of stimulus lengths. *Behavior Research and Therapy*, 1971, **9**, 209–217.

Wilkins, W. Desensitization: Social and cognitive factors underlying the effectiveness of Wolpe's procedure. *Psychological Bulletin*, 1971, **76**, 311–317.

Wilkins, W. Desensitization: Getting it together with Davison and Wilson. *Psychological Bulletin*, 1972, **78**, 32–36.

Wilson, G. T. Effects of false feedback on avoidance behavior: "Cognitive" desensitization revisited. *Journal of Personality and Social Psychology*, 1973, **28**, 115–122.

Wilson, G. T., and Thomas, M. G. W. Self-versus drug-produced relaxation and the effects of instructional set in standardized systematic desensitization. *Behavior Research and Therapy*, 1973, **11**, 279–288.

Wolpe, J. *Psychotherapy by reciprocal inhibition*. Stanford: Stanford University Press, 1958.

Wolpe, J. How can "cognitions" influence desensitization. *Behavior Research and Therapy*, 1969, **7**, 219.

Woody, R. H., and Schauble, P. G. Desensitization of fear by video tapes. *Journal of Clinical Psychology*, 1969, **25**, 102–103. (a)

Woody, R. H., and Schauble, P. G. Videotaped vicarious desensitization. *Journal of Nervous and Mental Disease*, 1969, **148**, 281–286. (b)

Woy, J. R., and Efran, J. S. Systematic desensitization and expectancy in the treatment of speaking anxiety. *Behavior Research and Therapy*, 1972, **10**, 43–49.

Yates, A. J. *Behavior therapy*. New York, Wiley, 1970.

CHAPTER 8

Biofeedback and Behavior Therapy

Psychologists who spend their time trying to bring the behavior of animals under stimulus control in the laboratory are usually chagrined when they visit the circus and discover the apparently miraculous degree of control exerted over the performing animals by trainers with no academic qualifications in comparative and physiological psychology. Contrary to the often-expressed saying, Skinner is not the best animal trainer in the busines. Similarly, psychologists who spend their time endeavoring to improve self-control in clinical patients or to teach various skills are chagrined when they see the quite extraordinary degree of control of the body exercised by other circus performers, such as trapeze artists, jugglers, and wire-balancers, as well as the equally extraordinary control over bodily functions that can apparently be exercised by people who allow needles to be driven through their skin without bleeding or who can maintain very uncomfortable positions for very long periods of time.

One reasonable interpretation of these wonders is that psychologists have barely scratched the surface in their attempts to explain control of behavior, whether externally or internally generated; a second reasonable deduction is that most humans could, if they wished to do so and practiced hard enough, obtain much more advanced control over their bodily functions than they customarily achieve. Biofeedback is basically concerned with the control exercised over behavior by feedback arising from that behavior—although there are difficulties with such a definition, especially with respect to just what constitutes *bio*feedback. The origins of biofeedback are first discussed, followed by a survey of the limited applications thus far in clinical practice, together with a glance at some possible future applications. The question of what is meant by the term biofeedback is then considered again.

ANTECEDENTS OF BIOFEEDBACK

The antecedents of biofeedback are generally traced to some startling experiments reported in the early 1960s by Neal Miller and his colleagues on the instrumental conditioning of autonomic functions in rats. The studies attracted particular notice, perhaps, because of the use of curare to induce paralysis of the skeletal system in an attempt to rule out the possibility that any autonomic conditioning obtained was artifactual, the autonomic changes merely following what was really skeletal learning (e.g., breathing rate might be what was really being conditioned, rather than heart rate, which was changing in step with the breathing but not actually being conditioned). However, as is usually the case, the antecedents of biofeedback are much older than this work, which merely served as a catalyst. Several important antecedents of biofeedback can be identified, each of which is discussed briefly in turn. No attempt is made to review the literature, but references are made to the major papers in which comprehensive reference lists may be found.

Autogenic Training and Relaxation Training

The work of Luthe (1969), which dates back to the first decade of this century, and the work of Jacobsen (1938, 1970), which dates back nearly half a century, are mentioned here only to pay respect to two pioneers who were apparently successfully training patients in progressive control of muscular and autonomic activities long before experimental psychologists became interested in biofeedback. In each case the aim of these workers was to sharpen the patient's awareness of internal responding and then to train him to control and modify that internal responding. Luthe and Jacobsen believed that muscular tension interfered with rational adjustment and that training the patient in relaxation would assist him to improve his adjustment to his environment. As we have seen, these approaches led eventually to systematic desensitization, with relaxation, as a therapeutic technique.

Instrumental Control of Autonomic Functioning

The animal studies carried out by Miller and his colleagues have been described in detail by Miller (1969). With the use of curare to paralyze skeletal functioning, for the reasons given before, these studies appeared to demonstrate that instrumental control of autonomic functioning could be demonstrated with respect to heart rate, blood pressure, intestinal contractions, peripheral vasomotor responses, the amount of blood in the stomach wall, and the formation of urine by the kidney. The importance of these findings lay in the flexibility of instrumental learning, as compared with classical conditioning. In the latter case, conditioning requires a precise unconditioned stimulus to elicit the response to be conditioned, whereas in instrumental learning almost any response can be strengthened by following it with any appropriate reinforcer. The relative neglect of autonomic learning resulted from the belief that autonomic responses could only be classically conditioned; if autonomic responding could be shown to be susceptible to instrumental learning, then a wide range of new possibilities was opened up. Unfortunately, the results dealing with heart rate and intestinal contractions, in spite of apparent replication in the early studies, have not been found recently in apparently identical studies, either by Miller and his colleagues or by other workers (Miller and Dworkin, 1974; Brener, Eissenberg, and Middaugh, 1974). This failure, of course, throws doubt on the other findings.

Nevertheless, these studies inspired others to carry out similar work (not, of course, involving the use of curare) with human beings, and the results here have been encouraging. Most of the work has been related to cardiovascular functioning, particularly heart rate and blood pressure (systolic and diastolic). The work of Schwartz (1973) and his colleagues can serve as an example. A new technique for automating blood pressure recordings was developed and binary feedback provided at each heartbeat for increases and decreases in blood pressure (i.e., the subject was provided with information that he had/had not, increased/decreased his blood pressure, but information was not provided concerning the magnitude of the change). In addition, what is described as an incentive or reward was given after the subject made a specified number of correct responses (the incentive usually consisted of a slide or token).

The principal findings obtained by Schwartz and his colleagues were that normal subjects were able to *raise* or *lower* systolic blood pressure within the course of a single session if they were given reinforcement for doing so, whereas subjects given noncontingent reinforcement did not change. The subjects were not told what bodily function was being studied, nor the direction of change required, and they were not aware they had controlled blood pressure, nor did they know the direction of change (Shapiro, Tursky, Gershon, and Stern, 1969; Shapiro, Tursky, and Schwartz, 1970a). A control study (Crider, Schwartz, and Schnidman, 1969) showed that these results *were not* due to nonspecific effects, such as instructions, feedback stimulation per se, reinforcement per se, or sitting quietly in a chair. Nor were they thought to be due to an *overall* increase in arousal level, because heart rate did not change in these studies. Similar results were obtained for diastolic blood pressure (Shapiro, Schwartz, and Tursky, 1972). It has also been shown that normal subjects may be trained to elevate or lower their heart rate, without affecting blood pressure (Shapiro, Tursky, and Schwartz, 1970b).

The fact that blood pressure rate and heart rate move in the same direction of change (increase or decrease) in the resting state only 50% of the time and that each can be trained to rise or fall under the control of the subject without the other changing in the same direction led Schwartz and his colleagues to investigate whether these two independent responses could be *integrated* on a learned basis; indeed, this has been shown to be possible. Subjects can voluntarily make heart rate and blood pressure change their rate in the *same* (Schwartz, 1972; Schwartz, Shapiro and Tursky, 1971) or *opposite* (Schwartz, 1972) directions— although it is apparently easier to move them simultaneously in the same rather than in the opposite direction (Schwartz, 1972).

Although the studies reported above constitute perhaps the most wide-ranging investigation to date of the possibility of instrumental control of heart rate and blood pressure, confirmation of these findings has not been lacking elsewhere. Blanchard and Young (1973) have provided a comprehensive review of all this work with human beings and have discussed the complex methodological problems involved. As the title of their paper uncompromisingly indicates, self-control of cardiac functioning represents a promise as yet unfulfilled. The promise, however, is there and, as is seen later, it is not confined to normal subjects.

Not a great deal has been accomplished or even attempted as yet in other areas of autonomic functioning, but two important strands of evidence may be mentioned. First, there now appears to be firm evidence that some subjects at least can voluntarily control peripheral skin temperature. Following the initial demonstration of this by Maslach, Marshall, and Zimbardo (1972), their results were successfully replicated and extended by Roberts, Kewman, and MacDonald (1973). They measured temperature from the pad of the middle finger of each hand and transduced this into an auditory tone signal that appeared to move from left to right in stereo headphones as the right-finger temperature rose; the reverse was found for a rise in the left-finger temperature. The tone also rose or fell in pitch as finger temperature moved in the appropriate or inappropriate direction. For reasons that are unclear, all but one of their subjects were highly hypnotizable, and temperature control was attempted only while the subject was hypnotized. The subject's task was to make his right-hand finger warmer (colder) than his left-hand finger in alternate sessions, which lasted 8 minutes. The dependent variable was the temperature difference between the two fingers at each 25" interval during each of three 8-minute trials.

The results are shown in Figure 1. One subject (S1) produced an overall mean difference of 2.96° C and a maximum difference of 5.6° C. Of the six subjects, four produced differences in the required direction at each of the 19 interval points; one subject began well but could not sustain control; one subject could not achieve control at all. Subsequently, the two best subjects did even better when auditory feedback was *not* provided. Qualitative analysis showed that various strategies were used to achieve the required temperature differential, such as making both hands

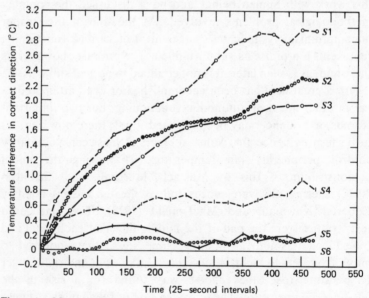

Figure 1. Mean temperature difference in the correct (specified) direction for nine alternating trials over three sessions with feedback. [Each subject is shown separately (N = 6)] (Source: Roberts, Kewman, and MacDonald, 1973.)

differentially warmer, keeping the temperature in one hand constant while warming the other, and so on. The subjects were not able to state clearly how they achieved control.

A second line of investigation to produce promising results is that dealing with voluntary control of salivation. Wells, Feather, and Headrick (1973) have summarized the few earlier studies and have provided new evidence that normal subjects can voluntarily control salivation. In their experiment they used sophisticated apparatus to collect saliva from the right-parotid gland and to transduce each drop into an auditory signal that was presented to the subject. The subject was under instructions to increase or decrease salivation as required, and the tone burst simply informed him of the rate of salivation. Wells incorporated many control procedures into the study (e.g., stabilizing salivary rate before each trial began, using baseline trials) and demonstrated that the subjects were able to *decrease* salivary rate significantly when feedback information was given immediately, but were not able to *increase* the rate voluntarily. When feedback information was delayed until the end of a trial, voluntary control of increase or decrease was absent.

The unidirectionality of the result obtained by Wells has also been found in some studies of heart rate. This fact is not necessarily surprising, given the different functions performed by increases and decreases in autonomic activity. Wells speculates that "at least in these response systems, sympathetic-like responses, i.e., HR increases and salivary decreases, are more easily conditionable than parasympathetic-like responses" (Wells et al., 1973, p. 508).

In summary, the studies of heart rate, blood pressure, peripheral body temperature, and salivation suggest that normal subjects may be able to control autonomic functioning to a significant degree. Important questions remain unanswered. For example, in the Schwartz studies the subjects were not informed what function was being studied, whereas in the temperature and salivary control studies the subjects were specifically instructed to utilize their own feedback and could "see" the results of their efforts at control. The relative contribution of the informational aspects of feedback as compared with reinforcement parameters remains quite unclear, although, as is seen later, the question is one of vital significance.

Control of Brain-Wave Activity

The apparent control that can be achieved over alpha and theta activity when these are displayed to the subject has attracted more attention in the popular press than any other aspect of biofeedback. However, this work is not reviewed here. The conclusion that self-control of the activity of brain waves has been truly achieved has been severely criticized by Grossberg (1972) on two grounds. The first is methodological: it appears that, for example, the enhancement of alpha rhythm under feedback display may represent disinhibition of blocking effects normally present under experimental conditions rather than genuine self-control. The second criticism is that much of the work appears to be based on the wish to utilize biofeedback merely as a device to explore those mystical aspects of human experience that have exercised such a fatal fascination for so long in psychology.

Classical Conditioning of Interoceptive Behavior

It is well known that the human black box is not empty, and to ignore what is happening inside it seems to be as foolish as the denial of the possibility of the circulation of the blood. Nonetheless, as is well known, a refusal to peer inside the black box is by no means uncommon among experimental psychologists in the Western world, a refusal that contrasts strangely with the attitude of Russian psychophysiologists, as Razran (1961) pointed out in his massive review of Russian research on interoceptive classical conditioning. This research (summarized in part also by Bykov, 1957 and, more recently, by Adam, 1967) cannot be covered in detail here. Only one or two examples are given to indicate the potential importance of interoceptive classical conditioning to biofeedback and behavior therapy, which is in no way lessened by the demonstration of the possibility of instrumental control of autonomic responding. As Razran points out: "Interoceptive conditioning may best be defined as classical conditioning in which either the conditioned stimulus (CS) or the unconditioned stimulus (US) or both are delivered directly to the mucosa of some specific viscus" (pp. 81–82). He distinguishes three basic forms of such conditioning:

1. *Intero-interoceptive* in which both CS and US are internal.
2. *Intero-exteroceptive* in which the CS is internal but the US is external.
3. *Extero-interoceptive* in which the CS is external and the US is internal.

Razran regarded only the first two forms as constituting genuine interoceptive conditioning, because they represent situations in which the viscera convey the conditioned information, whereas in the third kind this is not the case. Of the first two, he regards the second (intero-exteroceptive conditioning) as being the most significant and instructive (although this may merely be a function of technical difficulties—in principle, intero-interoceptive conditioning may eventually turn out to be the most important of all).

Razran also distinguishes five types of reaction that may be studied (visceral, skeletal, sensory-verbal, and the special cases of exteroceptive verbal stimuli in extero-interoceptive and intero-exteroceptive conditioning), giving a total of fifteen classes of interoceptive conditioning. He provides examples of each kind of study, both animal and human, from the Russian literature.

Mention should be made here of the important distinction made by Mowrer (1960) between nonresponse-correlated and response-correlated avoidance behavior. The former case can be illustrated by the example of the animal that escapes, then avoids a threatened shock (a tone) by moving from one compartment to another; the latter by the example of an animal proceeding up a runway towards a goal then stopping at a point associated with shock. In the former case the escape or avoidance behavior is associated with the occurrence of a conditioned stimulus not under the animal's control; in the runway situation, however, the conditioned stimulus arises internally in the animal from movements it makes in advancing up the runway. In the first instance the avoidance behavior is not produced by any specific prior behavior of the animal, because the occurrence of the conditioned stimulus is under the experimenter's control. In the latter case, however, the avoidance behavior results from stimulation arising from the animal's behavior itself (hence the terms nonresponse correlated and response correlated).

Voluntary Control of Individual Motor Units

Little attention has thus far been paid by biofeedback enthusiasts to a quite different series of studies that provide much more clear-cut evidence of the voluntary control of behavior than do the studies of instrumental control of autonomic functioning. These studies, which deal with the fine control of motor behavior, are, in fact, laboratory analogs of the astonishing control exercized by skilled performers in the world of entertainment. One of the most remarkable of these studies was carried out many years ago by Hefferline (1958), who was among the first to transduce muscle actvity and display the result to the subject in order to determine whether he could utilize the display to increase his control over muscle activity. Hefferline worked with the masseter (jaw) muscle because of its favorable innervation ratio, its accessibility, and the fact that eating and talking means that this muscle is continually active. Using three electrode placements and amplifications of one million, Hefferline recorded and displayed visually on a meter the average action potentials of the masseter muscle. The display was adjusted so that, at resting level, the meter gave a reading of zero. At a given signal the subject was required to close his mouth by the smallest possible amount while watching the meter needle and then try to make the needle to go midscale and hold it there for 10 seconds (several variations on this basic task were used). With practice some subjects were apparently able to discriminate muscle changes that, as reflected at the electrodes, were of the order of one-hundred millionth of a volt. He concluded on the basis of his experiments that proprioception is a "modality of such astonishing sensitivity as perhaps few have heretofore suspected" (Hefferline, 1958, p. 761). These results have been fully confirmed and extended by Basmajian (1962, 1963; Basmajian and Simard, 1967), and by Green, Walters, Green, and Murphy (1969). Basmajian (1963), for example, concluded as a result of his studies, using both auditory and visual feedback, that trained subjects could activate single motor units while inhibiting all others in the neighborhood and could even produce "special effects" such as rhythmic contraction in one unit, drum roll sequences, and so on.

Disruption of Feedback Control of Skilled Behavior

Although the work of Hefferline and Basmajian has demonstrated the extraordinary degree of control that can be gained over fine muscular activity, it is also apparent that this control can be rather readily disrupted with very severe effects on ongoing behavior of the subject. Such disruption of control is shown in the dramatic effects of delayed auditory feedback on the speech of normal subjects who may become quite incoherent under such conditions. In general terms it is evident that many of our behaviors are under the control of servomechanical systems in which the output feeds back a signal that is matched in a comparator against the expected feedback signal and appropriate adjustments are made to subsequent output. A detailed account of the operation of such servo systems with respect to the functions of the pupil, the lens, the eye, and the hand has been given by Stark (1968). A similar account has been provided for respiration by Defares (1964). Fender and Nye (1961) have described in detail a model for eye-movement control, together with supporting evidence; many other examples could be cited. One way, however, of demonstrating servomechanical control is to interfere experimentally with the control system by disrupting one of several feedback channels that are normally integrated and to examine the resultant effects. This method is what was done with delayed auditory feedback, of course, in which the airborne, bone-conducted, and proprioceptive feedback channels normally produce compatible information. With delay in the auditory or bone-conducted channel, the speaker now, however, receives conflicting information about the progress of his speech. Under such circumstances a servo system will either repeat the output or halt it altogether, phenomena that are found as effects of delayed auditory feedback.

In this regard the most informative and remarkable series of studies investigating the effects of perturbing feedback on behavior are those of K. U. Smith and his colleagues, which have been surprisingly neglected by biofeedback enthusiasts. Smith's work, of course, was developed from a long line of such research which he himself has reviewed in great detail (Smith and Smith, 1962). The initial work was carried out with the ingenious use of television cameras to produce a visual display that provided information about ongoing behavior which conflicted with proprioceptive feedback while the subject was performing various tasks such as writing letters, drawing triangles, or tracking targets. In later work Smith used a much more complicated setup in which subject output was transduced by analog-to-digital converters into digital form. The digital representation of output was then perturbed by operations carried out on the digital representation by a digital computer. The perturbed signal was then transduced back into analog form by a digital-to-analog converter and displayed to the subject. Smith has reported the results of his extensive experimentation in many publications, of which perhaps the most appropriate with respect to biofeedback therapy is that by Smith and Henry (1967) in which he presents his concepts in substantial detail, together with suggestions for their application to rehabilitation. As is seen later, this is an area in which biofeedback training promises to be exceptionally useful. It is impossible to convey here the richness and detail of Smith's work, but one example may be given to illustrate the possibilities that computer-controlled intervention provides. It is possible to arrange a setup in which finger tremor (apparent when the subject tries to depress steadily a lever of considerable sensitivity) is displayed as a pen recording visible to the subject. With practice, the finger tremor (manifested as variations around a hypothetical straight line followed by the pen) will stabilize. This record is then hidden, and the subject's output is fed through the digital computer and displayed with a delay of up to 3 seconds. Thus the subject now "sees" his finger tremor as it was 3 seconds earlier while at the same time receiving immediate proprioceptive feedback about his current finger tremor. Under these conditions (and provided, of course, the subject keeps his eyes open and looks at the visual record) the discrepancy provided by the two feedback sources produces a dramatic and sustained disruption of finger tremor control. Some subjects are able with practice to overcome the effect and reduce the perturbation (although rarely to normal levels), whereas other subjects are quite unable to do so. In this respect the results parallel the effects of delayed auditory feedback. The significance of Smith's work lies primarily in the enormous possibilities such a computer-controlled system provides for interfering with feed-back control systems—in principle, any response that can be recorded and transduced into digital form can be interfered with, and Smith himself has already investigated a very wide range of behaviors in this way.

As Smith himself has pointed out, it is impossible (if indeed not absurd) to try to account for these phenomena in terms of learning concepts. Finger tremor, breath pressure and other such behaviors involve literally thousands of separately detectable responses every minute, and changes occur instantaneously as feedback conditions change. It s evident that complex feedback control mechanisms are involved in which very fine adjustments are being made every second. Smith himself has developed a complex model of behavior regulation to encompass his experimental findings, involving three levels of closed-loop control corresponding to postural, transport, and manipulative adjustments, which are involved in varying degree in all forms of skilled behavior. Appropriate adjustments are made by means of neurogeometric detectors that are sensitive to *differences* in stimulation rather than direct stimulation per se. Again, the reader must be referred to the publications of Smith for an appreciation of the extraordinary comprehensiveness and richness of detail of his theoretical analysis. A somewhat similar analysis has been made by Whatmore and Kohli (1968) who coined the term dysponesis to refer to physiopathologic states made up of errors in energy expenditure within the nervous system. Whatmore stresses the importance of effort (ponesis) in normal behavior, that is, the role of very small muscular movements, often not detectable by ordinary means, in nearly all activities, whether physical or mental. Dysponesis consists of covert errors in energy expenditure via motor and premotor cortical neurons and pyramidal and extra-pyramidal tracts and their feedback pathways in attempting to cope with input. The action potentials constituting effort, when misdirected, interfere with adjustment because they feed signals into the reticular activating system, the hypothalamus, the limbic system, and the neocortex, producing excitatory and inhibitory influences inappropriate to the immediate objectives of the organism. These effort responses, of course, are appropriate in certain circumstances (such as response to attack) but may become a general way of responding to any perceived threat and thus maladaptive.

The fact that it is possible to *disrupt* ongoing behavior by interfering with one or more feedback channels suggests, of course, that it may be possible similarly to *improve* defective ongoing behavior patterns by appropriately intervening in the feedback system. Hence the importance of the work of Smith for biofeedback therapy can scarcely be overestimated.

Biofeedback Instrumentation

In a very real sense, knowledge is a function of the instrumentation available to collect data. The science of cryogenics became meaningful only when instruments and techniques were devised by means of which extremely low temperature could be achieved. In psychology the development of sophisticated instrumentation has produced a revolution in some areas of study that is only in its early stages. The most obvious example of this, of course, the use of on-line computer control of biofeedback studies, exemplified in the work of K. U. Smith, and now very widespread, indeed mandatory, in many areas in which otherwise data collection is virtually impossible because of the difficulty of reducing continuous human responding to manageable data displays. Because it is unnecessary to attempt a comprehensive review of biofeedback instrumentation here, examples are confined to illustrations of the kind of instrumentation used in the clinical studies to be reviewed in the next section.

The display of *blood pressure changes* is difficult, if not impossible with the use of the customary techniques for measuring blood pressure in clinical practice; whereas alternative techniques that are available are not practicable for work with normal subjects since the method involves surgical insertion of a pressure-transducing tube into an artery. Tursky, Shapiro, and Schwartz (1972) overcame the problem by developing an automated constant cuff pressure system to measure accurately median blood pressure. The technique involves placing a microphone at the distal end of the cuff over the brachial artery and listening for the presence or absence of the Korotkoff sounds which are heard whenever systolic pressure rises above cuff pressure but are absent when systolic pressure is lower than cuff pressure. With this equipment it is possible to set up a cuff pressure at which an equal number of beats are above and below cuff pressure.

Instrumentation for the display of *electromyographic activity*

(EMG) has been described in detail by Budzynski and Stoyva (1969). They describe how EMG activity may be transduced into an auditory signal in analog form, arguing that analog representation provides much more information to the subject than a digital readout (their argument is not necessarily valid for all feedback displays, and comparative studies are an urgent necessity). Their system provides the subject with a constant volume tone that varies in pitch as EMG activity changes. (Again, it should be noted that volume may be used as a transduced signal unless the intent is *relaxation* of a muscle, in which case increasing volume may, of course, impede relaxation). As EMG activity increases, the pitch of the tone gets higher; as the activity decreases, the pitch gets lower. The instrumentation allows the experimenter to shape the EMG activity of the subject by altering the demand characteristics of the analog signal so that to maintain an achieved lowered level of EMG activity the frequency of the tone must be lowered still further—in this way, muscle activity may be progressively reduced further and further. Full details of the technique are found in Budzynski and Stoyva (1969), and Leaf and Gaarder (1971) have specified in detail the criteria that must be met by instrumentation for clinical use. An interesting variant of these procedures has been described by Jacobs and Felton (1969). They transduced EMG feedback from the trapezius muscle into a dual-beam oscilloscope to provide two kinds of visual display of feedback. The first kind of display involved the integration of EMG activity over time, the integrated value being shown in the form of a vertical line on the oscilloscope. As EMG activity increased, the line moved to the right, and the subject's task was to keep the line as far to the left as possible. The second display showed the moment-to-moment EMG activity in the form of a horizontal line that splayed as a function of EMG activity. The subject's instructions were to keep the horizontal line as flat as possible. In the former case, of course, the information displayed to the subject fell somewhere between binary (intermittent) and continuous display, whereas in the latter it was continuous. Rubow and Smith (1971) have outlined the advantages and disadvantages of continuous versus integrated displays of EMG activity and have provided empirical evidence that the continuous moving-average technique of integration is superior to the technique of intermittent averaging. This makes sense in terms of findings by Smith and his colleagues, mentioned earlier, that delay in the display of feedback is a major factor in producing disruption of ongoing control of function. With respect to the techniques used by Jacobs and Felton (1969) this suggests that their integration technique (which involves much longer delays than either of the integration techniques studied by Rubow and Smith) may be less desirable than a continuous display. As Rubow and Smith point out, however, a subject may find it hard to discriminate signal from noise in a continuous display. It is possible that either of the integration techniques studied by Rubow and Smith would prove more satisfactory than that used by Jacobs and Felton, because the former techniques provide continuity with maximum reduction of noise. It should be added that commercial, portable versions of the EMG feedback apparatus have been developed (Budzynski, Stoyva, Adler, and Mullaney, 1973). A simple apparatus for transducing GSR into a continuously variable auditory tone has been described (Yonovitz and Kumar 1972).

These two examples, taken with the elaborate computer on-line control systems developed by K. U. Smith and others will suffice to illustrate the importance of instrumentation in fostering the development of interest in biofeedback. A similar comment could, of course, be made with respect to the elaborate and complex instrumentation required to study interoceptive classical conditioning, many examples of which are illustrated in the paper by Razran (1961).

CLINICAL APPLICATIONS OF BIOFEEDBACK

Training the patient to monitor and manipulate his own feedback has resulted in promising advances as yet in only three areas;

elsewhere, there is only very scattered evidence suggesting that biofeedback training may prove to be worthwhile. The three areas where real advances have already been made are the display of muscular activity, the display of temperature changes, and the display of heart rate and blood pressure. It is obvious that these are the three areas in which most of the basic research has been carried out.

Control of Muscular Activity in Abnormal States

Work in this area has been based on two assumptions, one of which is almost certainly valid, the other almost certainly invalid. The valid assumption is that if a disorder is associated with specific muscular tension, then reduction of the specific muscular tension will result in a reduction of the other abnormal characteristics of the disorder. The assumption that is probably invalid states that reduction of specific muscular tensions will generalize to other muscular systems and hence that, for example, generalized anxiety may be treated by reduction of any specific muscular tension present in the patient. The approach to *tension headache* represents an example of the first assumption. Preliminary work by Budzynski, Stoyva, and Adler (1970), which showed very promising results, has been followed by a much larger study by Budzynski, Stoyva, Adler, and Mullaney (1973), incorporating baseline recording of both EMG activity from the frontalis muscle and of headache activity and the use of appropriate control groups. This study involved 18 patients (only 2 of whom were male) between 22 and 44 years of age whose baseline frontalis muscle activity over a 2-week period was double the level of that of normal subjects. Following baseline assessment, the patients were allocated to one of three groups: EMG feedback training, involving the display of their own frontalis muscle activity; a feedback control group in which the patient was shown the feedback of another patient; and a no-treatment control group. The false feedback control group requires further description. The false feedback was not random but reflected the course of sequential reduction in muscle activity without, however, being correlated with anything the patient was achieving with his own EMG activity in the frontalis muscle. The control could be regarded as one way of allowing for expectancy of success, because the record suggested to the patient that he was succeeding in reducing his frontalis muscle activity. The feedback display involved auditory clicks, with the click rate decreasing as muscle tension decreased. Clearly, the control used by Budzynski was preferable to either random click rates or click rates going in the opposite direction to muscle tension.

Sixteen training sessions were given to the two treatment groups with an initial 3-month follow-up, after which the false feed-back training group and the control patients were offered the real-feedback treatment. The training consisted of 30-minute sessions during which the patient heard the auditory representation of the level of EMG activity in his frontalis muscle, recorded from electrodes taped to his forehead. Integrated rather than moment-to-moment feedback representation was used.

The results for frontalis muscle activity are shown in Figure 2. for the two experimental groups. It is clear that activity declined much more in Group A (true feedback) than in Group B (false feedback), and there was a corresponding difference in variability of feedback activity, with Group A showing a considerable reduction in variability. The difference in EMG activity was fully maintained at a 3-month follow-up.

The results for headache activity are shown in Figure 3 from which it can be seen that headache activity was reduced in Group A by the end of treatment and continued to decline during the follow-up period. The most impressive evidence for the success of the training, however, was the demonstration that the correlation between weekly headache activity and EMG activity during the baseline and training weeks for Group A was +.90, whereas for Group B it was −.05. It is not often that correlational analysis turns up such striking differences. There was some evidence of the kind of more general differences in Group A that

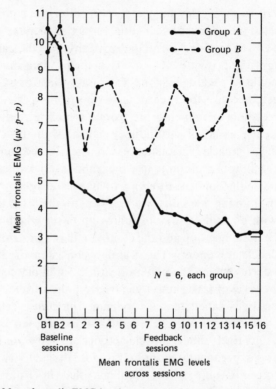

Figure 2.   Mean frontalis EMG levels across sessions. Group *A*—true feedback. Group *B*—pseudofeedback. (Source: Budzynski et al., 1973.)

might be expected as tension headaches became less frequent (less depression, less anxiety, reduction in insomnia, and so on), but these differences do not validate the second assumption, mentioned earlier. Just as importantly, Groups *A* and *B* showed striking differential changes in the amount of drug usage (to combat tension headache) following the initial treatment period, with Group *A* showing a significant decline in drug usage compared to Group *B*. Finally, at a later follow-up (18 months), four of the six true feedback patients were traced, and all remained apparently significantly improved.

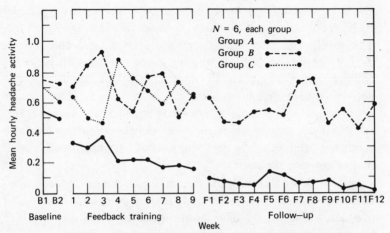

Figure 3. Headache activity during feedback training (all three groups) and during the 3-month follow-up (*A* and *B* only). Group *A*—true feedback. Group *B*—pseudofeedback. Group *C*—no treatment. (Source: Budzynski et al., 1973.)

In summary, then, this study constitutes one of the most successful applications of biofeedback therapy to date. The systematic within- and post-treatment changes on several relevant dependent variables (frontalis muscle activity, headache activity, drug usage), the use of appropriate control groups, the collection of baseline pretreatment data, and the differential correlation between EMG activity and headache activity in the two treatment groups, all suggest that the results obtained are significant and probably replicable.

These results have, in fact, been successfully replicated outside Budzynski's laboratory. Wickramasekera (1972) studied the effects of biofeedback training on five female patients with long histories of chronic tension headache. He used an A-B-C design involving baseline recording of EMG and headache activity[1] for 3 weeks, training with false but apparently relevant

---

[1]The paper is unclear on this point. Figure 1 in the paper suggests EMG *and* headache activity were recorded during baseline, but the text indicates only headache activity was recorded during this period.

EMG feedback for 6 sessions, and then training with genuine EMG feedback for six sessions, each session lasting 30 minutes. The results indicated no change in EMG or headache activity during the false feedback training as compared with baseline, followed by a significant decline in both EMG and headache activity when genuine feedback was provided. Very similar results were obtained in another study by Wickramasekera (1973) that followed a somewhat different course, omitting the false feedback training, but combining EMG training with verbal instructions in relaxation.

Budzynski et al. (1973) did not, so far as can be deduced from their procedure, train their patients in general relaxation, a procedure that would have confounded their results. It is not known to what extent training in muscular relaxation, whether general or specific to frontalis muscle activity but not involving feedback display, will significantly reduce EMG activity in this muscle, because surprisingly little attention has been paid to this disorder until recently by behavior therapists, even though it is very common. Tasto and Hinkle (1973) trained six students with tension headaches in muscular relaxation. They did not use hierarchies, and it is not clear to what extent the subjects concentrated on frontalis and neck muscle activity when practicing relaxation as compared with other parts of the body. The patients were given four training sessions over a 3-week period and were instructed to practice at home and whenever they felt a tension headache coming on. Two and one-half months after treatment ended they were asked to record the frequency and duration of headaches for 1 week. Four out of the six subjects reported no headaches during that week; the other two reported one headache each. However, these results can hardly be considered as reflecting unfavorably on the biofeedback approach. The subjects in the Tasto and Hinkle study were young, with short duration of tension headaches; frontalis muscle activity was not measured at any stage as a check on the subjective reports of frequency of headaches; and consequently there was no control whatever (by way, for example, of false feedback) for demand characteristics.

The application of biofeedback training to *chronic anxiety* has only just begun, but an important study by Raskin, Johnson, and Rondestvedt (1973) has indicated its potential value, at the same time making use of the second assumption, outlined before, which is almost certainly invalid. They hoped to alleviate *general* anxiety by training their patients to control a *specific* group of muscles, namely, the frontalis muscles. Their argument was that the frontalis muscle is difficult to train and that success in mastering the activity of this muscle would therefore have generally beneficial effects via, apparently, a general lowering of arousal level.

The patients in this study had suffered from severe anxiety over many years and had received many forms of treatment without success. They were trained in frontalis muscle relaxation with auditory feedback for a total of 40 hours of training. The criterion aimed at was practically zero motor unit firing, indexed by EMG activity averaging less than 25μV peak-to-peak levels for 25 minutes during a trial of 1 hour. In addition to EMG activity, the patients rated themselves on level of calmness at the beginning and end of each session; the therapist rated them in interview on anxiety, insomnia, and tension headache; a 65-item mood checklist was completed; and records of sleep and tension headache frequency, duration, and intensity were kept.

All the patients achieved deep relaxation as defined before over periods varying from 2 weeks to 3 months. At the start of the study the mean baseline activity of the patients was 14.1μV, and this was reduced by one-half to one-eighth following training. One intriguing phenomenon occasionally reported was the occurrence of profound subjective anxiety reported at a time when frontalis muscle activity was effectively zero. In general, in fact, EMG levels did not correlate with the patient's subjective rating of his anxiety level. Of the ten patients, six did not show any improvement in overall anxiety, but those who did reported that although they could not use their relaxation skills to *prevent* an attack (as appears to be possible with tension headache patients) they could reduce the severity of an anxiety attack that occurred while they were alone (only three patients had any success at all in reducing anxiety in social situations). Five out of six patients with insomnia found that the relaxation training did help them to get to sleep but did not prevent subsequent waking. Four of the patients suffered from tension headaches and, as might be expected, the training in frontalis muscle relaxation had a dramatic effect at least on this aspect of the patients' functioning.

The authors regarded their results as quite encouraging, given the severity of the disorder with which they were dealing. The fundamental error in this study, however, lies in the false assumption that training in relaxing one group of muscles will generalize to other muscular systems and hence that patients with generalized anxiety can be treated by training them to relax *any* group of muscles (it should be noted carefully that it is *not* being argued that *all* muscle groups must be trained in general anxiety. As is seen later, the problem is to identify the *particular* muscle activity or activities involved in a particular disorder, a problem that can only be resolved by individual patient analysis).

The same faulty assumption underlay the work of Davis, Saunders, Creer, and Chai (1973) who trained *asthmatic* children in frontalis muscle relaxation, one group being given biofeedback, the other group not being given it (a control group was told to relax and given reading material to peruse). The dependent variable was peak expiratory flow rate (PEFR) which measures the ease of expiration, the latter supposedly being facilitated by relaxation and inhibited by anxiety. The results of this study were not very clear-cut, and the differences obtained between nonsevere asthmatic children and the controls (a significant increase in PEFR following relaxation training with or without biofeedback) were not maintained. The study was experimental rather than clinical in nature. Alexander, Miklich, and Herschkoff (1972) have shown also that training in relaxation alone will increase PEFR, but the question of the effect of *appropriate* biofeedback training in this disorder remains unclear.

Thus the main conclusions from all this work must be that biofeedback will produce very encouraging amelioration of symptoms provided the muscular system being trained is specifically implicated in producing the disorder (as is the case with tension headache) but that the results will be negligible when no such correlation can be demonstrated, and it is simply hoped that specific biofeedback training will have a general effect.

Control of Peripheral Temperature in Abnormal States

It has long been known that *migraine* attacks involve autonomic nervous system functioning and that they are often accompanied by increased blood flow in the head (both vasodilation and vasoconstruction effects have been noted, the changes often being prodromal in nature rather than being present during the attack itself). Chance observation of a substantial peripheral temperature rise in an experimental subject experiencing spontaneous recovery from a migraine attack led Sargent, Green, and Walters (1973) to investigate the possible effects of peripheral temperature control training on the frequency and severity of migraine attacks. In their initial study they investigated 28 patients who suffered from either migraine attacks or tension headaches (the two phenomena, of course, are often found in the same person). Instruction was given in the use of a "temperature trainer" that indicated the magnitude of the difference between midforehead temperature and right-index-finger temperature. The subject rehearsed "autogenic" phrases which suggested relaxation and an increase in hand temperature and then visualized this state of affairs, at the same time receiving feedback concerning the difference in temperature between the midforehead and index finger. This difference score could, of course, result from either an increase in finger temperature with no change or decrease in forehead temperature. However, anecdotal evidence suggested that when the objective temperature difference was in the appropriate direction, the subjective report always indicated increased feeling of warmth in the hands with no change in forehead temperature. The clinical results suggested that increased temperature control was followed by a substantial reduction in both the frequency and severity of migraine headaches and in the use of drugs to control migraine. Unfortunately, no objective data were reported on the temperature changes, no controls of the kind utilized by Budzynski et al. (1973) were employed, and, of course, the autosuggestion technique used via the autogenic phrases was confounded with the attempt to control temperature. A more recent study by Sargent, Walters, and Green (1973) has reported on results with a larger sample of patients, but these difficulties remain. Nonetheless, the approach seems to have possibilities for the treatment of migraine. The temperature control training had no effect on the patients suffering from tension headaches, which was somewhat unexpected in terms of the authors' initial expectations, but is not at all unexpected if specific kinds of training are relevant only to specific kinds of disorders.

To date, the only other application of peripheral temperature control training has been in connection with Raynaud's disease which involves peripheral constriction and reduced blood flow—in severe cases the disorder can have very serious conconsequences, including gangrene and limb amputation. Schwartz (1973) described an attempt to treat one such patient with biofeedback involving training in peripheral blood flow increase; more recently, Surwit (1973) has summarized scattered (unpublished) case reports on five patients suffering from this disease. Although some success appears to have been achieved, the author is rightly extremely cautious in his conclusions; certainly it cannot be said that any notable degree of success has been achieved.

Control of Blood Pressure and Heart Rate in Abnormal States

It should be apparent that although work with normal subjects on an experimental basis and work with patients on a clinical basis has been reported in all the areas thus far discussed, there has been no reference to basic experimental studies with clinical patients. One exception is the study by Bleecker and Engel (1973a) in which they trained five patients suffering from *atrial fibrillation* (associated with rheumatic heart disease) to speed, slow, and then alternately speed and slow ventricular rate, the feedback being the onset of a light whenever the ventricular rate was above or below (as appropriate) the baseline rate. Two of the patients were also trained in control of the variability of ventricular rate. The results obtained are shown in Figure 4 which shows that all three functions (slowing, speeding, and alternately slowing and speeding) were brought under control by the patients; speeding up of ventricular rate was, however, more successfully accomplished than was slowing. Individual differences in the ability to achieve control were very marked. In each case four out of six patients succeeded in the assigned task.

Premature ventricular contractions (PVCs) are known to be associated with sudden death. Weiss and Engel (1971) attempted to train eight such patients to control their heart rate by providing visual feedback. After baseline procedures, trials were instituted in which the patient was required to try to speed, slow, or alternately speed and slow his heartbeat in the manner used by Bleecker and Engel (1973a). The procedure also enabled the patient to become aware of the occurrence of PVCs and his control over them by controlling heart rate. In advanced stages of training the feedback was gradually faded out in an effort to maintain control in the absence of visual feedback. Weiss and Engel found that all eight patients achieved some degree of control of heart rate, and five showed a decrease in PVCs in association with acquiring control over heart rate. Measurements taken on the ward showed some degree of control outside the

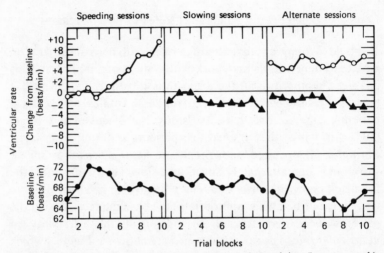

Figure 4. Mean baseline VRs for all patients during training (bottom graph); mean changes from baseline VR during training (top graph). VR during slowing is represented by ● and during speeding by o. Training has been divided into ten trial blocks by averaging temporally related training sessions. (Source: Bleeker and Engel, 1973a.)

experimental situation, and this control was maintained over follow-up periods of up to 21 months. Bleecker and Engel (1973b) have also reported some success in training patients with the *Wolff-Parkinson-White* syndrome (characterized by episodes of rapid tachycardia associated with dyspnea, syncope, and chest pains) to control the rate of beats and heart rate in general.

The other major work in this area has been with patients suffering from *essential hypertension* which refers to high blood pressure of unknown origin. Benson, Shapiro, Tursky, and Schwartz (1971), using the approach described earlier, successfully trained six out of seven patients with essential hypertension to reduce systolic blood pressure, the decrease achieved varying from as little as 3.5 mm Hg to as much as 33.8 mm Hg. Although Schwartz and Shapiro (1973) have reported failure to train patients with essential hypertension to reduce diastolic blood pressure, successful achievement of control has been reported by

Elder, Ruiz, Deabler, and Dillenkoffer (1973). They investigated 18 male patients aged 23–59 years who were regarded as suffering from essential hypertension. The patients were allocated to one of three conditions. In the first experimental condition a red light was made contingent on a reduction in diastolic blood pressure, using a shaping procedure in which the red light flashed on successive trials in which blood pressure was maintained below a previous criterion and then omitted if further lowering did not take place. The second experimental group was treated similarly except that verbal praise (graduated according to the amount of decline in blood pressure) was added to the visual signal. The third group was a control condition given no feedback. Blood pressure levels at time of hospitalization and just before treatment began were known, an important consideration because blood pressure levels can drop significantly following hospitalization. It should be noted that the patients were not required to distinguish systolic from diastolic blood pressure, being asked only to lower their blood pressure, but the feedback (verbal praise and/or signal light) was given only for change in diastolic blood pressure.

The results for diastolic blood pressure are shown in Figure 5 from which it is evident that the provision of informational feedback (light) alone produced significantly greater control of diastolic blood pressure in the final two trials (Group II versus Group I). However, the addition of verbal praise to the informational feedback produced decreases in diastolic blood pressure that were markedly different from the commencement of training as compared with informational feedback alone (Group III versus Group II); these differences were maintained at a 1-week follow-up. Although this study should be regarded as of experimental rather than clinical significance, the degree of control exercised indicated clinical applicability.

The control of tachycardia (abnormally high heart rate) has been studied by Scott, Peters, Gillespie, Blanchard, Edmunson, and Young (1973) and by Scott, Blanchard, Edmunson, and Young (1973). Although only four patients with chronic

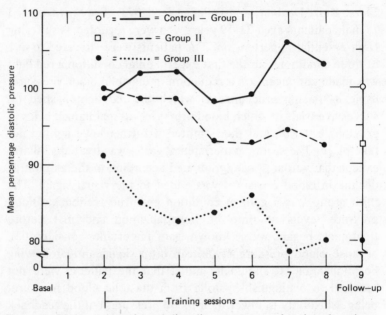

Figure 5.   Mean percent of basal diastolic pressure as a function of sessions. (Source: Elder, Ruiz, Deabler, and Dillenkoffer, 1973.)

tachycardia were involved, success in lowering and maintaining heart rate from an abnormally high level was achieved, using a variable criterion shaping procedure.

On the whole, therefore, the results from these three principal areas of biofeedback application indicate considerable promise, although they are less sensational than has been implicit in the amount of attention they have attracted.

Other Applications And Future Possibilities

The remaining applications to be considered must be regarded as thus far less well developed than the foregoing examples but are worthy of mention, for they indicate some exciting and important possibilities that will no doubt be extensively investigated in the near future. In some of the areas mentioned, no therapeutic work has thus far been carried out, and attention is drawn to them as possibly fertile sources of investigation. In most cases the appropriate technical devices are already in use, but have not yet been utilized to provide a feedback display to the subject.

Perhaps the most important area in which significant developments are likely to take place in the near future is that of *rehabilitation of physical function* following injury. Of course, in this area occupational and physical therapy techniques are well developed, but the addition of biofeedback techniques could produce very significant advances in effectiveness. One major example is already available. Jacobs and Felton (1969) studied the effects of visual feedback of myoelectric output from the trapezius muscle group in patients with neck injuries. Their patient group was required to practice relaxing the affected trapezius muscle, first of all without feedback and then with visual feedback, both integrated and moment to moment. Their performance was compared with that of a normal group of subjects under both conditions. In the absence of visual feedback, the patient group showed a much higher level of EMG activity than did the control group, being apparently unable to utilize proprioceptive and kinesthetic feedback to produce increased relaxation of the trapezius muscle. With visual feedback the control group was able to improve relaxation of the trapezius muscle, as would be expected from the results of studies reviewed earlier on relaxation of the frontalis muscle with feedback. More importantly, however, the patient group was able, with visual feedback, to improve control over the activity of the trapezius muscle to the *improved* level shown by the control group when provided with visual feedback. The very striking nature of these results is shown in Figure 6. Although Jacobs and Felton do not provide information about the correlation of these results with changes in the clinical status of the patients, the significance of these findings for a wide range of the consequences of physical injury are readily apparent. One important area would be the use of biofeedback to assist in the recovery of

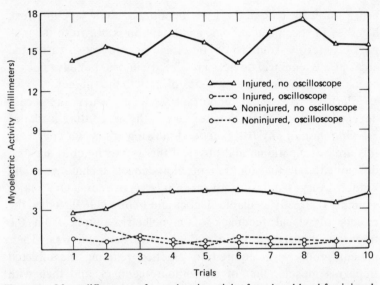

Figure 6. Mean differences of myoelectric activity from basal level for injured and noninjured subjects under visual-feedback and no-visual-feedback conditions. (Source: Jacobs and Felton, 1969.)

function in paraplegics and quadriplegics, at least in cases in which some degree of function is still available for use as a starting point.

An elegant study by Sachs, Martin, and Fitch (1972) has demonstrated the possibility of improving fine motor movement control in the *cerebral palsied child.* They fitted five metal tips to an 11-year-old child's fingers on each hand. The child's task was to touch each finger in turn to the thumb. Each touch activated a timer if the correct specified sequence were followed, enabling the total time for the sequence to be calculated, as well as individual finger latencies. Feedback was provided by means of a bank of four lights, which were activated only if the correct sequence were followed. An A-B-C-A-C design was used involving: baseline (no lights activated), noncontingent visual feedback (order of light activation randomized with respect to touch sequence), contingent visual feedback (lights sequentially lit contingent on correct sequence of touches), baseline, and contingent visual feedback again. In addition, one hand of the cerebral palsied child was used as a control on which no experimental manipulations were performed, and a further control was obtained by testing the child's normal 8-year-old sister under both experimental and control conditions. Although a practice effect producing improvement was found for the cerebral palsied child, an improvement attributable to the contingent visual feedback manipulation was found over and above the practice effect. In other studies Sachs and Mayhall (1971) have obtained similar improvement in the control of spasms in a cerebral palsied adult, and in the mastering of pursuit rotor performance, also in an adult patient (Sachs and Mayhall, 1972). It should be apparent that here, also, there are promising suggestions for improvement of training techniques with the cerebral palsied by the use of biofeedback techniques.

Mention may appropriately be made here of the work of Azrin and his colleagues on the *control of posture*. In one study, Azrin, Rubin, O'Brien, Ayllon, and Roll (1968) produced a dramatic reduction in slouching behavior by means of a portable harness that reacted to slouching behavior by activating a buzzer which Azrin described as an aversive stimulus. In a second study, however, O'Brien and Azrin (1970) used a vibrotactile stimulus as the indicator of slouching, and they concluded that the informational rather than the aversive properties of the stimulus could be the critical factor in reducing the amount of slouching behavior. This effect was because the stimulus was present constantly but was applied to one shoulder to indicate slouching and to the other to indicate normal posture—thus its aversive properties were equalized.

Finally, in this section, mention should be made of the use of biofeedback in attempts to control the frequency of *epileptic episodes*. Efron (1957) long ago illustrated the possibility of such control by the use of conditioning techniques, and more recently, Wright (1973) has reported success in the use of aversive conditioning to reduce the frequency of self-induced seizures in a

5-year-old child. Other conditioning approaches have been reviewed by Mostovsky (1972). The only biofeedback study thus far appears to be that of Sterman (1973). He attempted to capitalize on the fact that 12–14 Hz EEG activity is believed to be antagonistic to the occurrence of seizure activity by training four subjects to increase the rate of occurrence of such activity (called sensorimotor activity) by the provision of visual and auditory feedback. Sterman reported both a reduction in abnormal EEG activity and in frequency of actual seizures, but the improvement was maintained only as long as the training program was in operation.

A second area in which biofeedback might be expected to be a valuable approach is that of *speech disorders*. An unusual and interesting study by Roll (1973) illustrates one possibility. He investigated the modification of *nasal resonance in cleft palate* children by the provision of informative feedback. Nasality in speech is produced by the expulsion of air through the nasal cavity, with the mouth closed as a result of relaxation of the soft palate producing an opening between the pharynx and the nose. The nasal tone is the result of resonance of tissues in the nasal cavity. Nasality of speech is commonly found in cleft palate and may remain as a residual phenomenon after the cleft has been surgically repaired. The vibrations of the nasal cavity may be recorded by placing a contact microphone on the side of the nose. Roll transduced these vibrations into a binary information signal, a red light being on when the nasal cavity was vibrating and a white light being on when it was not. Roll treated hypernasality in two children by requiring them to produce continuous vowel sounds with and without informative feedback. The results were a striking reduction in hypernasality in one child but not in the other. Roll's study must be regarded as exploratory, but considerable possibilities are suggested by this kind of approach with respect to other disturbances in speech production.

The possibility of using biofeedback to modify *stuttering* does not yet appear to have attracted attention. Whether visual information via oscilloscope display or pen recording of stuttered and nonstuttered speech would be able to be utilized by a stutterer to reduce his stuttering behavior remains to be seen. However, an alternative approach may be mentioned based on recent work by Platt and Basili (1973). Working with three adult male stutterers (not necessarily typical of stutterers) Platt and Basili took EMG recordings from the right masseter muscle and the anterior suprahyoid group of muscles during the period 1400–400 msecs *before* the subjects spoke monosyllabic words beginning with /p/ and /b/. Tremor frequency (defined as the number of amplitude modulated peaks in each 1000-msec period) and tremor amplitude (defined as the average of voltage values for each EMG peak during each period) were measured, as well as the frequency and amplitude of isometric tremor while the subject voluntarily opened and closed his jaw without teeth contact (the intent being to determine whether muscle frequency matched isometric frequency).

A typical result is shown in Figure 7. Tremor frequency was

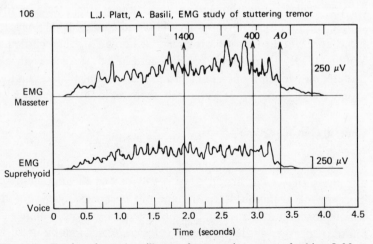

Figure 7.   Tracing of actual oscillogram for stuttering tremor of subject J. M. on word, pie. Line *AO* is erected at acoustic onset of word. Frequency and amplitude segment for analysis is demarcated between lines placed 400 and 1400 msocs prior to line *AO*. (Source: Platt and Basili, 1973.)

found to be similar across tasks (/b, /p/), both between and within subjects, and matched isometric frequency. For all three subjects tremor amplitude was greater for suprahyoid activity as compared with masseter activity, and this was so for isometric activity as well. Platt and Basili suggest that prestuttering jaw tremor may involve isometric muscular activity that prevents the normal execution of speech. It is evident that it would be worthwhile to explore the effects of displaying this prestuttering muscle activity to the stutterer visually or auditorily to determine whether the stutterer can reduce the activity in the same way that tension headache patients can reduce frontalis muscle activity. Whether such control would lead to a reduction in stuttering itself, of course, remains to be seen.

These examples indicate some of the exciting possibilities of biofeedback applications, and they are by no means exhaustive. Other areas in which instrumentation is already available but has not yet been used to display the subject's behavior to himself would include penile plethysmography, now widely used in the study of sexual disorders; writer's cramp; tics and other muscular disturbances; and alcoholism, in which the work in training the subject to monitor and recognize his blood alcohol level does, in fact, represent a form of biofeedback training. As Blanchard and Young (1973) said of blood pressure and heart rate, biofeedback training may indeed represent a promise as yet unfulfilled, but the promise is rich, even though the achievement is as yet small.

General Considerations

Finally, some mention should be made concerning fundamental questions that have arisen as a result of the development of biofeedback techniques for therapeutic purposes, questions to which no definitive answer can be given as yet but which will loom ever larger as the field is developed. Chief among these is the question: What exactly is meant by the term "biofeedback? The usual definition refers to stimulation arising directly from the behavior of the subject himself, stimulation which is not generated in his external environment. The feedback arising from speech represents a good example; the emitted sounds feed back directly into the brain via the airborne and bone conduction channels, whereas the movements of the lips, tongue, larynx, and so on also generate feedback stimulation. However, the situation is not so simple as it may seem to be. In the case of frontalis muscle relaxation training with feedback, the visual or auditory representation of the muscular feedback is, in a sense, produced by the experimenter, although it does not seem unreasonable to regard this as biofeedback, because there is a linear correlation between the muscular output and the visual or auditory representation of that output, provided at least that moment-to-moment activity is being displayed. Consider, however, the study by Heller and Strang (1973) on the reduction of bruxism (nocturnal teeth grinding) through automated aversive conditioning procedures (the terminology used by these authors being accepted for the moment). Heller and Strang recorded the sounds produced by teeth grinding by a student during sleep to estimate the frequency of teeth grinding and then arranged for a 3-second aversive sound blast to occur whenever grinding reached a rate of 3–5 per second. Using an A-B-A (baseline-aversive stimulation-aversive) design, they found that the sound blast condition reduced significantly both the rate and the intensity of teeth grinding in this patient. Heller and Strang did not use an arrangement in which the intensity of the noise varied continuously as a function of the rate (or intensity) of teeth grinding, but it is possible that, had they done so, the same linear relationship would have been obtained as was found between the visual or auditory display and EMG activity in tension headache. In the one case the EMG activity in a sense controlled the visual or auditory display; in the other case, the teeth grinding controlled the auditory display. The crucial differences between the two situations, of course, are that in the case of tension headaches the patient is awake and is voluntarily attempting to control the display, whereas in the bruxism case the patient was asleep and could scarcely be said to be bringing his disorder under voluntary control. Can the situation set up by Heller and Strang be described meaningfully as biofeedback therapy in the sense that the display of EMG activity can be so described? This problem leads to the second important point. It will be remembered that in the studies on the control of heart rate and blood pressure by Schwartz and his colleagues, the subject was deliberately not informed of the fact that changes in blood pressure and heart rate were the responses that produced changes in the visual or auditory correlate, and they were apparently not aware that these functions had changed. In clinical work with hypertension and other cardiac abnormalities, however, the patients were specifically instructed to try to change their heart rate. In the tension headache studies, of course, the essence of the technique is the instruction to the patient to change and control the visual or auditory analog of EMG activity. No doubt, in part, the intention of Schwartz and his colleagues was to obviate the kind of difficulty found with systematic desensitization studies in which demand characteristics or expectancy may lead to change in the required direction, and it is indeed well known that tension headaches of long duration may dramatically remit under a variety of placebo conditions. Nevertheless, the studies by Budzynski and his colleagues have successfully controlled for such placebo factors, and there seems to be a fundamental difference between a patient who will pick up' a snake on a behavioral avoidance test to please the examiner and a patient who reduces frontalis muscle activity significantly under specific instructions to try to do so. The essence of biofeedback does, indeed, seem to be in providing the patient with information he can utilize to control his own rate of responding, where under ordinary conditions such information is either not being used or is being used inappropriately.

A third important question relating to biofeedback is the role played by reinforcement in biofeedback training. There are scattered reports in the literature in which informational feedback alone is less effective than informational feedback plus reinforcement (e.g., Kohlenberg, 1973; Elder et al., 1973). But what exactly is the role played by reinforcement in such a situation? An example may help to indicate the nature of the problem. Consider the case of a person who does not possess the skill that would enable him to ride a bicycle and who then acquires that skill to a high degree of proficiency. Would it be possible, using operant techniques only, to return that person to his original status of not possessing the bicycle-riding skill? The feat has never been attempted and would appear to be impossible, using operant procedures. But it could be achieved, if the acquired skill is considered as involving servomechanical control systems, by disrupting permanently the feedback channels involved in the control of the skill. Spence long ago pointed out that when a rat is trained by reward to turn right in a maze, it is not being taught how to turn right for it already has that skill; similarly, in eyelid conditioning, the subject is not being taught how to blink. A fundamental distinction must be made between the control of the execution of a skilled response and the decision to perform that response. The bus driver may drive his bus because otherwise he will not get paid at the end of the week, but when he drives his bus round a tight corner, missing cars by inches, reinforcement or punishment plays no role whatever in determining whether he will successfully negotiate the corner or not. The successful exercise of the skill involves an incredibly complex sequence of interrelated movements that are integrated by feedback loops, on the one hand, and information emanating from the changing environment, on the other. Although not all forms of abnormal behavior may be comprehensible in servomechanical terms, it seems as if those disorders that are being treated by biofeedback training are best conceptualized in that way and that the role of reinforcement appears to be primarily to keep the subject in the situation and to heighten his attention to what is going on. The essence of biofeedback, therefore, is the provision of information about ongoing behavior on a continuous basis that will enable the subject to observe and monitor his performance and make appropriate adjustments.

This last point highlights one aspect of biofeedback training that serves as a partial answer to those critics of behavior therapy who have feared the controlling aspects of behavior therapy, especially insofar as they may seem to turn the patient into a person who is no longer a free agent. Now, it is true that the essence of a mature person may be regarded as stemming from a shift from being externally controlled as a child (by his parents, school teacher, and so on) to being self-controlled as an adult. It is true also that many behavior therapy approaches involve control over the patient's behavior being established by the experimenter and, perhaps, subsequently by society. One of the most important aspects of biofeedback training, therefore, lies in the degree to which the intent of the training is to display the patient's behavior to him in analog form so that *the patient himself* can bring the behavior under control. In a very real sense the intent is to help the patient achieve a degree of self-control that he has either never had or has lost. This does not mean, of course, that biofeedback procedures could not be abused, but this danger would not appear to be any greater than that involved in any kind of patient-therapist interaction, and the possible benefits in terms of increased independence through enhanced self-control for the patient are potentially greater than with any other kind of therapy.

The final point to be considered here relates to the specificity issue. The evidence thus far available suggests that when the biofeedback provided is appropriate to the disorder, then the patient will be able to utilize it to control and modify the activity producing the feedback and thus modify other aspects of the disorder. The obvious examples are the modification of frontalis muscle activity that leads to the control of the frequency, intensity, and duration of tension headaches (Budzynski et al., 1973), the modification of trapezius msucle activity in case of neck injury (Jacobs and Felton, 1969), and the modification of peripheral temperature in the case of migraine (Sargent, et al., 1973). In each of these instances, the display was appropriate to the disorder, and the modification of the display produced a corresponding change in the disorder. But Sargent et al. (1973)

found that peripheral temperature control training had no effect on tension headache; contrariwise, Raskin et al. (1973) found frontalis muscle control training was highly successful with tension headache but only moderately successful with chronic anxiety. This latter finding is particularly important, and the general point may be illustrated by reference to one of the major problems connected with the therapy of phobias. As is well known, three different criteria have been used to assess changes in strength of phobia before and after therapy: changes in physiological measures of various kinds, changes in verbal reports made by the patient of the degree of fear experienced, and changes in behavior as measured, for example, by the behavior avoidance test. It is equally well known that correlations between these three measures may be very often low; in particular, within the physiological category different physiological measures also tend to intercorrelate only moderately. What might this mean in terms of biofeedback therapy? Does it mean that biofeedback will not be useful for phobias (or generalized anxiety)? Such a conclusion would be premature. Given the generally accepted finding of the specificity of physiological response systems, it may well be the case that each individual's phobia (or group of phobias) is accompanied by one (or more) specific physiological correlates unique to that particular individual. Thus, as did Raskin et al. (1973), to focus on one particular physiological activity (in this case the activity of the frontalis muscle) in cases of general anxiety may be completely inappropriate. It is by no means impossible that the particular physiological system associated with anxiety or phobia in a particular individual is determined very often on a chance basis, according to the circumstances obtaining at the time the anxiety or phobia is acquired (whether this is very rapidly or very slowly). In that event, however, the role of biofeedback display becomes of vital significance. For the biofeedback display technique enables, as no other approach can, the therapist to *search* systematically for the *appropriate* physiological correlates in each *particular individual* patient. Assuming the correlate to exist, the therapist will then be able, having discovered it, to train the patient in control of that particular system. Whether the foregoing line of argument and recommended approach to general anxiety and phobias is valid or not is, of course, not yet known. If it is valid, it remains to be seen whether its systematic application would, in fact, revolutionize the therapy of general anxiety and phobias, as seems likely if the argument is valid. Certainly, however, the attempt should be made, for it represents a possible use of biofeedback therapy that would be quite unique.

The reader may have noticed that although this book is concerned with the relationship between theory and practice in behavior therapy, there has been virtually no mention of theory in this chapter. It is a striking fact about biofeedback that, to date, the therapist cannot instruct the patient in the rules he could follow in order to control the feedback display, nor can the patient, when he achieves such control, tell the therapist how he has achieved such control. The technique would therefore appear to be an excellent example of a purely technological approach that was not regarded favorably in the first chapter. The point must certainly be conceded with respect to the use of the kind of theorizing that characterizes the physical sciences in an advanced stage of development. As pointed out in the first chapter, however, psychology is in the preparadigm stage, and it would be unreasonable to expect the successful generation and use of universally accepted theories at this stage. As Kuhn pointed out, in the preparadigm stage of development there is no universally accepted base from which to proceed experimentally. However, the biofeedback work does illustrate the appropriateness of the other main point made in the first chapter. In light of the foregoing comments with respect to general anxiety and phobias and the need for exploring the feedback systems of the individual patient before proceeding with therapy, the approach advocated 100 years ago by Claude Bernard in physiology and revived more recently by Shapiro in abnormal psychology would appear to be especially relevant to biofeedback therapy. Thus the experimental analysis of the single case may well find its most appropriate field of application in this new and promising area of behavior therapy.

REFERENCES

Adam, G. *Interoception and Behavior.* Budapest: Akademiai Kiado, 1967.

Alexander, A. B., Miklich, D. R., and Hershkoff, H. The immediate effects of systematic relaxation training on peak expiratory flow rates in asthmatic children. *Psychosomatic Medicine,* 1972, **34**, 388–394.

Azrin, N., Rubin H., O'Brien, F., Ayllon, T., and Roll, D. Behavioral engineering: Postural control by a portable operant apparatus. *Journal of Applied Behavior Analysis,* 1968, **1**, 99–108.

Basmajian, J. V. *Muscles Alive: Their functions revealed by electromyography.* Baltimore: Williams and Wilkins, 1962.

Basmajian, J. V. Control and training of individual motor units. *Science,* 1963, **141**, 440–441.

Basmajian, J. V., and Simard, T. V. Effects of distracting movements on the control of trained motor movements. *American Journal of Physical Medicine,* 1967, **46**, 1427–1449.

Benson, H., Shapiro, D., Tursky, B., and Schwartz, G. E. Decreased systolic blood pressure through operant conditioning techniques in patients with essential hypertension. *Science,* 1971, **173**, 740–742.

Blanchard, E. B., and Young, L. D. Self-control of cardiac functioning: A promise as yet unfulfilled. *Psychological Bulletin,* 1973, **79**, 145–163.

Bleecker, E. R., and Engel, B. T. Learned control of ventricular rate in patients with atrial fibrillation. *Psychosomatic Medicine,* 1973, **35**, 161–175. (a)

Bleecker, E. R., and Engel, B. T. Learned control of cardiac rate and cardiac conduction in the Wolff-Parkinson-White syndrome. *Seminars in Psychiatry,* 1973, **5**, 475–479. (b)

Brener, J., Eissenberg, E., and Middaugh, S. Respiratory and somatomotor factors associated with operant conditioning of cardiovascular responses in curarized rats. In P. A. Obrist et al. (Eds.), *Cardiovascular psychophysiology.* Chicago: Aldine, 1974.

Budzynski, T. H., and Stoyva, J. M. An instrument for producing deep muscle relaxation by means of analog information feedback. *Journal of Applied Behavior Analysis,* 1969, **2**, 231–237.

Budzynski, T. H., Stoyva, J. M., and Adler, C. S. Feedback-induced muscle relaxation: Application to tension headache. *Journal of Behavior Therapy and Experimental Psychiatry,* 1970, **1**, 205–211.

Budzynski, T. H., Stoyva, J. M., Adler, C. S., and Mullaney, D. M. EMG biofeedback and tension headache: A controlled outcome study. *Psy-*

chosomatic Medicine, 1973, 35, 484–496.

Bykov, K. M. *The cerebral cortex and the internal organs*. New York: Chemical Publishing Co., 1957.

Crider, A., Schwartz, G. E., and Shnidman, S. R. On the criteria for instrumental autonomic conditioning. *Psychological Bulletin*, 1969, 71, 455–461.

Davis, M. H., Saunders, D. R., Creer, T. L., and Chai, H. Relaxation training facilitated by biofeedback apparatus as a supplemental treatment in bronchial asthma. *Journal of Psychosomatic Research*, 1973, 17, 121–128.

Defares, J. G. Principles of feedback control and their application to the respiratory control system. *Handbook of physiology*. Section 3 *Respiration*, Vol. I, Chapter 26, pp. 649–680. Washington, D. C.: American Physiological Society, 1964.

Efron, R. Conditioned inhibition of uncinate fits. *Brain*, 1957, 80, 251–262.

Elder, S. T., Ruiz, Z. R., Deabler, H. L., and Dillenkoffer, R. L. Instrumental conditioning of diastolic blood pressure in essential hypertensive patients. *Journal of Applied Behavior Analysis*, 1973, 6, 377–382.

Fender, D. H., and Nye, P. W. An investigation of the mechanisms of eye movement control. *Kybernetik*, 1961, 1, 81–89.

Green, E. E., Walters, E. D., Green, A. M., and Murphy, G. Feedback technique for deep relaxation. *Psychophysiology*, 1969, 6, 371–377.

Grossberg, J. M. Brainwave feedback experiments and the concept of mental mechanisms. *Journal of Behavior Therapy and Experimental Psychiatry*, 1972, 3, 245–251.

Hefferline, R. F. The role of proprioception in the control of behavior. *Transactions of the New York Academy of Science*, 1958, 20, 739–764.

Heller, R. F., and Strang, H. R. Controlling bruxism through automated aversive conditioning. *Behavior Research and Therapy*, 1973, 11, 327–329.

Jacobs, A., and Felton, G. S. Visual feedback of myoelectric output to facilitate muscle relaxation in normal persons and patients with neck injuries. *Archives of Physical Medicine and Rehabilitation*, 1969, 50, 34–39.

Jacobsen, E. *Progressive relaxation*. Chicago: University of Chicago Press, 1938.

Jacobsen, E. *Modern treatment of tense patients*. Springfield, Ill.: Charles C Thomas, 1970.

Kohlenberg, R. J. Operant conditioning of human anal sphincter pressure. *Journal of Applied Behavior Analysis*, 1973, 6, 201–208.

Leaf, W. B., and Gaarder, K. R. A simplified electromygraphic feedback apparatus for relaxation training. *Journal of Behavior Therapy and Experimental Psychiatry*, 1971, 2, 39–43.

Luthe, W. (Ed), *Autogenic Training*. New York: Grune and Stratton, 1969.

Maslach, C., Marshall, G., and Zimbardo, P. G. Hypnotic control of peripheral skin temperature: A case report. *Psychophysiology*, 1972, 9, 600–605.

Miller, N. E. Learning of visceral and glandular responses. *Science*, 1969, 163, 434–445.

Miller, N. E., and Dworkin, B. R. Visceral learning: Recent difficulties with curarized rats and significant problems for human research. In P. A. Obrist et al. (Eds.), *Cardiovascular psychophysiology.* Chicago: Aldine, 1974.

Mostovsky, D. I. Behavior modification and the psychosomatic aspects of epilepsy. In D. Upper and D. S. Goodenough (Eds.), *Behavior modification with the individual patient.* (Proceedings of the Third Annual Brockton Symposium on Behavior Therapy.) Nutley, N. J.: Roche Laboratories, 1972. pp. 57–71.

Mowrer, O. H. *Learning Theory and Behavior.* New York: Wiley, 1960.

O'Brien, F., and Azrin, N. H. Behavioral engineering: Control of posture by informational feedback. *Journal of Applied Behavior Analysis,* 1970, **3**, 235–240.

Platt, L. J., and Basili, A. Jaw tremor during stuttering block: An electromyographic study. *Journal of Communication Disorders,* 1973, **6**, 102–109.

Raskin, M., Johnson, G., and Rondestvedt, J. W. Chronic anxiety treated by feedback-induced muscle relaxation. *Archives of General Psychiatry,* 1973, **28**, 263–269.

Razran, G. The observable unconscious and the inferable conscious in current Soviet psychophysiology. *Psychological Review,* 1961, **68**, 81–147.

Roberts, A. H., Kewman, D. G., and MacDonald, M. Voluntary control of skin temperature: Unilateral changes using hypnosis and feedback. *Journal of Abnormal Psychology,* 1973, **82**, 163–168.

Roll, D. L. Modification of nasal resonance in cleft-palate children by informative feedback. *Journal of Applied Behavior Analysis,* 1973, **6**, 397–403.

Rubow, R. T., and Smith, K. U. Feedback parameters of electromyographic learning. *American Journal of Physical Medicine,* 1971, **51**, 115–131.

Sachs, D. A., Martin, J. E., and Fitch, J. L. The effect of visual feedback on a digital exercise in a functionally deaf cerebral palsied child. *Journal of Behavior Therapy and Experimental Psychiatry,* 1972, **3**, 217–222.

Sachs, D. A., and Mayhall, B. Behavioral control of spasms using aversive conditioning in a cerebral palsied adult. *Journal of Nervous and Mental Disease,* 1971, **152**, 362–363.

Sachs, D. A., and Mayhall, B. The effects of reinforcement contingencies upon pursuit rotor performance by a cerebral palsied adult. *Journal of Nervous and Mental Disease,* 1972, **155**, 36–41.

Sargent, J. D., Green, E. E., and Walters, E. D. Preliminary report on the use of autogenic feedback training in the treatment of migraine and tension headaches. *Psychosomatic Medicine,* 1973, **35**, 129–135.

Sargent, J. D., Walters, E. D., and Green, E. E. Psychosomatic self-regulation of migraine headaches. *Seminars in Psychiatry,* 1973, **5**, 415–428.

Schwartz, G. E. Voluntary control of human cardiovascular integration and differentiation through feedback and reward. *Science,* 1972, **175**, 90–93.

Schwartz, G. E. Biofeedback as therapy: Some theoretical and practical issues. *American Psychologist,* 1973, **28**, 666–673.

Schwartz, G. E., and Shapiro, D. Biofeedback and essential hypertenstion: Current findings and theoretical concerns. *Seminars in Psychiatry*, 1973, **5**, 493–503.

Schwartz, G. E., Shapiro, D., and Tursky, B. Learned control of cardiovascular integration in man through operant conditioning. *Psychosomatic Medicine*, **33**, 57–62.

Scott, R. W., Blanchard, E. B., Edmunson, E. D., and Young, L. D. A shaping procedure for heart-rate control in chronic tachycardia. *Perceptual and Motor Skills*, 1973, **37**, 327–338.

Scott, R. W., Peters, R. D., Gillespie, W. J., Blanchard, E. B., Edmunson, E. D., and Young, L. D. The use of shaping and reinforcement in the operant acceleration and deceleration of heart rate. *Behavior Research and Therapy*, 1973, **11**, 179–185.

Shapiro, D., Schwartz, G. E., and Tursky, B. Control of diastolic blood pressure in man by feedback and reinforcement. *Psychophysiology*, 1972, **9**, 296–304.

Shapiro, D., Tursky, B., Gershon, E., and Stern, M. Effects of feedback and reinforcement on the control of human systolic blood pressure. *Science*, 1969, **163**, 588–589.

Shapiro, D., Tursky, B., and Schwartz, G. E. Control of blood pressure in man by operant conditioning. *Circulation Research*, 1970, **26**, (Suppl. 1), **27**, I–27 to I–32. (a)

Shapiro, D., Tursky, B., and Schwartz, G. E. Differentiation of heart rate and blood pressure in man by operant conditioning. *Psychosomatic Medicine*, 1970, **32**, 417–423. (b)

Smith, K. U. and Henry, J. P. Cybernetic foundations for rehabilitation. *American Journal of Physical Medicine*, 1967, **46**, 379–467.

Smith, K. U., and Smith, W. M. *Perception and motion: An analysis of space-structured behavior.* Philadelphia: Saunders, 1962.

Stark, L. *Neurological control systems: Studies in bioengineering.* New York: Plenum Press, 1968.

Sterman, M. B. Neurophysiologic and clinical studies of sensorimotor EEG biofeedback training: Some effects on epilepsy. *Seminars in Psychiatry*, 1973, **5**, 507–525.

Surwit, R. S. Biofeedback: A possible treatment for Raynaud's disease. *Seminars in Psychiatry*, 1973, **5**, 483–490.

Tasto, D. L., and Hinkle, J. E. Muscle relaxation treatment for tension headaches. *Behavior Research and Therapy*, 1973, **11**, 347–349.

Tursky, B., Shapiro, D., and Schwartz, G. E. Automated constant cuff pressure system to measure average systolic and diastolic blood pressure in man. *IEEE Transactions on Biomedical Engineering*, 1972, **19**, 271–275.

Weiss, T., and Engel, B. T. Operant conditioning of heart rate in patients with premature ventricular contractions. *Psychosomatic Medicine*, 1971, **33**, 301–321.

Wells, D. T., Feather, B. W., and Headrick, M. W. The effects of immediate feedback upon voluntary control of salivary rate. *Psychophysiology*, 1973, **10**, 501–509.

Whatmore, G. B., and Kohli, D. R. Dysponesis: A neurophysiologic factor in functional disorders. *Behavioral Science*, 1968, **13**, 102–124.

Wickramasekera, I. Electromyographic feedback training and tension headache: Preliminary observations. *American Journal of Clinical Hypnosis*, 1972, **15**, 83–85.

Wickramasekera, I. The application of verbal instructions and EMG feedback training to the management of tension headache—preliminary observations. *Headache*, 1973, **13**, 74–76.

Wright, L. Aversive conditioning of self-induced seizures. *Behavior Therapy*, 1973, **4**, 712–713.

Yonovitz, A., and Kumar, A. An economical, easily recordable galvanic skin response apparatus. *Behavior Therapy*, 1972, **3**, 629–630.

Author Index

Subject Index